JUDICIAL LEADERSHIP

A New Strategic Approach

SIR ERNEST RYDER
&
STEPHEN HARDY

OXFORD
UNIVERSITY PRESS

UNIVERSITY PRESS

Great Clarendon Street, Oxford, OX2 6DP,
United Kingdom

Oxford University Press is a department of the University of Oxford.
It furthers the University's objective of excellence in research, scholarship,
and education by publishing worldwide. Oxford is a registered trade mark of
Oxford University Press in the UK and in certain other countries

Published in the United States of America by Oxford University Press
198 Madison Avenue, New York, NY 10016, United States of America

British Library Cataloguing in Publication Data
Data available

Library of Congress Control Number: 2019934667

ISBN 978–0–19–882933–1

JUDICIAL LEADERSHIP

for
Janette and Alice
&
Louise, Dominic and Will(iam)

With special gratitude and acknowledgement to the
Judicial College of England & Wales
for their permissions with regard to extracted and attributed materials
and
for their support as well as encouragement in the writing of this monograph
and future judicial training resource.

FOREWORD

The constitutional settlement agreed between 2003 and 2008 removed the Lord Chancellor as the Head of the Judiciary and imposed new obligations on the senior judiciary concerning the maintenance of the Rule of Law and the delivery of justice. The arrangements that were created involve statutory duties to be exercised by each of the principals (the Lord Chancellor, the Lord Chief Justice of England and Wales, and the Senior President of Tribunals) and the assumption of a large range of leadership responsibilities by the senior judiciary in respect of the effective, timely, and fair delivery of justice, ethical principles inherent in an independent judiciary, and arrangements for welfare, diversity, and change within the judiciary itself.

The Lord Chancellor had for many centuries been the linchpin between Parliament, the Executive, and the judiciary. With the fundamental reform in the office of Lord Chancellor, It became necessary for the judiciary to work directly with Parliament and the Executive and to handle their relationship with the media and the public – a task of some complexity given the imperatives of judicial independence and political neutrality.

In this new role, the judiciary had to confront a number of additional difficult issues: the public perception that justice was not central to the well-being of the state; justice in many areas was delayed and thus denied; acute problems arising out of the failure over many years to invest in those things necessary to deliver justice and to safeguard the Rule of Law had produced the real alternatives of wide ranging reform or managed decline; the far reaching implications of the Fourth Industrial Revolution to the delivery of justice had not been explored.

As in almost every other aspect of public life and business, leadership has been and remains the key. The judiciary had little experience of leadership in many aspects of the new responsibilities and virtually no training in leadership. That had to change. An indication of the scale of change necessary is provided by the first course on leadership training; I had to begin each course with a talk explaining to judges why such a course was needed and why they had been asked to come. Over the past decade a great deal has been achieved. As always much more remains to be done.

The aim of this book is to examine and delineate the responsibility of an emerging college of judges for safeguarding the Rule of Law and the delivery of justice. It does this in the context of the far reaching reforms made realizable by the Fourth

Industrial Revolution. It considers how to manage the relationship with the other powers in the state; how to ensure access to justice, open justice and the quality of decision making; the central importance of ethics; and the need for a strategic and consensual form of governance that will enable the judiciary to fulfil its role. The authors seek to identify the elements of a new approach to leadership that will deliver what is required in the 21st century.

Coupled with this pragmatic approach is an examination of what constitutes leadership and leadership styles within the context of the judiciary. As is made clear, it is important to identify what differentiates the judiciary from other organizations and institutions and to ensure that this is reflected in the way leadership is developed and practiced. The chapter on leadership in other institutions, including academia and the civil service, is therefore of great value; lessons are plainly to be learned – what should be adapted and what should be avoided at all costs. I always found that judges became much more interested in the topic of judges becoming actively engaged in leadership when the example of what had happened in the Health Service was discussed.

The authors have put together their own teaching materials from judicial training and academic education. They have a wealth of experience in leadership and teaching. This book will provide material for judges, academics, commentators, and legal practitioners to discuss and contribute to a debate that is important to the way the Rule of Law and the delivery of justice are safeguarded.

John Thomas, 15 May 2019
Lord Thomas of Cwmgiedd,
Lord Chief Justice of England and Wales 2013 to 2017

PREFACE

We live in the fourth industrial revolution, a digital era which involves rapid economic and political change, some of which is adverse to institutional structures and traditional checks and balances that inform fairness. This has profound implications for the private sector but most particularly for any part of the public sector that is not protected. Neither the judiciary nor the justice system are protected from these adverse influences notwithstanding their importance as the glue which holds society together. The judiciary have a vital role in safeguarding the Rule of Law by maintaining their independence and facilitating access to justice in a way that is open to scrutiny. In this book we shall examine the responsibility of an emerging college of leadership judges for the administration of justice. We will examine the partnerships in which they work with the legislature and the executive and we will describe the principles underpinning their independence which safeguard the rule of law. We will examine how the same principles both justify and underpin the decision-making of leadership judges which determines the efficiency and effectiveness of the justice system and we will argue for a strategic, collaborative, and consensual form of governance that ought to be the consequence.

The needs of the justice system in the twenty-first century have already led to the imperative which is, in times of austerity, to avoid managed decline. If the judiciary are to 'safeguard the rule of law by improving access to justice' by 'giving the administration of justice a new operating model with a sustainable and affordable infrastructure that delivers better services at lowest cost' they must be open to the challenge that change leadership presents not least to prevent price rationing and the encroachment of the executive and/or unconstrained populism into their independence. We will suggest that a more strategic approach towards judicial leadership will be necessary with a consequent enhancement in the skills of leadership judges who will be required to make decisions which must be made in accordance with long-standing principles that themselves underpin the rule of law. Furthermore, a more strategic approach will need:

- A greater understanding of the styles of leadership that might be applicable to the judiciary;
- A framework for decision-making and administering justice;
- Refreshed skills and evaluation tools for all judicial leaders; and
- A judicial leadership centre of excellence that supports those who seek to preserve the judiciary as a world class institution.

These objectives will be explored through the pages of this book. The discourse will not only detail alternative methods but will explore strategic approaches that are already being tried successfully. The sole agenda is the pursuit of a new approach to judicial leadership which is fit for a judiciary with new ways of working relevant to the twenty-first century and beyond.

We wish to take this opportunity to thank those who have made direct or indirect contributions to this project and to our many judicial, legal, and academic colleagues. Our families, most particularly our partners, live our day-to-day lives by default. Their contributions and the value of their advice and professional expertise should never be underestimated and we thank them and our children for their remarkable insights into what we do. Although it is invidious to identify individuals, there are some without whom the project could not have been completed. This book is based upon a collection of lectures, speeches, and teaching materials that both of the authors have used over recent years. Each of us has benefited from the considerable assistance of academic and judicial tutors with whom we have taught. Dr John Sorabji is the principal legal advisor to the Lord Chief Justice and the Master of the Rolls and Senior Fellow at the Judicial Institute at University College, London. His contributions to speeches and to the policy debate have been significant. Craig Robb is foremost among a generation of private secretaries whose political insight and advice to the judiciary is second to none. Drs Rashed Khan, Lisa Cove-Burrell, and Cornelius Tama and Professor Danny Morton are highly valued academic colleagues and intuitive commentators. Brian Walker is one of the last of a generation of judges' clerks who knows as much about the system of justice as any judge. Above all, we thank our publisher for her patience and direction. In particular, we thank the Judicial College of England and Wales, our fellow tutors Sir Stephen Irwin and Judge Brian Doyle and our educational advisors, Dr Kay Evans, Michelle Austin, and Trevor Elkin, for their inspiration and assistance in putting together the subject matter of this book.

Any omissions and/or errors are ours alone. The law is stated as at 1 October 2018.

Finally, we hope that your leadership journey is a positive experience both for you and for those around you.

Ernest Ryder and Stephen Hardy
Michaelmas 2018, London

CONTENTS

LIST OF FIGURES

LIST OF DIAGRAMS

TABLE OF CASES

TABLE OF STATUTES

LIST OF ABBREVIATIONS

ADR	Alternative Dispute Resolution
CPD	Continuing Professional Development
CRT	Civil Resolution Tribunal
DCJ	Designated Civil Judge
DFJ	Designated Family Judge
HE	Higher Education
HEA	Higher Education Academy
HEI	Higher Education Institution
HMCTS	Her Majesty's Courts and Tribunals Service
JC	Judicial College
JEB	Judicial Executive Board
JEGs	Judicial Engagement Groups
JoHs	Judicial Office Holders
LCJ	Lord Chief Justice of England & Wales
LFHE	Leadership Foundation for Higher Education
LLG	Local Leadership Group
LMD	Leadership & Management Development
MR	Master of the Rolls
NHS	National Health Service
ODR	Online Dispute Resolution
RJ	Resident Judge
RLG	Regional Leadership Group
RTJ	Regional Tribunal Judge
SPT	Senior President of Tribunals
TJEB	Tribunals Judiciary Executive Board
UKSC	United Kingdom Supreme Court
UT	Upper Tribunal

1

INTRODUCTION

We live in an age of transformations. They are more profound than any that we **1.01** have lived through in any period of our legal history. That is because of both the rapidity of transformation and the nature of change. The transformation from legal French to the use of English and, more recently, the Welsh language in our courts took several centuries to achieve, and its echoes continue to the present. The 1392 Pleadings in English Act did not accomplish its aim overnight. The transformation from common law forms of action and their confusion of substantive and procedural law took most of the course of the nineteenth century.

Transformation historically took time and considerable effort. It still takes re- **1.02** sources and considerable effort. But it no longer does or can take time; that is a simple fact of the technological age in which we live. There is a real risk here. Absence of time to get it right increases the chances of getting it wrong. It reduces the chance that we will plan properly; that we will implement those plans properly; and, that we will think about the consequences of what we may be doing properly. Rapidity creates risk. And where the delivery of justice is concerned risk must be minimized as far as it properly can. That is an important part of the task in which the judiciary of England and Wales are involved: safeguarding the Rule of Law by change while preserving our procedural and substantive protections. That is the leadership task with which we are involved and which is the concern of this book.

Let us then focus on the effect this age of transformations is having on our courts **1.03** and tribunals by considering: planning for change; securing greater access to justice; and improving the quality of justice which are the dominant themes of a judicial leader's work. Transformation cannot merely be concerned with moving from an analogue, paper-based, process-focused, justice system to a digital one. In this case the medium is not the message. It is and must only be the means to deliver the message better. And the message? Greater access to better quality justice. A justice system that best safeguards the Rule of Law in the twenty-first century.

1.04 When the Lord Chief Justice and the Senior President of Tribunals came to agreements with the then Lord Chancellor, Michael Gove MP in 2015, an aim was identified for a modernization programme for the courts and tribunals together with six principles. The aim was: *'to give the administration of justice a new operating model with a sustainable and affordable infrastructure that delivers better services at lower cost in order to safeguard the Rule of Law by improving access to justice'.* The six principles are the touchstone against which the judiciary check or validate each of the projects as they are tested and, if successful, implemented. They are:

1. Ensure justice is accessible to those who need it, that is to improve access to justice;
2. Design systems around the people who use them;
3. Create a system that is financially viable using a more cost-effective infrastructure, that is better IT, new working practices, and decent estate;
4. Eliminate the most common causes of delay;
5. Retain our national and international standing as a world class provider of legal services and in the delivery of justice;
6. Maintain the constitutional independence of the judiciary.

1.05 The imperatives that guided them and still inform them are: Access to justice as an indivisible right—there can be no second class even in, and we would suggest particularly so, an age of austerity, open justice so that the scrutiny necessary for the public's continuing trust and respect is ensured and ethical leadership (ie the administration of justice from ethical first principles that help guarantee the Rule of Law). Law administered through an independent judiciary requires effective and efficient governance and that necessitates continuing scrutiny of the efficacy of the institution that the senior judiciary are charged to lead to assure the respect that it needs to function. The consequence is that the senior judiciary cannot but look to modernize and reform the system. It is in that way that the judiciary are responsible for ensuring that our system is fit for purpose. They must do that by placing reliance on evidence-based and tested improvements to the judicial governance of the system and the quality of judicial decision-making. How are the judiciary approaching these aims and principles?

1.06 The courts and tribunals modernization programme involves change to the use of the estate; the provision of innovative and digital ways of working; changes and improvements to the way judges are led and workload is managed; and better support for the judiciary and users through registrars, legal advisers, and case officers;

the provision of assisted digital support for users who are digitally excluded, and especially those who are vulnerable; and a more diverse judiciary by the way the judges work, including in their recruitment and flexible deployment practices.

By way of example (and it must be emphasized that each jurisdiction is different and **1.07** that no one size fits all) the courts and tribunals intend to deliver the following projects:

- An online tribunal which provides a continuous online decision-making process, that is an asynchronous conversation leading to the determination;
- Separate online interfaces for users and judges;
- Intuitive online applications in place of forms;
- An online notifications and tracking system for each step of the process;
- E-filing and online document sharing;
- Online triage, pre-hearing supervision, and alternative dispute resolution opportunities;
- Online documentary management and case management;
- An assisted digital service for the digitally excluded;
- Online fee payment;
- Online identification;
- Online and video hearings, where appropriate;
- Online support services for judges and hearings that facilitate judge and estate bookings, allocation and listing by judges, leave and expense claims, and so on;
- Online services for face to face hearings including presentation equipment for documents and people who join remotely and for judgments and orders promulgation;
- Safeguards for open justice; and
- Safeguards for access to justice.

Such poses the key question: How are these aims going to be achieved? **1.08**

A. Judicial Ways of Working—2022

First, planning for change and Judicial Ways of Working 2022. Since 2005, the **1.09** constitutional settlement has been predicated on the idea that the delivery of justice is a partnership between 'two separate but equal branches working together to manage the courts': that is the government and the judiciary.[1] This interdependent relationship[2] is one that is manifested in a number of ways.

---

[1] Professor K Malleson, 'The Effect of the Constitutional Reform Act 2005 on the Relationship between the Judiciary, the Executive and Parliament' in House of Lords Constitution Committee, *Relations between the Executive, the Judiciary and Parliament* (6th Report of 2007) Appendix 3, 63 <https://publications.parliament.uk/pa/ld200607/ldselect/ldconst/151/151.pdf>.

[2] Lord Thomas CJ, 'The Judiciary within the State—The Relationship between the Branches of the State' (Michael Ryle Lecture, 15 June 2017) [18]ff <https://www.judiciary.gov.uk/wp-content/uploads/2017/06/lcj-michael-ryle-memorial-lecture-20170616.pdf>.

1.10   One way is that Her Majesty's Courts and Tribunals Service (HMCTS), the body which provides the support for the judiciary to carry out their constitutional role, is operated as a partnership between the Lord Chancellor, Lord Chief Justice, and Senior President of Tribunals.[3] Its board answers to these co-equal partners, the judiciary, and the executive, and is not, as it was historically, simply the means by which the Ministry of Justice and its predecessors manage the courts.

1.11   One consequence of that change in the constitutional settlement is that the duty long-placed on the judiciary to lead the modernization of our justice system is all the more acute today.[4] An example of this can be seen in the role played here by Lord Dyson MR's keen support for the work of Professor Richard Susskind. As the then Chairman of the Civil Justice Council, Lord Dyson was a prime mover behind the establishment of its Working Party on Online Dispute Resolution.[5] That report was the starting point for further work carried out by JUSTICE and then by Sir Michael, now Lord Briggs in his Civil Court Structure Review.

1.12   The foresight of each of the Heads of Jurisdiction who have commissioned, chaired, or implemented reviews has informed a series of documents that were distributed by the Lord Chief Justice and the Senior President of Tribunals, to all judges, tribunal panel members and magistrates at the beginning of May 2018: they are known as *Judicial Ways of Working—2022*. Among other things, they seek the judiciary's views on the modernization programme; on how and in what ways it should be used to simplify, clarify, and improve court and tribunal processes through digitization; to incorporate and expand the provision of alternative dispute resolution (ADR) and online dispute resolution (ODR); to increase the use of technology and online and video hearings; to increase access to justice; and provide a more flexible, diverse and skilled judiciary.

1.13   The documents seek judicial feedback. They are not a statement of a foregone conclusion. The duty to lead placed on the senior judiciary is a duty to lead effectively and efficiently (and in the case of the Senior President also to provide swift, expert, and innovative justice—no other head of jurisdiction in the UK has these additional duties). The senior judiciary have an obligation to lead the transformation that the justice system needs to prevent its decline. And that can only be done through listening effectively. They cannot lead in an echo chamber. They cannot lead without engagement: both with the public and with the judiciary.

---

[3] HMCTS Framework Agreement (Cm 882, July 2014) <https://www.gov.uk/government/uploads/system/uploads/attachment_data/file/384922/hmcts-framework-document-2014.pdf>.

[4] See further Sir Ernest Ryder SPT, 'Securing Open Justice' (Luxembourg, 1 February 2018) <https://www.judiciary.gov.uk/wp-content/uploads/2018/02/ryder-spt-open-justice-luxembourg-feb-2018.pdf>.

[5] See Civil Justice Council, Online Dispute Resolution for Low Value Claims (2015) <https://www.judiciary.gov.uk/wp-content/uploads/2015/02/Online-Dispute-Resolution-Final-Web-Version.pdf>.

Genuine leadership is properly informed. It is open, and open to and receptive of **1.14** criticism. We make better choices when they are informed choices. The present transformation of our justice system must be one that is carried out in the light of informed choices. We cannot shy away from scrutiny. Scrutiny, if we may borrow from Jeremy Bentham, is the best antiseptic. And to the extent that anyone involved in reform does shy away from scrutiny or is less open than they can properly be, reform is likely to be far less effective than it needs to be.

To make better choices, the heads of jurisdiction have sought the views of the judi- **1.15** ciary on the issues identified. It is important that we learn from their skills and experience. And we can then ensure, in the fast-moving technological world we live in today, that the reforms we pursue are the ones best calculated to deliver high quality justice.

B. Improving Judicial Leadership and Management

One essential feature of Judicial Ways of Working is the need to develop ways to **1.16** improve the leadership and management of the judiciary. If, as it discusses, we are to increase the degree to which judges can be deployed across jurisdictions and can have more flexible ways of working, if we are to continue to take a leading role in the modernization programme, we must review and continue to improve our governance structures.

This means that, as with any large-scale organization, we must review the way in **1.17** which we work. Do we have the right systems? Do we use the right processes? Do we have the right skills and training? Is, for instance, the present approach to the running of the courts and tribunals the optimum one? Is the judiciary's internal governance system the best for the demands of today? The great court reformers of the Victorian age did not shy away from the difficult questions. Nor should we. Business as usual, in particular our infrastructure and operations, must be improved before we digitize it.

This is all the more important if, as has been said—and as we are putting in **1.18** place—our courts and tribunals in the future will be digital by '*default and by design*[6] or, to be more accurate, will provide enhanced access to justice by being digital by default. To operate in this way we all need to be properly trained and we need to have the right governance systems in place. We cannot continue to manage the judiciary on an analogue basis. Looking at effective administration of justice from the perspective of first instance courts and tribunals, we must have regard to what Lord Browne-Wilkinson suggested over thirty years ago, a more

---

[6] M Briggs, 'Civil Courts Structure Review—Interim Report' (December 2015) 4.

collegiate leadership structure at all levels,[7] more engaged with civil society where it matters, for example in the essential collaborative arrangements with the legislature and the executive that at a national level are indispensable to the maintenance of the rule of law.

1.19 If we are to manage a digital workload and lead digital working practices we need better governance arrangements with HMCTS. That is the unfinished business of the 2005 constitutional settlement. We have to manage our functional and formal separation of powers. In any event, modernization casts a spotlight on our existing arrangements, that is the essential operational means by which we bring the digital world into the justice system. As judges involved in the governance of HMCTS we must do our utmost to inform, collaborate, and scrutinize what is done in our name and modernization will require better ways of undertaking that function. Leadership and management, in particular of innovation, are skills that some judges need if reform and its integration into business as usual are to succeed in a court or tribunal near you.

C. Increasing Accessibility and Open Justice

1.20 The reforms we have already embarked upon and which we should consider embarking upon have a common objective: to improve access to justice. This is a long-established constitutional duty placed on government and the judiciary to secure.[8] This means we must respond to the needs of digital society. When eBay can deal with 60 million disputes a year,[9] there is a pressing need to ensure that our justice system can operate to ensure that where the individuals involved in those disputes wish to do so, they can access the courts as readily as they can eBay's dispute resolution system. And there is a need to learn from those systems so that our courts and tribunals can operate as effectively. This is not to suggest that we seek to discourage settlement via ODR. It is to say that as a society we remain able to secure effective access to justice for all. Our systems must—as they are doing—change to meet the needs of today's society, today's citizens, and today's disputes. We cannot afford to create or countenance the existence of *digital outlaws*: individuals and businesses whose disputes are outside the law's protection.

1.21 Access to justice also demands that our reformed courts and tribunals, our new digitized systems, are accessible and accountable to the public. They must remain open to public scrutiny to maintain the health of the system, to maintain judicial accountability, and to ensure that arbitrary decision-making does not arise as it can when justice is said to be done outside the public gaze.

---

[7] Lord Browne-Wilkinson, 'The 11th FA Mann Lecture' [1988] PL 44, 56.
[8] *Attorney-General v Times Newspapers Ltd* [1974] AC 273, 307.
[9] E Katsh and O Rabinovich-Einy, *Digital Justice* (OUP 2017) 4.

Open justice and accessibility for today's disputes is necessary for another reason.   **1.22**
If we permit the creation of digital outlaws, we permit the subversion of our
substantive law. We do so because we acquiesce in some forms of disputes being
beyond the reach of the courts. In doing so we accept that some laws cannot be
interpreted, applied, or explained by the courts. Such laws become dead letters.
Their interpretation and application becomes a matter of private actors, not of
public fora. We thus accept a democratic deficit in our society. The modernization programme is the means through which we ensure that in a digital age we
do not permit the conversion of public laws, and the values they instantiate, into
private and privately interpreted guidelines. Hence the need to ensure that online
or video hearings, like telephone hearings at the present time, must be carried out
in public.

D. Improving the Quality of Justice

Improving the quality of justice must also be our constant endeavour. We are   **1.23**
all committed to providing the best quality of justice we can.[10] This does not,
as some have wrongly suggested, mean that we seek a blank cheque in terms
of the allocation of resources to the justice system. It does mean however that
the justice system must be provided with the resources to enable it to fulfil its
constitutional duty.

Quite some time ago, Guido Calabresi and Philip Bobbitt discussed the problem   **1.24**
of the tragic choices society faces when it needs to allocate scarce resources
among multiple demands.[11] Each is a valid, a necessary demand. How each society decides to allocate its resources is a statement of its fundamental values; it
is a statement of what and who we are as a society. In answering the question of
resource allocation to our courts and tribunals, to our justice system, we define
ourselves. We define our commitment to being a just society. So we must make
good choices.

Securing quality justice is not just a matter of resources. It goes wider than that.   **1.25**
Modernization must focus on how we are to improve quality. This has a number
of strands. One of the most important is the need to ensure that the steps we take
to improve the quality of justice are: systematic, evidence-based, and tested, for
example, there is data embedded to enable each project to be tested and improved
over time. Far too often in the past we have approached modernization as an exercise in ad-hocery. It is not been evidence-based, or at best it has been based on

---

[10] See further Sir Ernest Ryder SPT, 'The Role of the Justice System in Decision-Making for
Children' (Warwick, 9 April 2018) <https://www.judiciary.gov.uk/wp-content/uploads/2018/04/
spt-ryder-bapscan-april2018.pdf>.
[11] G Calabresi and P Bobbitt, *Tragic Choices* (Norton & Co 1978).

partial evidence. We have not tested reform. And we have not therefore learnt from such testing. Our civil justice system, for instance, provides a mechanism to test reform. It can introduce pilot schemes. It often does so, and learns the lessons of those pilots.

1.26 The modernization programme is making extensive use of pilots. Both in the courts and tribunals, pilots have been put in place: e-filing was piloted in what are now the Business and Property Courts; online divorce and probate pilot schemes are being tested in the family justice system; online civil money claims processes are being tested in the civil courts and online video hearings (otherwise known as virtual or fully video hearings) and continuous online hearings are being piloted in the tribunals alongside application and automatic notification systems. And the judiciary are learning from those pilots. Feedback is as important here as anywhere else.

1.27 More fundamentally, feedback does not stop at reform though. It is something which must be ongoing. Here we have traditionally faced a problem. It can be simply put: we have not had the evidence. Historically, the default position has been that we do not have sufficient, robust, and accessible evidence concerning the operation of our justice system. We do not therefore have the necessary material to enable us to assess where the causes of problems within the system lie. We have not been able to analyse our data on a continuing basis to inform reform when it needs to be carried out. Hence, we lurch from one major reform process, based on anecdote and impression, every ten years or so without genuinely knowing what target we are aiming at. So, therefore let us compare that with Canada and the Civil Resolution Tribunal (CRT). As is the case with ODR systems such as that operated by eBay, the CRT is able to obtain effective feedback on how it is operating. It can do so in real time. The online system has been designed to enable users—litigants—to provide feedback at every stage of the process. That feedback is then collated and—importantly—acted upon to refine and improve the system.[12] The same type of feedback process must be employed in the pilots of our court and tribunal reforms[13] to provide the means for the effective gathering and dissemination of data so that we can identify problems and cure them as they arise. Modernization must, and will, enable us to ensure that ongoing testing and refinement—and public scrutiny and hence accountability—is a feature of our justice system in the future. And it must enable us to work collaboratively with experts drawn from many different disciplines to ensure we can take a holistic, well-informed approach.

---

[12] See Tanja Rosteck, 'Happy First Birthday, Strata Solution Explorer!, and Solution Explorer Quarterly Update: 2017 Q4' <https://civilresolutionbc.ca/happy-first-birthday-strata-solution-explorer/>; <https://civilresolutionbc.ca/solution-explorer-quarterly-update-2017-q4/>.
[13] See Sir Terence Etherton MR, 'Civil Justice after Jackson' (15 March 2018) [33]–[35] <https://www.judiciary.gov.uk/wp-content/uploads/2018/03/speech-mor-civil-justice-after-jackson-conkerton-lecture-2018.pdf>.

Yet, improvements to quality also means improving the quality of judicial deci- **1.28**
sion-making. This is particularly important as we introduce greater use of ADR
and ODR into our justice systems. Judges are trained to determine rights. To
evaluate the merits of cases. Different skills and approaches are needed when mediation or facilitated negotiation is being carried out. Rights-based, evaluative,
approaches may and generally will not be appropriate to mediation and facilitated negotiation. Judges and court and tribunals officers who are involved in the
provision of mediation and facilitated negotiation need to be properly trained
so that they do not default to the rights-based approach. They must be adept at
identifying and applying problem-solving, interest-based approaches. We already
pioneer such approaches with our Employment Judges and we will need to put
more of their training into place as we modernize our approach. There is never a
finishing line to the approaches we can adopt to enhance the quality of judicial
decision-making.[14]

Justice is not something that is done to people. Nor is it a consumer service, as **1.29**
the Supreme Court in the *Unison* case felt moved recently to comment: a lesson
to us all in the role and purpose of courts; a lesson in the fact that courts and tribunals are not a consumer service.[15] It was right. And its lesson needs to be heard,
understood, and inwardly digested by everyone involved in the transformation of
our justice system, just as it does by everyone involved in the delivery of justice
generally. Justice is, as the opening line of *Justinian's Institutes* rightly noted a very
long time ago now, '*the constant and perpetual wish to render everyone [their] due*'.[16]
That wish is the duty cast on the State to ensure the effective delivery of justice.
The present transformation—modernization—of our courts and tribunals, of our
judiciary, is the means through which we can and must ensure that as a society we
can render everyone their due.

It is our task in the pages that follow to identify and discuss the ways in which **1.30**
judicial leaders can perform their vital roles and the principles they must use to
ensure that their leadership safeguards the Rule of Law.

E. Leadership Defined

Unsurprisingly, there is no universal definition for leadership. No text on **1.31**
'*Leadership*' can escape the toil of definition, since defining the touchstone concept is the natural starting place. Yet, within the concept of 'leadership', this is no
easy task and recognizing its importance is critical to its most basic appreciation.

---

[14] See Ryder (n 10).
[15] In particular see Lord Reed's judgment, *R (UNISON) v Lord Chancellor* [2017] UKSC 51,
[2017] 3 WLR 409 [68]ff.
[16] JAC Thomas (ed), *Justinian's Institutes* (Cornell University Press 1987).

1.32   Moreover, placing the key concept of leadership within the legal (judicial) context is a relative contemporary activity.

1.33   As Northouse[17] reports 'In a seminal work, Rost[18] analysed materials written from 1900 to 1990, finding more than 200 different definitions for leadership.'

1.34   This text takes up the challenge and sets off on a voyage of discovery—including something old and something new—in terms of the generic landscape of leadership.

1.35   This is, without exception, universally accepted throughout the subject-matter by all scholars. This is essentially due to its complexity. The longest and oldest debate about leadership being: whether leadership is innate or ascribed?

1.36   Given that it is widely acknowledged that there is no single agreed definition of the concept of leadership,[19] it has as a result however been possible to identify some common conceptual elements from the myriad of definitions put forward. At its most basic, leadership has been traditionally depicted as the way in which 'a leader influences followers'.[20] Nonetheless, Bass and Stogdill[21] proposed that the concept is commonly viewed from one or more of three perspectives; in terms of a group or team processes (involving the leader's influence); in terms of personality, skills, and traits of the leader; and in terms of behaviour of the leader. Further, in fact, Rost traced that leadership evolved in the twentieth century from its provenance as control and the centralization of power through to leadership influence in the 1930s. Thereafter, leadership converged into being defined by the behaviour of the individual, until during the 1950s when, upon reappraisal, leadership succumbed to group theory, though the latter was short lived, as 'goal theory' emerged. Again, the latter was short-lived when a new approach to leadership prevailed in the 1970s—the 'organized behaviour' theory. The reciprocal dimension of leadership was identified during this era.

1.37   As leadership definitions emerged, more leadership theories abounded. Accordingly, the 1980s hailed a ripe decade of scholarly scrutiny and exploitation which caused a raising of public consciousness in the subject. The latter period saw two decades filled with trait theory and transformational leadership. Whilst the concept of leadership entered into the twenty-first century—authentic, spiritual, and adaptive leadership were added to the volume of existing classifications, approaches, theories, and definitions.

---

[17] P Northouse, *Leadership: Theory and Practice* (7th edn, Sage 2016).
[18] JC Rost, *Leadership for the Twenty-First Century* (Praeger 1991).
[19] P Spicker, ' "Leadership": A Perniciously Vague Concept' (2011) 25(1) International Journal of Public Sector Management 34; G Yukl, *Leadership in Organizations* (8th edn, Pearson 2013).
[20] L Mullins (2013), 'Management and Organisational Behaviour' 11 edition (Financial Times).
[21] B Bass and R Stogdill, *Handbook of Leadership* (Free Press 1990).

In any event, 'leadership' has more commonly been defined based on personal **1.38** traits, whereby leadership is conceptualized based on 'special' character traits that some individuals possess.[22] These traits enable leaders to wield influence over others towards accomplishing tasks. According to Northouse[23], 'leadership' is a process by which a person influences others to accomplish an objective and directs the organization in a way that makes it more cohesive and coherent. Wouter et al (2010) earlier stated that leadership comes when people need to be shown a new way ahead with motivation, even if their instinct is to stick with the familiarity of the old tendencies. Northouse[24] adds that leadership should effect meaningful change for a particular course of action. This makes it different from normal management, which is usually misinterpreted to mean the same as leadership. According to Northouse,[25] leadership is far more critical for an industry or organization to realize more profits and achieve desired objectives as it is concentrated on vision, change, and strategies.

For the purpose of this monograph, Peter Northouse's seminal definition of lead- **1.39** ership is adopted. The rationale for this is because his definition comprises of three key components needed for leadership to occur. Thus, according to Northouse, 'leadership is a *process* of whereby an individual influences a *group* of individuals to achieve a *common goal*'.[26] Adopting such a Northousean tripartite definition ensures that leadership comprises of three components namely:

- influence,
- a group, and
- common goals.

Influence is primarily concerned with how a leader affects and relates with fol- **1.40** lowers. The leader could influence the emotions, behaviours, or opinions of group members/followers.

Northouse's seminal definition was further refined by Yukl[27], who sought to con- **1.41** ceptualize the relationships between the elements involved in leadership process. Whilst the first three elements relate to Bass and Stogdill's[28] three dimensions of leadership, the role of followers is identified as a separate element which influences both leadership input and output. Performance outcomes are also highlighted, without the assumption that these will need to be effective or successful.

---

[22] M Horner, 'Leadership Theory: Past, Present and Future' (1997) 3 Team Performance Management 4. <https://pdfs.semanticscholar.org/5d58/ef16eed47908583604a412efb091228727be.pdf?_ga=2.7246262.529058808.1552835588-387193996.1552835588>.
[23] Northouse (n 17).
[24] Northouse (n 17).
[25] ibid.
[26] ibid 3 (emphasis added).
[27] Yukl (n 19).
[28] Bass and Stogdill (n 21).

1.42   In addition to these elements, Yukl's model also acknowledges the influence of environmental variables on the leader and follower behaviours, as well as their interaction. Interventions relating to the leaders' traits and skills, for example—training and development techniques are not included as a moderator in the model.

1.43   Leadership takes place within the context of groups. Simply put, there is no leadership *without* followers. The sizes of these groups vary from very small groups, to communities and even entire organizations and nations. There ought to be a level mutuality between the leadership and followership as to the direction the group or organization is headed. The sense of mutual interests provides an ethical pulse which guides the relationship between the leadership and the followership in the quest for achieving targets and maximizing group efforts. As Burns aptly puts it, 'leadership is nothing if not linked to collective purpose'.[29] Having the constituent components of leadership, it becomes imperative to briefly examine leadership theories.

1.44   However, as this opening Chapter has already asserted, its central phenomenon—*leadership*—is to be regarded as a process which involves influence, as it occurs in groups and involves common goals. Therefore, leadership is a process where an individual seeks to influence a group of individuals to achieve a common goals or goals. Prior to examining such theories, this book will now map out the judicial context of leadership.

---

[29] J Burns, *Leadership* (Harper & Row 1978).

2

THE ORGANIZATION OF LEADERSHIP IN THE JUDICIARY

We have briefly appraised leadership more generally in the Introduction to this **2.01** book—so is it possible to say what traits, styles, or models judicial leaders adopt? Is judicial leadership the same as or different to other concepts of leadership? And/ or, is judicial leadership essentially a species of its own?

All of these questions beg imperative answers. Similarly, they suggest that 'judicial **2.02** leadership' is from the outset distinct from other forms of leadership. If so, why is that?

In the pages of this monograph we will consider the principles and values which **2.03** give rise to the traits, styles, and models of leadership adopted by the judiciary. We will emphasize the importance of those principles and values to the essential judicial function: safeguarding the rule of law—the function which gives an in-dependent judiciary its mandate in a democratic state. We will argue that it is the principled basis of their decision-making as judicial leaders, a basis that is coinci-dent with and just as important as their independent decisions in individual cases, that marks them out and makes them distinct from other leaders.

A. What is 'Judicial Leadership'?

Leaders are expected to demonstrate their professional ethics and integrity but **2.04** the demands of judicial leadership go much further and deeper into constitu-tional norms, the very bases of the Rule of Law and the statutory powers and duties which constrain and enable leadership judges to facilitate the administra-tion of justice in a way which we will suggest is susceptible of scrutiny from first principles.

2.05 In an era of wide-ranging reform to the administration of justice, the need for enhanced judicial leadership is patent. Most particularly, since the constitutional settlements of 2004 to 2008 and the creation of what is now Her Majesty's Courts and Tribunals Service (HMCTS), and the heads of jurisdiction (the chief justices and Senior President of Tribunals (SPT)) as heads of their own judiciaries and presidents of their courts and tribunals, there is a new model for the administration of justice by judges which carried with it new responsibilities. No longer can the senior judiciary leave the administration of justice to others: it is central to their statutory functions and it involves a constitutional partnership with the executive and a practical collaboration between all three limbs of the state.

2.06 The constitutional settlement has led to the participation of the judiciary in the administration of the justice system in a way that is not entirely new. It had been prefaced by Sir Nicholas Browne-Williamson, the then Vice-Chancellor in his 1987 Francis Mann Lecture.[1] That no doubt influenced Lord Woolf CJ in the proposals that he first made as Lord Chief Justice (LCJ) in 2003 but it was not until the subsequent and unplanned constitutional settlement of 2004–05 that the new Concordat gave birth to the Constitutional Reform Act 2005, the Framework Agreement that sets out the constitutional partnership between the LCJ, the SPT, and the Lord Chancellor and the joint venture HMCTS Board that is independently chaired and has a majority of non-executive and judicial directors. Over the same period, the constitutional settlement was broadened to encompass the tribunals judiciary with the enactment of the Tribunals, Courts and Enforcement Act 2007 and the 'organisation of the judiciary' began to take on a more developed form in the way that its executive boards (the Judicial Executive Board and the Tribunals Judiciary Executive Board) and advisory councils operate at a national level.

2.07 The present focus on judicial leadership has its causes not just in the constitutional settlement but in the effects of austerity after the 2008–09 financial crisis and the prospect of unaffordability giving rise at best to the managed decline of the justice system or at worst a form of price rationing that is the antithesis of access to justice. No responsible judge, let alone one charged with leading their judiciaries, would contemplate those consequences while continuing to purport to exercise their statutory duties. The consequence was an agreement between the Lord Chancellor, the LCJ, and the SPT backed by the Treasury for the modernization of the courts and tribunals—a £1Bn reform programme which aims to transform the ways in which justice is delivered by 2022 using new technology funded in part by the sale of redundant estate. The vision document and strategic plan are agreements that mark a turning point by the involvement of the senior judiciary in change leadership and decision-making with significant strategic and

---

[1] Entitled: 'The Independence of the Judiciary in the 1980s' [1988] PL 44.

operational implications. The basis for that decision-making and the principles and methodologies involved have informed much of the content of this book.

In more limited or perhaps different social contexts judges have always been en- **2.08** gaged in 'out-of-court work' (ie the judiciary do *not* just try cases). It has always been the case that judges in different and perhaps more limited contexts across the global economy are led within administrative systems which evoke 'judicial leader' roles. To that extent, it is universally accepted across many legal jurisdictions that judicial leadership is a hierarchical platform which requires leaders to relate to others within and outside the organization, to recognize how they view themselves and their position, whether or not they are successful as leaders.[2]

All judicial leaders need to reflect on how the task is to be accomplished, that is **2.09** how does a judicial leader set out to get it done? If an emergency arises, how does a judicial leader handle it? If the organization needs the support of the community, how does a judicial leader go about mobilizing it? At the end of this monograph we will bring together ideas with practical examples. All of these depend for their success both on the application of principle to decision-making and the leadership style adopted. Factors that also influence the style to be used include: how much time is available; whether relationships are based on respect and trust (or on disrespect); who has the information, you, your colleagues (both judicial and civil service), or both; how well your colleagues are trained and how well you know the task; internal conflicts; stress levels; the type of task, whether it is structured, unstructured, complicated, or simple; and laws or established procedures and training plans. As a preface to the principles which are in play we set out the present organization of the judiciary and examine the leadership styles that are available to be adopted by judicial leaders.

B. Judicial Office Holders

The Constitutional Reform Act 2005 made the LCJ the President of the **2.10** Courts of England and Wales and Head of the (courts) Judiciary in England and Wales. The LCJ's principal responsibilities are: Making representations to Parliament and representing the views of his judiciary to Ministers and more widely; the making of arrangements for judicial welfare, guidance, and training; and arrangements for the deployment of judges and the allocation of work in the courts of England and Wales. In fact, under the 2005 Act, the LCJ has some 400 statutory duties. The LCJ also sits on important criminal, civil, and family cases. The LCJ gives guidance judgments and makes practice directions in many of the most important issues that come on appeal or before the

---

[2] P Northouse, *Leadership: Theory and Practice* (7th edn, Sage 2016).

Divisional Court. The LCJ has a non-delegable duty to take steps to encourage judicial diversity and shares responsibility with the Lord Chancellor for conduct, discipline, and sanctions.

2.11 The SPT has broadly similar duties and functions in respect of the administration of justice in tribunals and as head of the tribunals' judiciary in the UK. His office is independent of other leadership judges with the consequence that there are duties of mutual cooperation with the geographic chief justices.

2.12 The organization of the judiciary has rapidly developed since 2003, although not with the coherence which may be required to meet the needs of the digital age and a rapidly changing political, economic, and justice landscape. The heads of jurisdiction in England and Wales (civil, crime, and family) are now coincident with the Heads of Division of the Court of Appeal and the High Court: the Master of the Rolls, the President of the Queen's Bench, and the President of the Family Division of the High Court. The Chancellor of the High Court presides over a modern collaboration of jurisdictions; the Business and Property Courts of England and Wales, is arguably the most concerted effort to meet real business need. But the lack of any Head of Administrative Justice and the poorly defined relationships between the tribunals in the UK and the courts arguably prevents the development of a strategic vision across all jurisdictions and effective planning for cross-jurisdictional deployment and career progression.

2.13 The most recent description of the organization of the judiciary is a public document agreed on 1 June 2017 by the Judicial Executive Board (JEB) and the Tribunals Judiciary Executive Board (TJEB). Save for the delegation of the role of Head of Criminal Justice to the President of the Queen's Bench by the LCJ (a delegation that is foreshadowed in the document) the description remains accurate. Given the clarity which the document was intended to provide, it is wise to repeat its contents verbatim:

> *The Constitutional Reform Act 2005 and the Concordat set out the responsibilities of the Lord Chief Justice (LCJ), as Head of the Judiciary of England and Wales and as President of the Courts of England and Wales, in respect of the judiciary.*
>
> *The LCJ carries out these responsibilities through the Judicial Executive Board (JEB) and the Judges' Council.*
>
> *The Tribunals, Courts and Enforcement Act 2007 sets out the responsibilities of the Senior President of Tribunals (SPT), as head of the unified tribunals judiciary across the United Kingdom. Tribunals outside the unified system established under the 2007 Act fall under the judicial leadership of the relevant Chief Justice in England & Wales, Scotland or Northern Ireland respectively.*
>
> *The SPT carries out these responsibilities through the Tribunals Judicial Executive Board (TJEB).*
>
> *The LCJ, the Heads of Division and the SPT sit for the greater proportion of their time. Spread over the term the LCJ spends 2/3 days a week on judicial cases; the Heads of Division and the SPT spend 3 days a week on judicial cases.*

The Judicial Office, headed by its Chief Executive, mirrors the responsibilities assigned to the judiciary. It is a significant office with over 200 staff. Full support is provided for the judges with administrative and leadership responsibilities through their private offices. The Judicial College, Judicial HR team, the Judicial Communications Office and the Judicial Conduct Investigations Office are also part of the Judicial Office.

I. THE JUDICIAL EXECUTIVE BOARD

(a) Function

The primary function of the Judicial Executive Board (JEB) is to make executive decisions in relation to:

1. the provision of leadership, welfare, direction and support to the judiciary of England and Wales;
2. determining the structure, roles and responsibilities of the judiciary;
3. approving policy and other matters in relation to Her Majesty's Courts and Tribunals Service (HMCTS), including the Reform Programme, as are within the responsibility of the LCJ and SPT under the Framework Agreements, including the agreement with the Lord Chancellor of the budget of HMCTS;
4. developing policy and practice on judicial deployment, authorisations, appointment to non-judicial roles and general appointments issues;
5. developing policy and practice on increasing the diversity of the judiciary;
6. developing policy and practice on the welfare support for the judiciary;
7. directing the judicial communications strategy through the Judicial Communications Office, including on matters arising from the HMCTS reform programme;
8. directing the work of the Judicial College in the provision of training for the judiciary;
9. managing the judiciary's overall relationship with the Executive branch of Government and Parliament, international relations with other jurisdictions and with other bodies, including the legal profession;
10. considering and developing judicial-led improvements to the justice system;
11. agreeing the approach to issues arising from other Government initiatives affecting the judiciary;
12. close oversight and responsibility for the performance of the courts and tribunals;
13. considering and making recommendations on financial priorities, and plans as they affect the judiciary and the financing and resources for the courts and tribunals system;
14. approving the annual budget and business plan for the Judicial Office and approving the agreement with the Permanent Secretary on resources for the Judicial Office;
15. setting clear objectives, priorities, and standards for the Judicial Office and monitoring its performance.

(b) Composition

Composition of the Judicial Executive Board is set by the LCJ with the assent of the Board. At present, the Board comprises the holders of the following judicial offices:

- Lord Chief Justice, Chair
- Master of the Rolls
- President of the Queen's Bench Division

- President of the Family Division
- Chancellor of the High Court
- Vice-President of the Queen's Bench Division
- Judge in charge of recruitment and diversity
- Senior President of Tribunals
- Senior Presiding Judge
- Chair of the Judicial College
- Chief Executive of the Judicial Office

The secretariat is provided by the Judicial Office.

The Judicial Executive Board may from time to time invite additional members to work with it on particular issues or to attend particular meetings.

Officials from the Ministry of Justice (MoJ) and HMCTS are invited to attend the Board and discuss issues as appropriate.

(c) The conduct of business

The Judicial Executive Board generally meets monthly, on or about the penultimate Thursday of each month.

Weekly 'informal' meetings take place most Wednesdays (where there is not a full meeting) where immediate matters can be considered.

Board members will debate issues reflecting their individual responsibilities. The overriding aim of the JEB is to reach conclusions that are best for the judiciary as a whole and then to act on them.

The JEB endeavours to reach a decision by consensus; in default of consensus on an issue, the decision on that issue is for the LCJ.

The responsibilities of the secretariat are to:

- agree the agenda with the LCJ and circulate, with accompanying papers, to Board members one week in advance of the meeting;
- prepare a Forward Programme of key issues to be considered by the Board in each financial year;
- keep the minutes; and
- maintain an action log, shared with those responsible for taking matters forward, and ensure that all actions are completed.

(d) Leadership responsibilities

Members of the JEB, supported by the appropriate teams within the Judicial Office, take responsibility for leading and overseeing the overall strategy in a number of specific areas:

- Civil Justice (except the day to day operation of the High Court): Master of the Rolls with the Judicial Civil Justice Board and the Civil Executive Team;
- Business and Property Courts: Chancellor of the High Court, in consultation with the President of the Queen's Bench Division;
- Criminal Justice: LCJ or President of the Queen's Bench Division with the Criminal Justice team;
- Family Justice: President of the Family Division;
- Tribunals: Senior President of Tribunals;
- HMCTS, including the reform programme: Senior President of Tribunals and Senior Presiding Judge; the Judge in charge of Reform attends as necessary;

- Pay and Pensions: Chancellor of the High Court;
- Recruitment, and diversity: a Lord Justice of Appeal, currently the Vice-President of the Court of Appeal (Criminal Division);
- Talent management, succession planning and High Court deployment: Vice-President of the Queen's Bench Division;
- Training: Chair of the Judicial College;
- International relations: Chancellor of the High Court;
- Cross-jurisdictional performance and deployment below the High Court, and welfare policy: Senior Presiding Judge, with assistance from the Deputy Senior Presiding Judge as appropriate.

The JEB will also have oversight of communications and engagement matters as they affect the judiciary.

The JEB will receive regular (at least annually) reports on the overall strategy for each of these areas for review and approval. The timetable will be set out in the forward programme. More immediate issues should come before the Board in the usual way.

(e) Annual strategy meetings

The JEB will hold an annual strategy meeting, organised by the Judicial Office, at which broad and strategic issues relating to the judiciary are discussed.

II THE TRIBUNALS JUDICIAL EXECUTIVE BOARD

(a) Function

The primary function of the Tribunals Judicial Executive Board (TJEB) is to provide leadership, strategic direction and support to the tribunals' judiciary in the following areas:

1. manage the tribunals judiciary's overall relationship with HMCTS, MoJ and other jurisdictions, Departments and bodies;
2. provide comment and advice to HMCTS (through the SPT's membership of the HMCTS Board) and MoJ from the judicial perspective on any programmes, projects and/or initiatives relating to or impacting on tribunals, their judicial office holders and/or their users;
3. discuss with HMCTS and MoJ spending review and allocations priorities, targets and plans as they affect the tribunals judiciary and the financing and resources of tribunals;
4. represent tribunals interests to the Judicial Executive Board and the Judges' Council (respectively through the Senior President of Tribunals' membership, and TJEB/judicial representation on standing committees);
5. ensure appropriate cross border relationships are maintained and promoted;
6. maintain relationships with the Judicial Appointments Commission and MoJ and hold discussions on specific competitions and forecasting where necessary;
7. ensure effective provision and delivery of judicial training in tribunals through representation on the Board of the Judicial College and the Tribunals Committee;
8. oversee the implementation of the programme to increase judicial diversity at all levels including proposals for evaluation; and
9. oversee the provision of publications, on-line services and other reference materials for judicial use and agree allocation of the publications budget.

(b) Composition

The TJEB comprises the holders of the following judicial offices:

- Senior President of Tribunals (Chairman);
- Chamber/Pillar Presidents or their nominees
- Chairs of the judicial sub-groups (see below)
- Chair of the Tribunals Procedure Committee
- Representatives of 'cross-border' interests (respectively for Wales, Scotland, and Northern Ireland)
- Other tribunal judicial office holders by invitation of the Chair

The secretariat is provided by the SPT's office.

(c) Conduct of business

TJEB has a formal meeting every two months, except during August and September.

(d) Leadership responsibilities

Designated members of the Board will report, respectively, on matters of interest to the Board, including but not limited to:

- Tribunals Judicial Activity Group;
- Tribunals Judicial IT Group;
- diversity;
- appraisals;
- estates;
- publications;
- communications;
- judicial security; and
- training.

III THE JUDGES' COUNCIL

(a) Function

The primary function of Judges' Council is to be a body broadly representative of the judiciary as a whole which will inform and advise the Lord Chief Justice and the JEB. The Judges' Council:

1. is consulted to obtain a wide perspective on matters which concern more than one discrete judicial grouping;
2. considers and conveys views, ideas or concerns of the wider judicial family;
3. provides detailed analysis and consideration of specific matters on which judicial views are sought; and
4. develops policy in matters within its areas of functional responsibility.

(b) Composition

With the exception of the Chair and the JEB, all members of the Council should be selected by the judicial group which they represent.

The usual period of membership is three years (subject to terms of appointment to President or Secretary roles) with a power to extend for an additional year in specific circumstances.

The Council can co-opt members for specific purposes.

The Judges' Council comprises the following:

- Lord Chief Justice, Chair;
- other members of the JEB;
- a Justice of the Supreme Court;
- a Presiding Judge;
- a High Court Judge of the Chancery Division;
- a High Court Judge of the Family Division;
- a representative of the High Court Judges' Association;
- the President and Secretary of the Council of HM Circuit Judges;
- the President and Secretary to the Association of HM District Judges;
- a District Judge (Magistrates' Court);
- a member of the Association of High Court Masters;
- a senior tribunal judge;
- a tribunal judge;
- a member of the Magistrates' Association;
- a member of the National Bench Chairmen's Forum.

There are also three co-opted members: the senior judge who represents the Judges' Council on the European Network of Councils for the Judiciary (ENCJ); a judicial member of the Board of HMCTS; and, the liaison judge to the Judicial Council for Scotland.

The Chief Executive of the Judicial Office also attends meetings. The secretariat is provided by the Judicial Office.

(c) Conduct of business

The Judges Council meets at least 4 times a year with ad hoc meetings as necessary.

The Council has a specific statutory responsibility for appointing three members of the Judicial Appointments Commission under the Constitutional Reform Act 2005. An ad hoc committee of the Council is established when such appointments are required.

The Council does its work largely through working groups and committees. These are established as and when required but currently comprise:

- Standing Committee on Communications;
- Diversity Committee;
- European Committee;
- Judicial HR Committee;
- Library Committee;
- Resources Committee;
- Security Committee;
- Tribunals Committee;
- Wales Committee.

IV THE ALLOCATION OF DAY TO DAY RESPONSIBILITIES

This section sets out the allocation of the day to day responsibilities of the following leadership roles:

1. The Lord Chief Justice
2. The Master of the Rolls
3. The Heads of Division
4. The Senior President of Tribunals

The Lord Chief Justice

The Lord Chief Justice presides over leading cases across each jurisdiction.

As well as the responsibilities conducted through the JEB, as set out above, the LCJ is responsible for:

1. the protection of judicial independence and the cohesion of the judiciary;
2. maintaining relationships with the Parliament, the Government, specifically through regular meetings with the Lord Chancellor and other Ministers of the Crown, and the Welsh Assembly on issues that affect the judiciary as a whole;
3. representation of the judiciary with heads of other jurisdictions and judiciaries, the professions, other related bodies (such as institutions, universities, the media and individuals);
4. promoting a greater public understanding of the role of the judiciary and the administration of justice, and the international standing of the courts and common law of England and Wales;
5. appointments to and within the judiciary, including reviewing and approving the appointment of all judges below the level of the High Court, chairing or sitting on panels for the most senior appointments and appointing judges, after consulting the Lord Chancellor, to senior leadership posts;
6. swearing in new judges;
7. judicial conduct and disciplinary decisions, in consultation with the Lord Chancellor and with the support of the Judicial Conduct Investigations Office;
8. overall responsibility for the Judicial Office;
9. overall responsibility for HMCTS in conjunction with the Lord Chancellor under the Framework Agreement;
10. responsibilities as President of all the Courts of England and Wales, including responsibilities as President of the Court of Appeal Criminal Division;
11. the LCJ is assisted in the responsibilities as President of the Sentencing Council and Chairman of the Criminal Procedure Rules Committee by the Chairman of the Sentencing Council and the Deputy Chairman of the Criminal Procedure Rules Committee.

The Master of the Rolls

The Master of the Rolls (MR) is President of the Court of Appeal Civil Division and Head of Civil Justice. The MR presides over and decides on the allocation of the leading and most significant cases in the Court of Appeal Civil Division.

The MR is responsible for:

• supporting the judges of the Court of Appeal in pastoral care and career development, and overseeing their deployment;
• modernising the procedures of the Court of Appeal;
• considering and making decisions on recommendations from the Standing Committee of the Court of Appeal; and
• sitting as a member of the selection panel for new members of the Court of Appeal.

The Heads of Division

i. The President of the Queen's Bench Division

The President of the Queen's Bench Division presides over leading criminal, civil and administrative law cases in the Court of Appeal and the Divisional Court.

The President is responsible for:

- where the role rests with the LCJ, supporting the Head of Criminal Justice on the policy and operation of the criminal justice system, including maintaining relationships with other participants in the system;
- supporting the judges of the Queen's Bench Division in pastoral care and career development, and overseeing their deployment;
- overseeing the allocation of cases, and the just and timely dispatch of work, in the Administrative Court;
- the appointment of the lead judges in charge of the courts within the Queen's Bench Division;
- general consultation over the civil business of the Queen's Bench Division and with the Chancellor over the Business and Property Courts.

ii. The President of the Family Division

The President of the Family Division is Head of Family Justice. The President sits on first instance cases in the Division and presides over leading family and other cases in the Court of Appeal.

The President of the Family Division is responsible for:

- deployment of High Court Judges of the Family Division and assignment of judges to High Court family work;
- appointment of Family Division Liaison Judges;
- support for the judges of the Family Division in pastoral care and career development;
- authorisations for types of family work, e.g. public law cases, which are from time to time agreed with the Lord Chancellor, and;
- chairing the Family Procedure Rule Committee.

The PFD is also President of the Court of Protection and is supported in this leadership role by a Vice President.

iii. The Chancellor of the High Court

The Chancellor of the High Court sits on first instance cases in the Chancery Division and presides over leading Chancery and other cases in the Court of Appeal.

The Chancellor of the High Court is responsible for the:

- deployment of High Court Judges of the Chancery Division (in conjunction, where appropriate, with the President of the Queen's Bench Division, and the Vice- President of the Queen's Bench Division) and assignment of judges to High Court civil work;
- appointment of the Supervising Judges of the Business and Property Courts; and
- support for the judges of the Chancery Division in pastoral care and career development.

The Senior President of Tribunals

The Senior President of Tribunals (SPT) is the judicial leader of the unified tribunals across the United Kingdom. The office of Senior President is a distinct from that of any other leadership judge. In carrying out the functions of that office, the SPT is not subject to the direction of any other judicial office holder.

The SPT's responsibilities are derived from the Tribunals Courts and Enforcement Act 2007, and broadly mirror the core leadership functions vested in the Lord Chief Justice (E&W) in respect of the unified tribunals judiciary, including:

- identical responsibilities to those of the Lord Chief Justice (E&W) in respect of training, welfare and guidance for judicial office holders across the unified tribunals, within the envelope of resources made available by the Lord Chancellor;
- powers relating to appointments and assignments of judicial office holders;
- presiding over the Upper Tribunal and the First-tier Tribunal (including allocation of cases within them), as well as powers (exercised with the concurrence of the Lord Chancellor) in respect of the organisation of both of those tribunals into Chambers;
- powers over the allocation of work between respective Chambers (subject to consultation with the Lord Chancellor);
- responsibility for representing the views of the unified tribunals judiciary to Ministers and to Parliament, including in respect of matters of importance to the judiciary or otherwise to the administration of justice by tribunals; and
- reporting to the Lord Chancellor, at least annually, on matters relating to the work of the tribunals that the SPT or the Lord Chancellor wish to be brought to the attention of the other (such report having to be published by the Lord Chancellor)

The Senior President and the LCJ have a duty of mutual co-operation in relation to their responsibilities for the training, welfare and guidance of the judiciary. The SPT has equivalent shared duties with the Lord President of Scotland and the Lord Chief Justice of Northern Ireland also.

V ORGANISATION OF JURISDICTIONAL RESPONSIBILITIES

Criminal Justice

Under the Constitutional Reform Act 2005, the LCJ is Head of Criminal Justice. This can be delegated to a Head of Division or a judge of the Court of Appeal, subject to consultation with the LC, if the LCJ chooses.

The Head of Criminal Justice has lead responsibility for:

- criminal justice policy issues;
- rules;
- practice directions;
- overall liaison on criminal justice with the Lord Chancellor, Home Secretary and Attorney General and their respective departments, including legal aid and advocacy standards relating to criminal justice;
- the development of substantive criminal law and criminal procedure; and
- certain appointments to the Criminal Procedure Rule Committee.

The Head of Criminal Justice is also responsible for:

- in conjunction with the Vice-President of the Court of Appeal (Criminal Division), the overall conduct of the business of and deployment in the Court of Appeal Criminal Division, including allocation of cases and liaison with the Registrar of Criminal Appeals, the list office and other senior staff. The day to day running of the court is carried out by the Vice-President of the Court of Appeal Criminal Division;

- authorisations for sitting in the Court of Appeal Criminal Division and for trying murder and attempted murder cases, in conjunction with the Vice-President of the Court of Appeal Criminal Division and Senior Presiding Judge respectively;
- the appointment of Resident Judges in conjunction with the JAC (for Senior Circuit Judge roles), the SPJ and Presiding Judges; and
- in conjunction with the SPJ, authorisations for criminal cases, including murder, attempted murder and serious sexual cases.

Civil Justice (except the day to day operation of the High Court)

As Head of Civil Justice, the Master of the Rolls is responsible for:

- civil justice policy issues;
- rules;
- practice directions;
- overall liaison on civil justice with the Lord Chancellor, Ministers, officials in the Ministry of Justice, the professions and institutions in the UK and internationally;
- the development of substantive civil law and procedure;
- chairing the Judicial Civil Justice Board;
- chairing the Civil Justice Council, ensuring it fulfils its statutory role in keeping the civil justice system under review and making recommendations aimed at ensuring the system is fair, accessible and efficient;
- chairing meetings of, and recommending appointments to, the Civil Procedure Rule Committee; and
- appointment of Designated Civil Judges, in conjunction with the JAC (for Senior Circuit Judge roles) and in consultation with the Deputy Head of Civil Justice, the Senior Presiding Judge and Presiding Judges.

The **Deputy Head of Civil Justice** is responsible for:

- chairing the Civil Executive Team;
- de facto chairing the Civil Procedure Rules Committee and acting as Deputy Chairman of the Civil Justice Council, with a responsibility for implementation of major Rule changes;
- oversight, in consultation with the SPJ, Presiding Judges and Designated Civil Judges, as appropriate, of civil justice operational matters in the county courts;
- leadership of civil justice reform matters, including through the HMCTS Reform programme, the implementation of the Civil Courts Structure Review, the development of new online rules and other initiatives as appropriate;
- agreeing the necessary authorisations of judges to hear civil work;
- arranging the annual conference of Designated Civil Judges; and,
- overseeing the Senior Courts Costs Office.

The Business and Property Courts

The **Chancellor of the High Court** takes day to day responsibility for the conduct of business in the Business and Property Courts of England and Wales, and in the Business and Property Courts outside the Royal Courts of Justice through the Supervising Judges of those courts.

The Chancellor is also responsible, in consultation with the President of the Queen's Bench Division, for co-ordinating the overall work of the specialist civil business heard at the Royal Courts of Justice, and jointly with the PQBD in relation to the operation of the specialist jurisdictions in the Business and Property Courts that are within the Queen's Bench Division.

The Chancellor is responsible for liaison with the Lord Chancellor and City and other institutions and bodies in relation to the business of the business and property courts and for the promotion of the international business of those courts.

Family Justice

As Head of Family Justice, the President of the Family Division is responsible for:

- family justice policy matters;
- rules;
- practice directions;
- chairing the Family Procedure Rule Committee and the Family Justice Council;
- appointment of Family Division Liaison Judges;
- appointments of Designated Family Judges, in conjunction with the JAC (for Senior Circuit Judge posts) and following consultation where necessary with the Senior Presiding Judge;
- appointments to Family Procedure Rule Committees and to Family Justice Council;
- agreeing the necessary authorisations for judges to undertake family work;
- overall supervision of the responsibilities of the Family Division Liaison Judges for the deployment of District Judges (Magistrates' Courts) when sitting in family work, in liaison with the Senior Presiding Judge and the Senior District Judge (Magistrates' Courts).

The Head of International Family Justice is responsible for:

- international family law issues arising in individual cases, including in cross-border public law (care) cases relating to children, and in international child abduction and relocation cases;
- issues arising under Brussels IIA, the 1980 Hague Convention and the 1996 Hague Convention as well as other European regulations and international conventions; and
- considering developments in European and international family law, practice and policy.

Tribunals

The Senior President of Tribunals responsibilities broadly mirror those of the Lord Chief Justice. These responsibilities are summarised above.

Other Leadership Roles

The Vice-President of the Civil Division of the Court of Appeal is responsible for:

- the business of and deployment in the Civil Division, subject to the overall supervision of the MR, and day to day liaison with the Head of the Civil Appeals Office, the list office and other senior staff;
- monitoring timely delivery of judgments in the Civil Division; and
- collating judgments where criticism is made of a judge in respect of which action needs to be taken and taking forward;
- chairing the Standing Committee of the Court of Appeal and making recommendations for change/improvement to the Master of the Rolls.

The Vice-President of the Criminal Division of the Court of Appeal is responsible for:

- the business of the Criminal Division including allocation of cases and day to day liaison with the Head of the Criminal Appeals Office, the list office and other senior staff;
- overseeing the appointment of s9 judges for the Criminal Division;
- monitoring timely delivery of judgments in the Criminal Division; and,
- collating judgments where criticism is made of a judge in respect of which action needs to be taken and taking forward.

The Vice-President of the Queen's Bench Division is responsible for:

- cross-Divisional deployment, in conjunction with the Heads of Division, to meet the needs of the business and offer a wide range of sitting options to judges of the High Court;
- such other aspects of the work of the QBD as agreed with the PQBD.

The VP also, in conjunction with the PQBD, assists with personnel and monitoring issues for High Court Judges within the Queen's Bench Division.

The **Chairman of the Judicial College** is responsible for:

- advising the LCJ and SPT on the provision and sponsorship of training; and
- providing leadership and direction to the Judicial College, including the Directors of Training.

The responsibilities of **the Senior Presiding Judge (SPJ) and the Deputy (DSPJ)** are to be shared between them, as agreed in each case with the LCJ:

- ex officio member of the Board of Her Majesty's Courts and Tribunals Service;
- day to day oversight of operational criminal justice issues, working with officials from the MoJ, HMCTS, Home Office, CPS etc;
- overall supervision of the responsibilities of the Presiding Judges (who work with the Supervising Judges of the Business and Property Courts and Family Division Liaison Judges) who are responsible on a day-to-day basis for:
  - i. deployment in and the business of the Crown Court and the county courts, including allocation of work;
  - ii. the requirements for judicial appointments below the level of the High Court, including District Judges (Magistrates' Courts);
  - iii. personnel issues for judges below the High Court;
  - iv. judicial appraisal schemes;
  - v. the work of the magistrates' courts (as set out below); and
  - vi. the Local Leadership Groups.
- liaison, at national and local level, with the Council of Circuit Judges, the Association of District Judges, the Magistrates' Association, the National Bench Chairs Forum and the Justices' Clerks Society;
- overall supervision of the responsibilities of the Senior District Judge (Magistrates' Courts) for deployment, personnel and monitoring issues for District Judges (Magistrates' Courts);
- appointment of Resident Judges, in conjunction with the JAC (for Senior Circuit Judge roles), the Head of Criminal Justice and Presiding Judges;

- in conjunction with the Head of Criminal Justice, authorisations for criminal cases, including murder and attempted murder and serious sexual offences;
- recommendations for the appointments to Boards and Committees dealing with Criminal Justice in conjunction, with President of the Queen's Bench Division; and
- ongoing liaison with the Judicial Appointments Commission on appointments-related matters.

For the duration of the HMCTS Reform Programme, leadership of judicial engagement and oversight of the programme will rest with the SPJ/DSPJ/Judge in Charge of Reform.

The **Nominated Judges**, appointed by the LCJ, advise the LCJ and the Lord Chancellor (LC) as to whether a complaint about a judge's behaviour amounts to misconduct and if it does, recommend a disciplinary sanction. Complaints are received and considered by the Judicial Conduct Investigations Office (JCIO). If there is no evidence of judicial misconduct the complaint is dismissed by officials. Where the JCIO considers that the behaviour complained of may amount to misconduct, the complaint is referred to a NJ for his or her view.

A number of roles are also filled by other judges of the **Court of Appeal and High Court**. These include but are not restricted to:

- the Deputy Chairman and High Court Judge member of the Judicial Appointments Commission;
- the judges with responsibility for IT and Modernisation/Reform;
- the judge with responsibility for international relations;
- heads of specialist courts, including the component jurisdictions of the Business and Property Courts, the Administrative Court and the Queen's Bench list.
- the judges responsible for liaison with the Legal Services Board and other regulators.

VI THE JUDICIAL OFFICE

The role of the Judicial Office is to support the Lord Chief Justice, the Judicial Executive Board, the Judges' Council and the judges exercising their leadership functions set out above.

The Chief Executive of the Judicial Office:

- provides strategic leadership for the Judicial Office, ensures the Judicial Executive Board is properly supported and that the work of the leadership judges is co-ordinated;
- provides a high-level official link to MoJ, HMCTS and other Government Departments on issues of interest to the judiciary;
- has a strategic role in providing advice and an interface on policy issues and in ensuring that decisions of the Judicial Executive Board are taken forward; and
- is responsible for the budget of the Judicial Office.

The work of the Judicial Office is organised through four teams, each headed by a Deputy Director.

The **Judicial HR Team** provides support and advice to the judges responsible for the following issues:

- judicial welfare and personnel matters;
- mentoring, career development, succession planning and diversity;
- judicial leadership, in conjunction with the Judicial College;
- liaison with the Senior Salaries Review Board and with the MoJ on judicial terms and conditions, pay etc;
- judicial appointments, in conjunction with the JAC, MoJ and HMCTS;
- magistrates' issues;
- authorisations for judicial work; and
- identifying judicial resource needs as required, particularly in relation to new initiatives.

The team is also responsible for the maintenance of judicial records (on the eHR system) and for holding and controlling access to the personal files of judges.

The Executive Director of the **Judicial College** also has oversight of the JO **International and Business Support Teams**. Working with the lead judges in each area, the role of the teams is to:

- advise on and provide high quality training for all judges across all jurisdictions, including coroners. This training should meet the induction requirements for new judges, promote continued professional development and support the implementation of new initiatives;
- support the development of international judicial relations and the delivery of training overseas;
- produce spending bids, plans and budgets for the JO and monitor performance during the year; and
- provide support on other corporate matters for the JO.

The **Jurisdictional and Private Office** teams work closely together to ensure that the Lord Chief Justice, MR, Heads of Division, SPT, SPJ and Chief Coroner are supported in all other areas. In addition, the JO HMCTS Reform Team will provide support to all JEB members for the duration of the HMCTS Reform Programme.

The teams provide assistance with:

- policy, operational, legal, strategic advice and support for the senior judges;
- secretariats for judicial governance bodies;
- deployment of judges; and
- advising on working with government, parliament and others.

The secretariats to the Civil Justice Council and Family Justice Council are provided by the MR's and PFD's private offices respectively.

The Private Office of the Lord Chief Justice supports the Lord Chief Justice as Head of the Judiciary and calls upon the expertise of the other offices when the Lord Chief Justice is dealing with the particular jurisdiction in question.

The **Head of the Judicial Conduct Investigations Office** is also responsible for oversight of the **Judicial Communications and Press Teams** and for the **Judicial Library Services Team**. Their responsibilities can be summarised as:

- advising the LCJ and LC on disciplinary matters;
- developing and advising on the policy on judicial misconduct;
- providing advice and support on press, media and internal communications issues;

- increase understanding of the judiciary's work and value;
- promoting judicial outreach to the public;
- procuring and providing books and online subscriptions for all courts and tribunals judges; and,
- managing the Royal Courts of Justice library collection.

VII ORGANISATION OF THE COURTS AND TRIBUNALS

The Crown, County, Family and Magistrates' Courts

Below the High Court, the **Presiding Judges (PJJ)**, **Family Division Liaison Judges (FDLJJ)** and **Business and Property Courts Supervising Judges (BPJJ)** have general responsibilities for the judiciary on their circuit. For the **Crown, Family and County Courts**, these include:

- Appointments: determining with the Delivery Director the requirements for the number and type of new appointments, consultation on new appointments, making, in consultation with the Delivery Director, the arrangements for the deployment of newly appointed judges; and swearing in District Judges;
- Deployment: oversight of deployment of Circuit and District judges; recommendations for authorisations and board etc appointments; assignment and release of the more serious civil and criminal cases and decisions on part- time working;
- The business of the courts: the general supervision of the Resident Judges and Designated Civil and Family Judges in the discharge of their responsibilities for the conduct of the judicial business of the Crown and county courts; and
- HR and welfare issues: arrangements for career development, mentoring, conduct, welfare matters etc.

At **Magistrates' courts** level, the PJJ, with the FDLJJ, have general responsibilities for the judiciary and magistracy on their circuit, their deployment and the business of the courts which include:

- Appointments: determining the numbers of magistrates needed; consultation on the appointments of District Judges (Magistrates' Courts) in conjunction with the Senior District Judge (Magistrates' Courts); nominating an interview panel member for the appointment of Justices' Clerks;
- Deployment: overall supervision of the business of the magistrates' courts and the work of the Magistrates' Liaison Judges; deployment of District Judges (Magistrates' Courts) in conjunction with the Senior District Judge (Magistrates' Courts); and a supervisory role in the establishment of dedicated courts and in the settlement of any disputes over listing policy; and
- The business of the courts: general supervision of the conduct of the judicial business of the magistrates' courts, including through liaison with Justices' Clerks, Legal Advisers etc.

In each of these areas, the PJJ, FDLJJ and BPJJ are supported by the Regional Support Unit. The RSUs are part of the office of the Delivery Director and its staff, accommodation and running costs are met by HMCTS. Staff are appointed and remain in the line-management chain of the Delivery Director although, on a day to day basis, they often act under the authority and instructions of the PJJ, FDLJJ and CSJJ in the discharge of the statutory responsibilities delegated to them by the Lord Chief Justice.

Resident, Designated Civil and Designated Family Judges

Each Crown Court Centre will have a Resident Judge. Designated Civil and Family Judges are appointed to oversee the work of groups of civil and family courts. The responsibilities of Resident, Designated Civil and Designated Family Judges mirror those of the PJJ, FDLJJ and CSJJ as appropriate. They are entitled to administrative support, as appropriate, which is provided by HMCTS.

The Tribunals

The two-tier tribunal system (for those tribunals operated through HMCTS) is split into Chambers. Each Chamber is headed by a President, who is supported by an office provided by HMCTS. The responsibilities of a Chamber President are:

• appointments: determining the number of judges needed for their Chamber;
• deployment;
• the business of the tribunals:
• HR and welfare issues, including investigation of conduct complaints against members of their tribunal.

Arrangements for more local judicial management and discussion

The Regional and Local Leadership Groups consider and implement locally nationally agreed principles and decisions arising from the reform programme and other policy areas.

Outside the leadership judiciary who sit on JEB, the senior judiciary in England **2.14** and Wales is comprised of the judges of the Court of Appeal and the High Court, almost all of whom will have leadership functions in respect of the first instance judiciary in the specialist courts and in the Crown Court, the County Court, and the Family Court. There are judges in charge of specialist courts and lists in London and presiding judges and their equivalent for the whole of England and Wales. The courts hierarchy is administered across seven regions which are co-terminus with the ancient Circuits (the Northern, the North Eastern, the Western, London (and) the South East, the Western, and Wales). There are two presiding judges for each circuit (and four for the South East) and each serve for four years with a period of two years where their appointments overlap. In addition, the Chief Magistrate is the Senior District Judge (Magistrates Court) responsible for leading her judges across England and Wales. Each circuit also has a Family Division Liaison Judge drawn from the Family Division (three for London and the South East), a Business and Property Supervising Judge drawn from the Chancery Division or the Queen's Bench Division, and a Queen's Bench Liaison Judge drawn from the Administrative Court of that division who supervises regional administrative court lists. The leadership of the presiding judges and the administration of justice regionally is delegated by the LCJ to the Senior Presiding Judge and her Deputy to the extent that it is not a direct responsibility of the Head of Civil Justice, the Head of Family Justice, and the Head of the Business and Property Courts. In practice, there is a significant need for collaboration and cooperation between senior leadership judges in respect of those functions that are identified in the 'organisation of the judiciary'.

2.15 The local administration of justice is in the hands of Resident Judges (RJ) in the Crown Court (the most senior of whom hold the title of honorary recorder of a major city), Designated Civil Judges (DCJ), and Designated Family Judges (DFJ). There are also regional judges who lead regional lists of the specialist courts either as Specialist Senior Circuit Judges or, for example, as the regional judge of the Court of Protection. Each has a responsibility for leading their judicial colleagues within a discrete jurisdiction under the supervision of the relevant senior judges and for dealing with the majority of day-to-day difficult problems concerning work allocation, listing, the estate, IT, welfare, guidance, liaison with the magistracy, relations with HMCTS, outreach, and informal discipline and grievance.

Types of Tribunals

2.16 The Reserved Tribunals of the UK are organized on a national basis. Some tribunals cover the whole of the UK, others Great Britain or England and Wales only and some only in one national geographic jurisdiction, most with an appellate route to the Upper Tribunal. Northern Ireland has a partially implemented devolved tribunal system within which dedicated resources including, importantly, Commissioners who are Upper Tribunal judges, sit in reserved jurisdictions. The complex organization of the tribunals which has been developed out of their different traditions of administrative decision-making, the employment jurisdiction, and party determinations such as those in property and lands, is described pictorially in Diagram 2.1.

2.17 The First-tier Tribunal comprises the Health Education and Social Care Chamber, the Immigration and Asylum Chamber, the Social Entitlement Chamber, the Tax Chamber, the Property Chamber, the War Pensions Armed Forces Compensation Chamber, and the General Regulatory Chamber. The Upper Tribunal, which is a specialist appellate superior court of record with all the powers and duties of the High Court, is grouped into four chambers: the Administrative Appeals Chamber, the Immigration and Asylum Chamber, the Tax and Chancery Chamber, and the Lands Chamber. The Upper Tribunal is a cadre of specialist judges who possess both a statutory appeals jurisdiction and the power in defined circumstances to undertake judicial review. Alongside the reserved tribunals the Employment Tribunals of England and Wales and of Scotland and the Employment Appeal Tribunal provide a Great Britain-wide specialist resource which is administered as a separate specialist jurisdiction with its own procedures and rules (known as the separate pillar).

2.18 As a general principle, the tribunals judiciary have national judicial leads—the Chamber Presidents. Each of the fourteen First-tier and Upper Tribunal Chambers is headed by the equivalent of a senior circuit judge who is the Chamber President or in the case of the Upper Tribunal a High Court judge. Depending on whether a chambers' judiciary is large or small, there will be a judicial leadership and

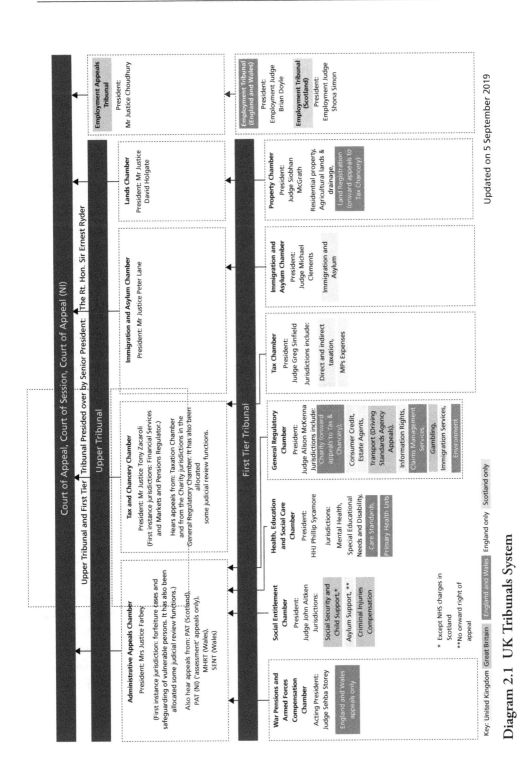

Diagram 2.1 UK Tribunals System

management structure consisting of a president with various combinations of vice presidents, deputy presidents, principal judges, regional or resident judges, and designated judges. All reserve jurisdiction tribunals in the UK including the Employment Tribunals (and Employment Appeals Tribunal (EAT)) are the responsibility of the Senior President and are represented on the TJEB.

2.19 The tribunals are known as a 'managed service'. That does not mean that leadership judges influence or interfere in the determination of individual cases but that the management of workload by the matching of supply with demand and the allocation of case load by complexity between salaried and fee paid judges and panel members is a function reserved to the leadership judiciary. The leadership judiciary are assisted in that task by jurisdictional boards which bring First-tier and Upper Tribunal jurisdictions together to consider outcome measures, priorities, and the allocation of resources. Although mirrored in some parts of the courts jurisdictions by business authorities or their equivalent, the involvement of leadership judges in the tribunals in the administration of justice is more significant. In particular, the responsibility for listing policy, judicial assignment (deployment), allocation, and both volume listing and listing of sensitive and complex cases is in the hands of the Chamber President, his nominated deputy, and/or his regional judges. An important aspect of the leadership function within the tribunals relates to the panel members, that is the body of specialist judicial office holders who sit with the legal chair in many tribunals jurisdictions and provide a part of the specialist knowledge required to administer tribunals justice. Examples of their value can be found in the specialist juries of employment panel members and in medical, disability, surveyor, and valuer members who work across a range of specialist tribunals. The identification and allocation of panel members for cases is a leadership skill which is exercised by the leadership judiciary. It is also of note that the majority of tribunals judges are fee paid which has the additional consequence that there needs to be management of a constantly changing practitioner base and their regular appraisal.

2.20 The relationship between the tribunals' leadership judiciary, their jurisdiction boards, national and regional offices, and the HMCTS regions is a relatively recent phenomenon. HMCTS provides a specialist link through its Heads of Civil, Family, and Tribunals in each region. In order for there to be effective participation by the tribunals as a national structure in a regional environment that is courts dominated, it has been necessary to appoint regional tribunal presidents and regional tribunal liaison judges to sit in regional leadership groups with the presiding judges, their equivalents from other divisions of the High Court and the most senior of the local leadership judges.

2.21 Regional leadership groups in each circuit/region are an essential collaborative arrangement to ensure that different courts and tribunals jurisdictions are adequately resourced and that the local estate, information technology support, and service support is appropriate to the many different ways in which the jurisdictions come together in buildings across the UK. At a local level, leadership judges come together in any number of different formal and ad hoc arrangements to implement reform, to discuss business as usual issues, and to liaise with cluster and operations managers in HMCTS in order to discuss strategic and long-term leadership issues with regional delivery directors and their heads of service. It is in the nature of the way that tribunals are led and managed that national jurisdictional and regional issues are brought together via jurisdiction boards and the Chamber Presidents to the Senior President and the TJEB.

Given the historic legal framework of the justice system in England and Wales and its extension into the UK for tribunals, an inherent hierarchical series of responsibilities underpins the judiciary and explicitly informs judicial leadership. Once unpicked from the web, it is plain that the indicators of judicial leadership are 'being in charge/responsible for something' and/or 'taking the lead on something'. Although these are managerial colloquia, within the judicial context this is characterized as deployment/assignment, welfare, disciplinary and grievance, supervision and mentoring, appraisal, development and training and/or liaison with those who provide or are responsible for the essential support services for the jurisdictions. Those functions find their way in to the job descriptions of the LCJ and the SPT and each leadership judge below them. These functions are the characteristics that distinguish judicial leaders from other judicial office holders. The characteristics should never be confused with the operational management of HMCTS but they are nevertheless the indicia of an operationalized judicial administration in the UK. **2.22**

All judicial office holders have duties, whether statutory or derived from their office. Those translate into core skills and abilities. Some judicial office holders undertake ancillary duties outside of the hearing of individual cases, for example in the provision of mentoring, training, or outreach. Those judicial office holders who undertake leadership duties, including the deployment and assignment of their colleagues, discipline, grievance, and welfare are the judicial leaders. **2.23**

The separation of duties and functions in this way is key to the maintenance of the critical independence of the judiciary. While all judicial office holders are stewards of the rule of law, and in particular access to justice and procedural fairness in the individual case, only judicial leaders have the power and duty to design and implement judicial policy and practice in the administration of justice. Judicial leaders must accordingly have the ability to acknowledge that, as the third limb of the state, judicial leaders are embedded in the social, political, economic, and technological contexts of society that are dynamic and constantly changing. **2.24**

1. The HMCTS regions

Each region has an HMCTS Delivery Director. The regions are divided into clusters and each cluster has a manager. RJs, DCJs, and DFJs will have more regular **2.25**

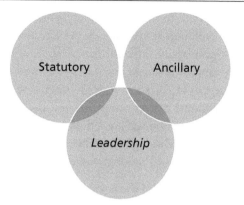

Diagram 2.2 Distinguishing between JoHs and judicial leaders
Source: Authors (2018)

contact with their cluster manager(s) than with the Delivery Director whose role tends to be strategic and financial. There are also Heads of Service for Crime and for Civil, Family, and Tribunals who advise upon and implement national HMCTS policies and who are available to assist Resident and Designated Judges just as much as the Delivery Directors and cluster managers. A cluster manager may cover an area and have responsibility for all courts (criminal, civil, and family) within the area. Alternatively, in the large conurbations a cluster manager may have responsibility just for criminal courts or a combination of civil, family, and/or tribunals. The cluster manager is responsible for the general management of the courts and tribunals within the cluster, in particular the deployment of staff and other resources within the cluster.

2.26 The local leadership judiciary of the courts and the tribunals will need to liaise regularly with the cluster manager in relation to deployment of resources with the disposition of more senior staff at his/her court(s) being of particular significance. Each court and hearing centre (or, in the case of smaller courts, group of courts) will have an operations manager. The operations manager is responsible for all day-to-day management issues. The local leadership judges will be in more or less daily contact with the operations manager. It will be through the operations manager that the leadership judges will be aware of the performance of the court or tribunal (both managerial and judicial) and will agree measures to improve outcomes and working practices. The relationship of the local leadership judge with the operations manager is central to the exercise of his/her leadership and management functions. Every court (or group of courts) will have dedicated listing officers through whom the courts' leadership judges will exercise their listing functions. The relationship of the judge to that HMCTS official is also key to his leadership and management functions. As previously explained, the leadership functions of tribunals judges include significantly greater emphasis on allocation and listing so that the importance of listing officers is, in some jurisdictions, replaced by an enhanced role for the judiciary.

2. Where next in judicial leadership?

The tripartite delineation of functions that we have briefly illustrated demon- **2.27**
strates the multi-faceted nature of the art of judging and highlights the importance of judicial leadership. More significantly, it suggests that without judicial
leadership the administration of justice would fail through a lack of coherence
both in terms of the integrity of the system, its organization, and the consistency
of the executive decisions made within it. It can of course be demonstrated that
the correlative of the powers and duties that are vested in the leadership judiciary
is the acknowledgement of their colleagues that they should participate in ancillary functions as well as their core functions so that judicial leadership becomes a
collaborative and collegiate exercise of those powers and duties.

Leadership theories and styles are of significant importance to the notion/concept **2.28**
of judicial leadership and we shall discuss this further in Chapters 4 and 5 of this
book. In the next chapter we analyse the different theoretical perspectives which
underpin leadership and evaluate their interface with judicial leadership.

3

THEORETICAL PERSPECTIVES

Judicial leaders, as with all other types of leaders, adopt leadership theories. **3.01**

Therefore, various theories on leadership exist and are propounded by numerous **3.02** theorists. However, below, are the basic frameworks universally respected which provide a platform for understanding how individuals interact within the context of organizations.

A. Theories of Leadership

1. Trait theory

Trait, or '*Great Man*' theories of leadership are premised on the assumption that **3.03** some individuals possess an inherent capacity to lead, and therefore are 'born to lead'. According to proponents of this theory, the focus was to identify the intrinsic qualities possessed by socio-political and military leaders. The emphasis of the trait theory was on the combination of charisma, confidence, intellectual dexterity, and courage which set certain individuals apart as leaders and differentiated them from followers.[1]

---

[1] B Bass, *Bass and Stogdill's Handbook of Leadership: A Survey of Theory and Research* (Free Press 1990).

3.04 Critics of the trait theory of leadership contend that it is too leader focused and does not take account of the role of the followership within the group or organization. Furthermore, it fails to consider the influence of environmental and situational factors on the level of effectiveness of a leader. To that extent, it is accepted that the trait theory provides a narrow understanding of leadership theory.[2] In terms of the judiciary, given its hierarchical nature, plainly it has leaders and followers and therefore, the trait theory is inherently applicable.

2. Situational (contingency) theories

3.05 In response to the criticisms of the trait leadership theory, there was a renewed impetus towards understanding the behaviour of leaders across different contexts and situations as opposed to their individual characteristics. This led to the emergence of behavioural leadership theories including the contingency, situational, and path-goal theories.

3.06 The contingency theory of leadership posits that there is no best way to be a leader. Instead, good leadership is contingent upon how well a leader understands the contexts within which he/she is leading and applies the appropriate leadership style. This approach opened the door to the possibility that leadership could be different in different situations. Such situational leadership theory proposes that a good leader should be able to adapt their leadership style to the demand of their situation. Therefore, depending on the demand of the situation, the leader could be either authoritarian and hands on with group members or democratic and laissez-faire.[3]

3.07 Another dimension to the contingency and situational leadership theories is whether the leadership is task oriented or relationship oriented. Task-oriented leadership focuses on establishing procedures and structures to ensure the completion of certain tasks. Task-oriented leadership tends to lean towards an autocratic style of leadership and consequently may pay less attention to the motivation of team members and followers. Relationship-oriented leaders on the other hand place more emphasis on team cohesion and bonding, prioritizing the welfare of group members and providing support to individuals to achieve desired objectives. Critics of relationship-oriented leadership argue that in the process of building relationships with group members, attention to the task at hand may be lessened. Applied to the judicial context, such a situational approach fits with a task-orientated scheme.

---

[2] P Northouse, *Leadership: Theory and Practice* (7th edn, Sage 2016).
[3] Bass (n 1).

3. Path-goal theory

Similarly, the path-goal theory, which suggests that the leadership has the pri-   **3.08**
mary responsibility of facilitating the development of certain behaviour within
the followership that will enable the achievement of desired goals, fits within
any judicial system. However, the role of the followers becomes more prominent
with the path-goal theory.[4] This leadership theory is premised on the expectancy
theory, which suggests that employees are more likely to be motivated if they
think they are capable of undertaking their roles and responsibilities with successful outcomes and commensurate payoffs. The challenge for the leader based
on this theory is to fill the behavioural gap evident within the workplace and
at the same time provide opportunities for subordinates for self-attainment and
self-actualization.[5]

4. Transformational leadership

Transformational leadership theory as defined by Burns is primarily focused on   **3.09**
leadership that shapes the motives of followers in order to reach the collective
goals of both leaders and followers.[6] Transformational leadership is deontological
in nature—as the leader pays attention to the motives of followers—since it develops a deep connection with the followership and treats them as full human be-
ings. This consequently leads to the raising of motivation and morality in both the
leader and follower.[7] The transformational leader tries to help followers achieve
high levels of self-actualization. Transformational leaders are sceptical of the status
quo and tend to innovate even when the status quo guarantees success for the
organizations they lead.[8]

Bass extended Burn's initial ideas and adapted them from the political sphere into   **3.10**
organizational settings and identifies three key attributes that transformational
leaders possess: charisma, intellectual stimulation, and individualized consideration. He argues that leaders who are able to provide these attributes within the
workplace are able to foster productivity and effective performance.[9]

Tourish is critical of the transformational leadership and argues that this theory   **3.11**
of leadership tends to be an extension of the trait theory of leadership and largely
depends on the leader influencing followers with his views and values which could

---

4 Northhouse (n 2).
5 Bass (n 1); Horner M, *Leadership Theory—Past, Present & Future* (1997).
6 J Burns, *Leadership* (Harper and Row 1978).
7 Northhouse (n 2).
8 Alice H Eagly, Mary C Johannesen-Schmidt, and Marloes L van Engen, 'Transformational,
Transactional, and laissez-Faire Leadership Styles: A Meta-Analysis Comparing Women and Men'
(2003) 129(4) Psychological Bulletin 270.
9 B Bass, 'From Transactional to Transformational Leadership: Learning to Share Vision' (1990)
18 Organizational Dynamics.

ultimately lead to catastrophic consequences. For instance, charisma, which is a key attribute of transformational leaders, is innately possessed by individuals in varying measure and is ultimately leader-centred. He contends that in adopting the transformational approach of leadership, the unintended consequence is that leaders and organizations have extended powers in increasingly intrusive directions.[10]

3.12 Yet, it is important to recognize that whilst much judicial work is considered to be transactional, transactional leadership differs from transformational leadership in the sense that the relationship between the leader and subordinates is a form of trade by barter, with both parties acting on appeals to their self-interests. Transactional leadership involves leaders 'clarifying subordinates' responsibilities, rewarding them for meeting objectives, and correcting them for failing to meet objectives'.[11] Transformational leadership tends to be reliant upon charisma and is directive in nature such that where there is good work and positive outcomes, subordinates are rewarded.[12] Conversely, a failure to meet mutually agreed upon goals leads to 'punishment' (ie discipline) until the problem is rectified. It is leadership that involves the use of corrective criticisms, negative feedbacks, and negative reinforcement to achieve a set objective. Accordingly, applied to the judicial context, transformational leadership may have its place when change management is required.

3.13 Overall, all of these theories show the multi-dimensional nature of leadership theory. Applied to judicial leadership, these theories also illustrate the complex relationship between leadership theory, culture, and organization theory. To that end, whilst judicial leaders readily engage with organizational and cultural issues, as do all judicial office holders, the core underlying responsibility of the judicial leader is to direct and supervise others to meet common goals.

B. Leadership Styles

3.14 Whilst the leadership theories evaluated above set out the hallmarks for leaders, the variant leadership styles encompass how the leader behaves. To that end, in order to reassess judicial leadership, we must not only understand the classifications, definitions, and theories, but also the variant styles adopted by judicial leaders.

---

[10] D Tourish, *The Dark Side of Transformational Leadership: A Critical Perspective* (Routledge 2013).
[11] Eagly et al (n 8) 571.
[12] J Antonakis, 'Transformational and Charismatic Leadership' in D Day and J Antonakis (eds), *The Nature of Leadership* (Sage 2012) 119–51; J Antonakis and R House, 'Instrumental Leadership: Measurement and Extension of Transformational—Transactional Leadership Theory' (2014) 25(4) The Leadership Quarterly 746.

1. Autocratic leadership

Autocratic is a classic/tactical model of 'military' style of leadership termed, 'com- **3.15**
manding', probably the most often used because the objective is very clear, such
as 'defeat the enemy', but the least effective. Autocratic management style operates
with the manager in control and issues orders because he/she feels more knowledgeable. Subordinates are given some level of flexibility in carrying out their
work, but within specific limits and procedure (Bass, 2008). The communication
in groups led by autocratic leaders is top-down and individuals are promoted on
favouritism and office politics.

2. Bureaucratic leadership

According to Bass (2008), the bureaucrat knows the rules of the institution and has **3.16**
the team abide by them. When there are rigid policies and guidelines in place, the
bureaucrat makes sure that they are maintained and used to the best of their ability.
Northouse[13] shows that leaders in organizational departments that used coercive/
directing and bureaucratic styles of leadership had low productivity. This seems to
be in line with what the author is arguing that these are routine responsibilities in a
similar organization and not effecting meaningful change for inter-agency functions.
This is an approach often related to in connection to the NHS (see Chapter 4).

3. Collaborative leadership

Collaborative leadership is about leading as a peer, not as a supervisor, to excite **3.17**
and influence a group to achieve a shared goal. 'Collaborative leadership' refers
to taking a leadership role in a coalition, organization, or other enterprise, where
everyone is on an equal footing and working together to solve a problem or create
something new. This is often the nature of the UK's Higher Education sector (see
Chapter 5). It has more benefits of money savings, increased capacity, waste is
reduced, and investment can be made once so that the wheel is not re-invented.
Collaborative leaders usually have no formal power or authority and they exercise
leadership in what is perhaps the most difficult context.

All of these styles will be applied and evaluated in relation to the judiciary in the **3.18**
following chapters.

C. Organizational Culture

Although the concept of organizational culture was popularized in the early 1980s, **3.19**
its roots can be traced back to the early human relations view of organizations that

---

[13] Northouse (n 2) 100.

originated in the 1940s. Human relations theorists viewed the informal, nonmaterial, interpersonal, and moral bases of cooperation and commitment as perhaps more important than the formal, material, and instrumental controls stressed by the rational system theorists. The human relations perspective drew its inspiration from even earlier anthropological and sociological work on culture associated with groups and societies.

3.20   To the extent that research on organizational culture survived, its focus shifted to its more measurable aspects, particularly employee attitudes and perceptions and/or observable organizational conditions thought to correspond to employee perceptions (ie the level of individual involvement, the degree of delegation, the extent of social distance as implied by status differences, and the amount of co-ordination across units). In fact, 'organizational climate' studies were prominent during the 1960s and 1970s (Denison, 1990). The renewed interest in organizational culture that emerged in the late 1970s and resulted in a deeper, more complex anthropological approach was necessary to understand crucial but largely invisible aspects of organizational life. This renewed interest in organizational culture represented a return to the early organizational literature but it went far beyond this literature in contributing important new insights and ways of thinking about the role, importance, and characteristics of organizational culture. Also, research on the effect of culture on organizational performance and investigations into how organizational cultures are created, maintained, and changed received greater attention. The main difference was that organizational culture was now viewed less as a natural, organically emergent phenomenon and more as a manipulable and manageable competitive asset.

3.21   The traditional view of organization cultures can be identified as follows:

3.22   **Power.** This culture's descriptors include centralization; individual power and decision-making; autocratic, patriarchal power; fear of punishment; and implicit rules. The values are control, stability, and loyalty.

3.23   **Bureaucracy.** This culture's descriptors include a hierarchical structure; emphasis on formal procedures and rules; clearly defined role requirements and boundaries of authority; minimized risks; impersonal and predictable work environment; employees as cogs or slots; and positions more important than people. The values include efficiency, predictability, production, and control.

3.24   **Achievement and innovation.** This culture's descriptors include an emphasis on the team, a strong belief in the mission of the organization; organized work of task requirements; worker autonomy and flexibility; decision-making pushed to lower ranks; and the promotion of cross-functional knowledge and skills. The values include creativity, adaptability, risk taking, and teamwork.

3.25   **Support.** This culture's descriptors include egalitarianism; nurturance of personal growth and development; usually non-profit organizations; a safe environment;

and a non-political workplace. The values include commitment, consensus, and growth.

Most notably, in Schein's view, fundamental assumptions constitute the core and most important aspect of organizational culture. Accordingly, he offers the following formal definition of organizational culture: **3.26**

> A pattern of shared basic assumptions that the group learned as it solved its problems of external adaptation and internal integration, that has worked well enough to be considered valid and, therefore, to be taught to new members as the correct way to perceive, think, and feel in relation to those problems.[14]

Whilst the deeper levels may have been somewhat invisible in the past, this may no longer be the case. As a result of greater attention being directed at managing culture, organizations are recognizing the importance of articulating and stressing their fundamental assumptions. This is similar to what later happens with knowledge management—greater attention becomes directed at making the tacit knowledge within an organization more explicit and accessible. This suggests a general trend towards more explicitly managing what previously was considered largely unmanageable.   **3.27**

Although all organizations have cultures, some appear to have stronger, more deeply rooted cultures than others. Initially, a strong culture was conceptualized as a coherent set of beliefs, values, assumptions, and practices embraced by most members of the organization. The emphasis was on: (1) the degree of consistency of beliefs, values, assumptions, and practice across organizational members; and (2) the pervasiveness (number) of consistent beliefs, values, assumptions, and practices. Many early proponents of organizational culture tended to assume that a strong, pervasive culture was beneficial to all organizations because it fostered motivation, commitment, identity, solidarity, and sameness, which, in turn, facilitated internal integration and coordination. Some, however, noted that a strong culture might be more important for some types of organizations than others.   **3.28**

Culture was initially seen as a means of enhancing internal integration and co-ordination, but the open system view of organizations recognized that culture is also important in mediating adaptation to the environment. The traditional view of a strong culture could be contrary to the ability of organizations to adapt and change. Seeing culture as important for facilitating organizational innovation, the acceptance of new ideas and perspectives, and needed organizational change may require a different, or more nuanced, view of organizational culture.   **3.29**

---

[14] Edgar H Schein, *Organizational Culture and Leadership* (Jossey-Bass Publishers 1992) 418 pages.

3.30 As Schein[15] affirms a strong organizational culture has generally been viewed as a conservative force. However, in contrast to the view that a strong organizational culture may be dysfunctional for contemporary business organizations that need to be change-oriented, he argues that just because a strong organizational culture is fairly stable does not mean that the organization will be resistant to change. It is possible for the content of a strong culture to be change-oriented, even if strong organizational cultures in the past were typically not. He suggests that the culture of modern organizations should be strong but limited, differentiating fundamental assumptions that are pivotal (vital to organizational survival and success) from everything else that is merely relevant (desirable but not mandatory). Today's organizations, characterized by rapidly changing environments and internal workforce diversity, need a strong organizational culture but one that is less pervasive in terms of prescribing particular norms and behavioural patterns than may have existed in the past.

3.31 Handy,[16] well known for his characterization of four dominant types of leaders as corresponding to gods of Greek mythology, distinguishes key types of organizational cultures that correspond to different organizational forms. He asserts that clearly distinguishable organizational cultures give rise to four types of leaders, which he characterizes as: Zeus, Apollo, Athena, and Dionysus. These distinct cultures (just as clan-based, hierarchy-oriented, market-based, and adhocracy-based cultures) are associated with organizations that have congruent attributes across multiple technical/functional dimensions.

3.32 In contrast to identifying distinct types of organizational cultures, there has been a growing tendency to recognize and emphasize cultural complexity (Denison et al, 1990). One approach to incorporating greater cultural complexity is to recognize that most organizations today will have some aspects of all of these cultures. This view of culture focuses on the need to balance and manage the mix. The problem with this view is that culture tends to lose any sense of coherency. It is difficult to see culture, in this sense, as providing meaning or motivating/inspiring organizational members to behave in particular ways. There is an alternative approach to cultural complexity that avoids the problem that culture will fail to provide meaning and a sense of corporate identity.

3.33 This approach moves beyond differentiating cultures in terms of technical/functional orientation (ie external versus internal orientation, stable versus change orientation, control versus individual discretion, directive versus participative, autocratic versus democratic, task-oriented versus relationship-oriented,

---

[15] ibid.
[16] C Handy, *Understanding Organisations* (4 edn, Penguin 1995).

integrative versus adaptive, same-ness versus differentiation, transactional versus transformational). Rather than seeing the role of organizational culture as balancing competing technical needs and, thus, becoming a complicated mix of cultural types, organizations are viewed as consisting of multiple, differentiated cultural orientations directed at critical ways of thinking and behaving as a member of the organization. These cultural orientations can include ways of thinking and behaving with respect to change, diversity, conflict, innovation, organizational learning, knowledge management, partnership or alliance building, relationship formation, and corporate responsibility. This cultural differentiation perspective sees cultures being developed around various critical organizational aspects rather than based on competing orientations. The key is to identify and effectively manage key cultural orientations, develop synergies between them where possible, and prevent them from conflicting with one another. Although, in many cases, these various orientations can be highly interrelated and mutually reinforcing, there is not necessarily a need for a single overarching culture that incorporates everything.

As Schein[17] suggests, organizational culture is even more important today than **3.34** it was in the past. Increased competition, globalization, mergers, acquisitions, alliances, and various workforce developments have created a greater need for coordination and integration across organizational units in order to improve efficiency, quality, and speed of designing, manufacturing, and delivering products and services.

In addition to a greater need to adapt to these external and internal changes, **3.35** organizational culture has become more important because, for an increasing number of corporations, intellectual as opposed to material assets now constitute the main source of value. Maximizing the value of employees as intellectual assets requires a culture that promotes their intellectual participation and facilitates both individual and organizational learning, new knowledge creation and application, and the willingness to share knowledge with others.

Further, Schein (1992) argues that leadership today is essentially the creation, the **3.36** management, and at times the destruction and reconstruction of culture. In fact, he says, 'the only thing of importance that leaders do is create and manage culture' and 'the unique talent of leaders is their ability to understand and work within culture'. Leaders must be able to assess how well the culture is performing and when and how it needs to be changed. Assessing and improving organizational culture as well as determining when major cultural transformations are necessary is critical to long-term organizational success. Managing differentiated cultures and creating synergies across these cultures is also a critical leadership challenge.

---

[17] Schein (n 14).

Effective culture management is also necessary to ensure that major strategic and organizational changes will succeed. Basically, culture management is a key leadership and management competency.

3.37 Therefore, critical instrumental mechanisms for changing and managing culture include:

- Strategic planning and the identification of necessarily cultural requisites;
- Ensuring consistency of culture with mission, goals, strategies, structures, and processes;
- Creating formal statements of organizational philosophy and values;
- Establishing consistent incentives, recognition systems, and performance measurement;
- Maintaining appropriate error-detection and accountability systems;
- Coaching, mentoring, informal and formal training, and identifying role models;
- Embracing appropriate rites, rituals, symbols, and narratives;
- Taking advantage of the growth of sub-cultures; and,
- Managing and promoting strong communities of practice.

3.38 Within the judicial context cultural and change management are now everyday issues. Accordingly, strategic planning is at the core of what all judicial leaders do.

D. Culture and Leadership

3.39 In the field of international business management, scholars raise the following questions:

- What does it mean by culture?
- Do people differ according to their cultural background?
- Is there any influence of cultural differences on international organizations?
- What do international managers do in a diverse culture situation?

3.40 Notably, some scholars in leaderships think that managers can be encouraged by cultural norms to put a screen over race, sex, and ethnicity and make them able to see people as only individuals and consider just their professional skills. This approach creates confusion between recognition and judgement. When a leader/manager understands that individuals with various cultural backgrounds have different conducts and because of this difference the relationship between individuals and the organization gets affected, then recognition occurs. On the other hand, usual judgement is that individuals from one culture are not naturally better or worse than the individuals from another culture since they are just different. It is an unproductive idea for an organization to ignore cultural differences. Judgments about diversity of culture can cause unacceptable, racially prejudiced, sexist, and ethnocentric ways of behaving while recognizing diversity of culture has the opposite effect.

Moreover, numerous scholars[18] claim that in an organization, prospects and wide-ranging structure for the expansion of human resources' technical and interactive skills can be provided by the help of organizational culture. This makes sense because decent behaviour is motivated by moral principles. An organizational culture can influence its employees' behaviour.   **3.41**

Organizational culture helps to keep employees consistent and make them familiar with the objectives of the organization. The impact of culture on organizational performances through human resource development programmes can be demonstrated by the giving gift certificates, vouchers, and prizes instead of paying cash for the same sort of activities. This means that organizational cultures may vary from one organization to another, but ultimately they help to develop human resources and organizational performances. Also, organizational culture may affect corporate performance by providing free medication facilities, cheap cafeteria, paid sick calls, and so on. As well as corporate culture influences human resource management (HRM) by controlling individuals' decisions and behaviour. According to Adewale and Anthonia (2013) 'culture is pervasive and operates unconsciously'.   **3.42**

Organizational culture therefore can automatically guide employees directly or/ and indirectly. Further, organizational culture plays a role like a social adhesive that ties individuals together and lets them feel part of the organization. It also satisfies people's needs for social identity; as a result employees are motivated to adopt the organization's leading culture. And at end of the day this social adhesive attracts new individuals and keeps them as the best treated staff.   **3.43**

A proper corporate culture has an excellent communication system which helps individuals to understand their responsibilities easily and promptly, particularly when they have been assigned a task so that they do not need to waste time to figure out what is expected of them. In this culture employees share a common mentality and as a result they can more proficiently cooperate and communicate with each other (Adewale and Anthonia, 2013). Finally, organizational culture has a significant effect on the recruitment and selection process of an organization. An organizational culture that achieves a good name attracts a better quality of recruits. With the help of the organizational culture new starters can more rapidly get to know about the organizations. New employees also know why their organization is different from others through the organizational culture. In a nutshell, culture has a significant influence on the overall HRM system, especially   **3.44**

---

[18] G Hofstede, *Culture's Consequences: International Differences in Work-related Values* (Sage Publications 1980).

on the recruitment and selection process, training and development events, compensation, and performance management of an organization. These norms impact upon leadership of all forms.

3.45 Judicial leadership in plain terms has to administer justice in such a way that it ensures justice is accessible to those who need it. Access to justice is an indivisible right—there can be no derogation from this. That requires its own checks and balances which we suggest can be derived from the principles that underpin the rule of law. Law must be administered through an independent judiciary and that in turn requires effective and efficient governance and more significantly, a fully-trained and equipped judiciary, led by effective judicial leaders. It is in that way that the judiciary are responsible for ensuring that our system is fit for purpose. We must do that by placing reliance on evidence-based and tested improvements to our governance of the system and the quality of our decision-making, including that judicial leaders have all the necessary skills and training. The primary duty to lead placed on the senior judiciary is a duty to lead efficiently. However, genuine leadership across the judiciary requires it to be properly informed. That is, it is open, and open to and receptive of criticism. As judicial leaders, if not leaders more generally, we make better choices when they are informed choices. One essential feature of the modernization programme is the need to develop ways to improve the leadership and management of the judiciary. If, as this book canvasses, we are to increase the extent to which judges can be deployed across jurisdictions and can have new and more flexible ways of working, the need for greater leadership and management skills within the judicial system becomes more pressing. Leadership and management, in particular of innovation, are skills that some judges need if reform and its integration into business as usual are to succeed in courts and tribunals across the UK. There is never a finishing line to the approaches we can adopt to enhance the quality of judicial decision-making in an open justice system. Having flagged the importance of open justice principles to the way judges lead, it is now convenient to describe them in greater detail.

E. Securing Open Justice

3.46 Open justice is therefore central to our justice systems. It is more than that. It is, through our courts and justice systems, of fundamental importance to democratic government. Borrowing from Woodrow Wilson, our courts are the 'balance-wheel' of our constitutions. They are 'the ultimate safeguard alike of individual privilege and of governmental prerogative'. They maintain 'political liberty', and the rule of law.[19] Without effective open justice they would not be able to be so.

---

[19] W Wilson, *Constitutional Government in the United States*, cited in HP Lee and E Campbell, *The Australian Judiciary* (2nd edn, CUP 2013) 1.

This might seem, at first glance, rather a bold claim for what many may take to **3.47** be no more than the principle of publicity common to our justice systems and articulated in article 6 of the European Convention on Human Rights. It is not a bold claim, in that sense, in so far as this book suggests that such is the importance of the principles to the administration of justice that they must inform the way in which the judiciary perform their constitutional functions, that is the way in which leadership judges secure the effectiveness of the justice system and the way in which they protect the independence of the judiciary in their individual decision-making. Open justice is not simply another way of referring to the principle of publicity. On the contrary, it encompasses three related principles; related because they depend upon each other for their general efficacy.

First, open justice incorporates the principle of equal access to a court: the con- **3.48** comitant of access to justice, a common law constitutional right in the UK.[20] Unless courts are genuinely open to all those, whether individuals, businesses, state entities, governments local and central, who need to vindicate their rights, our commitment to democratic government is at best weakened and at worst simply not made good. In the UK this point has recently and forcefully been expressed by the Supreme Court. In the case of *R (UNISON) v Lord Chancellor*, Lord Reed explained, not that it should need explanation, how without 'unimpeded access' to the courts, 'laws are liable to become a dead letter'. In turn, as he put it, that renders 'the work done by Parliament ... nugatory, and the democratic election of Members of Parliament ... a meaningless charade'.[21]

Notably, for democracy to be meaningful, the courts—justice—must be open to **3.49** all. To emphasize this in the clearest terms in our highest courts, as Lord Reed did, is a starting point. To ensure it is a reality is entirely another thing. We need only recall the pioneering work of Cappelletti and Garth to know that.[22] It is, unfortunately, a continuing truism that for large numbers of individuals and businesses the doors of our courts and tribunals remain closed; the right of access theoretical. To the extent that they are, we can say, following Lord Reed, that there is a democratic deficit. We are taking steps to remedy this problem in the UK through bold, systemic reform and digitization of our court and tribunal processes, to which we return later in this work. It is, however, particularly important that we do so for another reason. For instance, in their recent book on the continuing and possible future development of online dispute resolution, *Digital Justice*, Ethan Katsh and Orna Rabinovich-Einy[23] outline the sheer number of disputes that are

---

[20] *Attorney-General v Times Newspapers Ltd* [1974] AC 273; *Bremer Vulkan Schiffbau und Maschinenfabrik v South India Shipping Corp* [1981] AC 909, 979.
[21] [2017] UKSC 51, [2017] 3 WLR 409 [68].
[22] See, for instance, M Cappelletti, 'Alternative Dispute Resolution Processes within the Framework of the World-Wide Access-to-Justice Movement' (1993) 56 The Modern Law Review 282.
[23] E Katsh and O Rabinovich-Einy, *Digital Justice* (OUP 2017).

being resolved online by private dispute resolution services, such as those used by eBay and Amazon. The numbers are staggering: eBay, for instance, resolves 60 million disputes per year.[24] These systems are effective in the sense that they produce settlements that the parties are happy with, and they provide procedures which are intuitive, that is both intelligible and comprehensible to the user. There are serious arguments underpinning their work that our justice systems could not properly deal with the number of disputes these digital systems deal with, nor provide an equivalent user experience. At the moment, those arguments are at least likely to have some merit. There is also a persuasive argument that, from a public policy perspective, we should not encourage all such disputes to come before the courts. Peaceful, mutually agreed settlement is in the public interest, albeit that we must be astute not to diminish the rule of law by diversion. Therefore, it is one thing to accept that there is a public interest in the promotion of settlement. It is, however, quite another to accept that such disputes are not, or could not be made, capable of being brought before the courts. To accept the second proposition is to accept that we are moving towards a society where there are *digital outlaws*—individuals and businesses whose disputes are outside the law's protection and control. We would thereby improperly accept that dispute resolution should be outsourced by the state to algorithms designed to the specifications of private actors. We would be acquiescing in the privatization of justice; or to borrow from Owen Fiss, it would be 'capitulation to the conditions of [digital] society'.[25]

3.50 Therefore, if we are properly committed to open justice in the first sense outlined, we cannot accept that this is, or should be, the case. On the contrary, if we are—as Lord Browne-Wilkinson once put it—to ensure that courts and tribunals meet society's current demands for justice we cannot but configure them so that such claims are capable of being tried and adjudicated effectively.[26] If we do not, as he went on to rightly conclude, we undermine both judicial independence and the rule of law. This places a significant onus on the judiciary as an institution of state to act.[27]

3.51 Open justice's second aspect is the one with which we are all immediately familiar. It is that courts and their judgments must be open to scrutiny by the public, and the media. Followers of Bentham will know why. It is that publicity—openness—is the great antiseptic. That it is, as Bentham had it, 'the very soul of justice. The keenest spur to exertion, and the surest of all guards against improbity. It keeps the judge ..., while trying, under trial.'[28] A judge observed while judging is

---

[24] ibid 4.

[25] O Fiss, 'Against Settlement' (1984) 93 Yale LJ 1073, 1075.

[26] Lord Browne-Wilkinson, 'The Independence of the Judiciary in the 1980s' [1988] PL 44.

[27] ibid 45.

[28] J Bentham, 'Draught for the Organization of Judicial Establishment' in *The Works of Jeremy Bentham* (ed Bowring) (William Tait 1843) Vol 4, 316.

an attentive judge. A judge observed is, as Lord Neuberger MR observed in the case of *Al-Rawi*, a democratically accountable judge.[29] When justice slips out of sight, this is lost and the prospect of arbitrary, incompetent, or unlawful conduct raises its head. Again, if we simply accept the argument that private online dispute resolution is the way in which the majority of disputes, and in some areas all disputes, may be resolved in future we accept this loss of accountability; we further accept the growth of a democratic deficit. And the same is the case if we divert public justice to an unobservable online forum. Our digital courts must be open courts. Thus, open justice's third aspect again is one we are all familiar with. Open justice, through accessibly written public judgments, are the means through which the courts fulfil their role of, again if we can borrow from Owen Fiss, explicating and giving 'force to the values embodied in authoritative texts such as [our] Constitutions and statutes'.[30] They interpret, communicate, and develop our public social values. Finally, and again as most recently emphasized in the UK by Lord Reed, judgments help to provide clarity and certainty in terms of our legal framework—the framework without which the social and economic development of society would not be able to take place effectively.[31]

Moreover, open judgments create the shadow of the law within which we order **3.52** our lives. And again, linking back to both the first and second aspects of open justice, access to the courts and public scrutiny provide for the judicial process to be carried out properly and ensure that that framework can be properly challenged, articulated, and developed both through the legal process and through stimulating public, democratic debate. The importance of this latter aspect, a concept we shall call 'observational justice', should not be underestimated in the face of the tendency otherwise to irrational populism or at least populist propositions that are incapable of empirical validation. Against this background, we focus on the question of what steps the judiciary should take to secure open justice. In doing so we want to look particularly on:

• The judiciary's duty to secure open justice; and
• How that duty should be implemented.

Consequently, the judiciary has a clear, constitutional duty to secure open **3.53** justice. This is not a matter of debate. It was recognized as such by to the House of Lords in its seminal decision in *Scott v Scott* [1913] AC 417.[32] It is inherent

---

[29] *Al-Rawi v Security Services* [2010] EWCA 482, [2012] 1 AC 531, 543.
[30] Fiss (n 25) 1085.
[31] *R (UNISON) v Lord Chancellor* [2017] UKSC 51 at para 70, [2017] 3 WLR 409 at 'Every day in the courts and tribunals of this country, the names of people who brought cases in the past live on as shorthand for the legal rules and principles which their cases established. Their cases form the basis of the advice given to those whose cases are now before the courts, or who need to be advised as to the basis on which their claim might fairly be settled, or who need to be advised that their case is hopeless.'
[32] *Scott v Scott* [1913] AC 417.

in the duty placed on courts by section 6 of the Human Rights Act 1998 not to act in ways incompatible with article 6 of the Convention. It is inherent in the long-established common law constitutional principle of the rule of law, which in the UK has been explicitly recognized in statute since 2005.[33] It was affirmed by the Supreme Court in *Al-Rawi*, when the court held that the courts could not, in developing the common law, do so in a way that permitted the creation of secret hearings, ones which admitted of no public participation or accountability and contravened fundamental aspects of party participation in proceedings.[34]

3.54 Accordingly, these and other such decisions, of which there are many, affirming the constitutional right of access to justice are however focused on what the judiciary is required to do in exercising its judicial functions. It might be said that they do not provide a *basis* for the judiciary taking active steps to secure this constitutional right outside the court room. The judiciary's duty is not limited in this way. As Lord Diplock put it:

> ... in any civilised society, it is a function of government to maintain Courts of Law to which its citizens can have access for the impartial decision of disputes as to their legal rights and obligations towards one another individually and towards the State as representing society as a whole. The provision of such a system for the administration of justice by Courts of Law and the maintenance of public confidence in it, are essential if citizens are to live together in peaceful association with one another"[35]

3.55 Different countries can take different approaches to how their government carries out this duty. The way in which our constitutional settlement now operates, and has done since the Constitutional Reform Act 2005 and the Concordat between the Lord Chancellor and Lord Chief Justice (LCJ)[36] which both preceded it and was implemented by it, is one of active partnership between the executive and judiciary in running the courts.

3.56 As Professor Malleson rightly noted in evidence to the House of Lord Constitution Select Committee in 2007, the post-2005 settlement was one that envisaged 'two separate but equal branches working together to manage the courts and judiciary'.[37] As Lord Thomas, then LCJ put it in 2017, the relationship between the branches of

---

[33] Constitutional Reform Act 2005, s1.

[34] *Al-Rawi v Security Services* [2010] EWCA 482, [2012] 1 AC 531.

[35] *Attorney-General v Times Newspapers Ltd* [1974] AC 273, 307.

[36] Department of Constitutional Affairs, 'Constitutional Reform—The Lord Chancellor's Judiciary-related Functions: Proposals' (January 2004); also see the Concordat between the Ministry of Justice and the UK Supreme Court <https://www.supremecourt.uk/docs/concordat-with-ministry-of-justice-150113.pdf>.

[37] Professor K Malleson, 'The Effect of the Constitutional Reform Act 2005 on the relationship between the Judiciary, the Executive and Parliament' in House of Lords Constitution Committee, *Relations between the executive, the judiciary and Parliament* (6th Report of 2007) Appendix 3, 63 <https://publications.parliament.uk/pa/ld200607/ldselect/ldconst/151/151.pdf>.

the state is one of interdependence.[38] This interdependence—working together—is manifested in a number of ways, each of which emphasizes the active role the judiciary must play in securing the proper administration of justice, of open justice. Let us outline the specific aspects of this duty and the manner in which it is carried out in partnership with the other branches of the state.

First, as a matter of the common law it is the judiciary that exercises the court's **3.57** inherent jurisdiction to govern the court's processes. This was the historic power to issue Practice Directions governing the courts procedure and practice. It was, and remains, additional albeit subordinate to, any rules of court approved by Parliament. Today, it is a power that is usually only exercised by the senior judiciary in partnership with the executive, although its basis remains the court's common law jurisdiction.[39] This jurisdiction permits the senior judiciary to prescribe both rules in the broad sense, governing practice in the courts, but equally enables it to make provision for the effective administration of the courts.[40]

Second, the judiciary in partnership with the executive and Parliament is responsible **3.58** for the administration of the courts and tribunals. This is carried out in England and Wales by way of an express partnership between the Lord Chancellor, for the executive, and the LCJ for the courts and Senior President of Tribunals (SPT) for the tribunals.[41] The Lord Chancellor is under the specific statutory duty to provide sufficient court and tribunal buildings and staff and secure, from Parliament, sufficient funds to secure the proper administration of justice.[42] The LCJ and SPT are under statutory duties requiring them to secure the effective deployment of the judiciary; to provide effective training, guidance, and welfare provision for the judiciary; and to represent their views to the executive and Parliament.[43] In Scotland, there is no Lord Chancellor and the partnership in respect of tribunals is between the SPT and the Parliaments. The constitutional partnership in England and Wales is carried into effect by Her Majesty's Courts and Tribunals Service (HMCTS), the body which provides and runs the courts and tribunals on a day-to-day basis.[44]

---

[38] Lord Thomas CJ, 'The Judiciary within the State—The Relationship between the Branches of the State' (Michael Ryle Lecture, 15 June 2017) [18]ff <https://www.judiciary.gov.uk/wp-content/uploads/2017/06/lcj-michael-ryle-memorial-lecture-20170616.pdf>.

[39] *Bovale v Secretary of State for Communities and Local Government* [2009] EWCA Civ 171, [2009] 1 WLR 2774.

[40] *Attorney-General of the Gambia v Pierre Sarr N'Jie* [1961] AC 617, 630. A recent example would be Lord Philips CJ's Practice Direction effecting a change to judicial court dress: Practice Direction Court Dress (No 5) of 2008 <https://www.barcouncil.org.uk/media/61240/1508_court_dress_pract_dir.pdf>.

[41] HMCTS Framework Agreement (CM 882, July 2014) <https://www.gov.uk/government/uploads/system/uploads/attachment_data/file/384922/hmcts-framework-document-2014.pdf>.

[42] Courts Act 2003, ss1–3; Tribunals, Courts and Enforcement Act 2007, ss 39–41.

[43] Constitutional Reform Act 2005, ss 5, 7; Crime and Courts Act 2013, s 21; Tribunals, Courts and Enforcement Act 2007, sch 1, part 4.

[44] On the broader approach to cooperation in leadership between the LCJ and the SPT see, for instance, R Carnwath SPT, 'Justice in a Cold Climate' (17 November 2010) <http://webarchive.nationalarchives.gov.uk/20131203071215/http://www.judiciary.gov.uk/Resources/JCO/

3.59 Finally, the Lord Chancellor, LCJ, and SPT have joint and several responsibility for the appointment of judges, for promoting diversity within the judiciary, and judicial discipline.[45] Equal access to justice cannot but mean that the judiciary is not a cloistered profession, but one to which any member of society can be appointed on merit. Open justice requires an open judiciary, one in which every part of our democratic societies can see they have a stake. We must therefore ensure that proper and properly open processes are in place to implement these responsibilities. Therefore, if we draw these various strands together, they demonstrate an inescapable conclusion: the judiciary cannot sit on its hands. On the contrary, it is under a wide range of specific duties, each of which in its own way requires the judiciary to secure open justice in each of its facets. As such they are aspects of a wider general duty which, as the former LCJ, Lord Thomas recently reiterated, requires judges to 'engage in the reform and modernisation of the system of the delivery of justice'.[46] To do so judges 'must be proactive in reform. They must also provide the leadership in the major changes that will soon come to legal education and legal practice consequent upon the technological revolution.' And as he noted there was nothing new in this leadership role, Lord Mansfield CJ was a vigorous leader of reform in the eighteenth century and Lord Bramwell was equally vigorous in the nineteenth century. Even if it requires the judiciary to engage to a certain degree in policy issues where the proper administration of justice is concerned, the judiciary cannot but be involved.[47]

3.60 It is all very well to note that judges have actively led reform in the past. The past is a different country. How best to implement the duty today? There are two areas in which the judiciary must act: governance and policy; and reform.

3.61 First, governance. During the course of two public lectures in 2017—examples of the judiciary communicating its views in a democratic society outside of individual judgments—Lord Thomas outlined the basic requirement: that judiciaries have both 'internal cohesion' and 'good governance'.[48] Without such structures the judiciary would not be able to carry out its duty effectively. We have flexibility to devise our own structures. Respective LCJs and SPTs have done so. It is of central importance that those structures are subject to principled review. As with any large-scale organization, systems can become outmoded or inadequate; as times

---

Documents/Speeches/spt-speech-justice-in-a-cold-climate.pdf>; Lord Chief Justice and Senior President of Tribunal's Diversity Statement, 5 October 2012 <https://www.judiciary.gov.uk/about-the-judiciary/who-are-the-judiciary/diversity/message-from-lcj-judicial-diversity/>.

[45] Constitutional Reform Act 2005, ss108, 137A, sch 14; Tribunals, Courts and Enforcement Act 2007, s 47; Equality Act 2010, ss 50–51.

[46] Lord Thomas, '*The Rule of Law, the Executive and the Judiciary*' (31st Sultan Azlan Shah Lecture, Kuala Lumpur, December 2017) [24]. See also Lord Thomas CJ, *Michael Ryle* lecture (n 37).

[47] Lord Thomas was not alone in this view, see Lord Browne-Wilkinson (n 26) 56.

[48] Lord Thomas, *Lionel Cohen lecture* at [9]. <https://www.judiciary.uk/wp-content/uploads/2017/04/lcj-speech-national-judges-college-beijing-april2017.pdf>; <http://s3-eu-west-2.amazonaws.com/lawcom-prod-storage-11jsxou24uy7q/uploads/2017/06/lcj-speech-scarman-lecture-20170626.pdf>.

change systems also must change. Two questions arise here; and these are as applicable to the UK as they are to the Administrative Office of the United States Courts or Councils of the Judiciary and their equivalents throughout Europe.

The judiciary must ask the question: is the structure in place optimal? In the **3.62** courts the Judicial Executive Board (JEB) supports the LCJ. It is comprised of the Heads of Division of the High Court and the heads of jurisdiction: criminal, civil, family, and tribunals but until recently not business and property and still not administrative law. In the tribunals, the Tribunals Judiciary Executive Board (TJEB) supports the SPT. It is constituted of the fourteen independent Presidents of First-tier and Upper Tribunals from across the UK including the Presidents of the Scottish Tribunals, the Welsh Tribunals, and the senior commissioner from Northern Ireland. Within the tribunals, correlative jurisdictions are grouped together into Chambers whose leadership is provided by Chamber Presidents and deputy Chamber Presidents and by regional leadership judges. Are these structures still appropriate today? The more the judiciary as an institution must take policy decisions further to its duty to secure open justice, does this remain the right structure? Might it need to be expanded into, as was suggested over thirty years ago by Lord Browne-Wilkinson, a more *collegiate body of judges*.[49] Should it include representatives of the legal profession and civil society among its membership? The benefits of non-executive directors are well-recognized in government, just as they are in business. Ought we not to consider drawing on those benefits to improve our governance, and through this form of engagement with wider society, our accessibility? The tribunals have recently responded to these questions by forming an Administrative Justice Council to advise both the judiciary and government which is chaired by the SPT. It is administered independently of the executive and Parliament with an academic board to advise upon governance and policy in the law, a pro-bono panel to advise on the quality of outcomes in administrative justice, and a broad council of interested organizations and independent commentators from across the administrative law community.

Secondly, is the management right? The senior judiciary in England and Wales **3.63** is very fortunate to be supported by a cadre of excellent civil servants, who form the Judicial Office. It is, in essence, a department for the judiciary in miniature. It comes under the aegis of the Ministry of Justice, but consistent with the principle of judicial independence, its members work for the judiciary and not the Lord Chancellor. Should we not also be taking steps to consider whether and in what ways we may need to reform the structure of support we receive? Is the structure right? It does not extend to the regions (which are administered as circuits by HMCTS) where the majority of leadership judges work. What might we learn from the latest management techniques? Is the training right? Do we need

---

[49] Lord Browne-Wilkinson (n 26) 56.

to ensure that all those who support the judiciary are properly familiar with the digital world? If our courts and tribunals are to be, and they will be in the future, digital by 'default and by design',[50] we all need to be properly trained and supported. If, for instance, an Executive Board is to consider properly policy decisions concerning the redesign of a jurisdiction or the support the judiciary receive, its advice must be fully informed; greater experience in the digital world will not only ensure that our advice is up-to-date, but equally it will enable those giving advice to be able to go beyond reviewing material. It will enable them to see connections, propose further developments and improvements, that would not otherwise come to light. Just as any company or industry must learn from the latest management techniques, must keep abreast of the latest technological developments and invest accordingly in them, so must the judiciary. The judiciary are practised in the incremental development of the common law which is an analogous process but we are judges, we are not historically trained in leadership and management—a point which Richard Posner has recently and interestingly written about. As he put it, 'Management skills are often not positively correlated with judicial ability.'[51] You do not have to engage in the esoteric delights of the economy of law to readily see the truth in that statement. That must change. So that in order to better enable the judiciary to discharge its governance responsibilities, we need the right structure and the right support; but that is not enough. There are also questions about transparency and accountability. First, transparency. It is important that the public can understand the role that the judiciary plays in society. That judicial independence is, in some parts, being viewed as something which is a matter of judicial self-interest is as dangerous as it is worrying. That judicial independence is not understood to exist, as it does, for the benefit of the public, for society as a whole, is a matter which needs to be combated if we are to maintain our commitment to the rule of law. It is also, however, important that society understands how the judiciary is run and organized. Transparency, in so far as it does not impair judicial independence—and that is an important caveat—will help understanding. In doing so it may also improve scrutiny. Scrutiny may well prompt debate concerning our leadership and management structures; it may point out issues that—looking at matters internally—we have missed or downplayed. It will help inform the judiciary as much as it will the public. And that of course will be of benefit to all.

3.64 Second, accountability. It is well-established that the courts and judiciary are accountable in a number of ways: appellate accountability for decisions; explanatory accountability on the part of the LCJ and SPT as leaders of our respective judiciaries in the justice system and in our respective powers to report to Parliament; remedial accountability, to ensure we lead reform; democratic accountability,

---

[50] Lord Briggs, 'Civil Courts Structure Review—Interim Report' (December 2015) 4.
[51] R Posner, *Divergent Paths—The Academy and the Judiciary* (Harvard 2016) 222.

through public procedures and judgments and through disciplinary accountability. We are accountable in many ways. As the judiciary as an institution enters
more into the policy arena, it becomes difficult not to grapple with the question
of how it is to be accountable for policy decisions. Equally, as the judiciary as an
institution works in partnership, as it does through HMCTS, the courts and tribunals service, the question has arisen as to our accountability for implementing
decisions taken by government.

Historically, the answer to the first point would have been to say that as head of **3.65**
the judiciary and a government minister, the Lord Chancellor was accountable to
Parliament for any such policy decisions. He was accountable as a minister not as
a judge, even if it was not entirely clear on what basis any particular policy was
being considered or implemented. When Lord Browne-Wilkinson considered the
creation of a college of judges to take policy decisions, that remained the answer.
It is not one available today. As the 2005 and 2007 constitutional and tribunal reforms laid the foundation for increased responsibility on the judiciary to develop
policy for the administration of the courts and justice generally, they reformed
the Lord Chancellor's role. If, as they do, the judiciary have leadership duties,
so must they have responsibilities. So must they be accountable. Accountability
must however continue to be informed by the principle of judicial independence;
it cannot undermine institutional independence. Is it perhaps time then for consideration to be given to the adoption of the US model of accountability, as operates through the Administrative Office? Is such a step perhaps more consistent
with both the changed role of the judiciary and the duty to secure open justice?

Constitutional purists may revolt at the idea that the judiciary should involve **3.66**
itself in policy decisions. They may take the view that the judiciary should not
be involved in the implementation of government-led reforms. Two points need
to be made. First, such points assume—and wrongly assume—that the judiciary,
government, and Parliament are and must be hermetically sealed away from each
other. They are not. They must and do work together. They are interdependent,
albeit they must all be careful to ensure that they do not over-reach into the
others' exclusive provinces. Developing and implementing policies concerning
the effective administration of justice do not over-reach; ensuring judges are
trained properly; ensuring judges' welfare is properly supported; ensuring judges
are deployed to the right courts and tribunals, and have the right level of support
within the financial settlement provided by the government and Parliament; ensuring that our courts and tribunals are open to the public. All these are matters
well within the judicial province. A failure to develop proper policies to secure
them would be an abdication of responsibility. Second, our constitutional settlement gives joint responsibility for the courts and tribunals to the government
and the judiciary. As it does so, it cannot but be the case that the judiciary works
in partnership with the government to effect relevant reform. The judiciary may
not, and should not, be responsible or involved in the formulation of government

policy, or legislation. That would be over-reaching. Once that policy has been established, and we must not forget both the government and Parliament are democratically accountable for policy decisions they take, partnership requires the judiciary to work with the government.

3.67 The end result, by acting in this way, is that the judiciary must however be guided by principle. It was once said by Lord Palmerston, that Britain had no permanent allies, no permanent enemies, only permanent interests.[52] The judiciary has and only has permanent interests. They are, as ought to be obvious in the light of what has already been said, to secure the effective administration of justice; or in the words of the judicial oath to 'do right to all manner of people after the laws and usages of this realm, without fear or favour, affection or ill will'. That interest is what must guide and determine any and all policy choices that the judiciary makes through its leadership and management structures.

3.68 How practical is it to apply this principle and by what means? It is suggested that the concept of 'Proportionality' is our practical guide. If that is right then the achievement of our aim can be done through an application of the approach explained by Lord Bingham in *Huang v Secretary of State for the Home Department* [2007] 2 AC 167 (at para19) and subsequently adopted by Lord Wilson in *(R) Quila v Secretary of State for the Home Department* [2012] 1 AC 621 (at para 45). As Lord Bingham put it, and adapting them for present purposes, four factors must be applied:

• First, does the policy objective further open justice?
• Secondly, are the proposed implementation measures designed to implement the objective rationally connected to it?
• Thirdly, are they no more than necessary to accomplish the objective?
• Fourthly, do they strike a fair balance between the rights of the individual and the interests of the community.

3.69 We can see that these same questions have underpinned the introduction of proportionality, and the more distributive form of justice it entails, into the civil, family, and tribunal justice systems in England and Wales through the concept of the 'overriding objective' in our procedural rules.[53] In examining our future approach to managing the justice system, to developing and implementing policies relating to it, we must adopt clear guiding principles such as these and apply them. They should be our rule of reason.

3.70 A clear statement of the judiciary's permanent interests and the test by which it carries out its duties to further those interests will not only better enable the

---

[52] For the exact quotation see D Brown, *Palmerston and the Politics of Foreign Policy—1846–1855* (Manchester University Press2002) 82.
[53] As explained by Lord Dyson MR, 'The Application of the Amendments to the Civil Procedure Rules' (2014) 33 CJQ 124.

public and the other branches of the state to understand what is done and why. It will also provide a means by which the judiciary can test its own internal structures, and it will also secure principled continuity in its long-term governance. It will ensure that governance does not wax and wane, as equity was said to do, with the length of the Lord Chancellor's—or Senior President's—foot.

The development and application of principle and up-to-date management **3.71** methods is of fundamental importance to reform. Historically reform has been the province of Royal Commissions or individual judges. Some have been advanced based on evidence. Others have not. Some have taken as their basis the idea that a judge knows best how the system operates, how it fails to meet its objectives, and what must be done. Some reforms have succeeded. Others have not. And others still simply create problems for future generations to solve—a point Professor Resnik knows only too well. As she has rightly pointed out, 'The history of procedure is a series of attempts to solve the problems created by the preceding generation's procedural reforms'.[54]

Nevertheless, we are now in a world where such an approach is, quite simply, no **3.72** longer acceptable. Reform based on the views of a single judge or group of judges, based on anecdote or impression, or even on a certain amount of evidence drawn from willing parties, can no longer be the way we approach the matter. Judges, while adept at researching the law, are not by and large trained in the skills of empirical, scientific research. They are not well-versed in dispute systems design. They do not necessarily understand or appreciate the connections, or potential connections, between the courts, the legal profession, ombuds schemes, and so on. They are not necessarily at home in the digital world, in terms of design and implementation. Sir Michael Briggs, whose excellent report is ushering in the digitization of our civil courts, is perhaps the last judge who will be in a position to carry out a detailed review of the historic type.

We are now in a new, digital world. It is one that will and does require the judi- **3.73** ciary to take a more considered approach. We cannot lead reform as an exercise in the ad hoc. In order to understand, to design, and to test reform we must engage far more than we have in the past with academia, with management experts, digital experts, with the professions, regulators, ombudspeople, and wider society. Reform must be based on proper research, robust and tested. It must consider the latest design techniques. It must be open to scrutiny, and communicated clearly and readily to the judiciary, government, Parliament, the professions, and the wider public. It must require us to consider whether our processes are sufficient to modern conditions. There is no point, for instance, being wedded to personal service of process, when we are moving to a digital world where secure service can

---

[54] J Resnik, 'Precluding Appeals' (1985) 70 Cornell LR 603, 624.

be effected at the touch of a button. Which of our processes must change, which may fall by the historical wayside? No question can be out of bounds. If we are to secure open justice, all questions must be capable of being asked and examined, but examined properly. The judiciary must therefore support, promote, and commission research. Just as the unexamined life is one not worth living,[55] the unexamined and unresearched reform may not be worth taking.

3.74 One point needs particular emphasis. At the present time, there is a lot of talk about digitizing or rebooting justice.[56] Online dispute resolution (ODR) has transformed mediation and negotiation. It is also increasingly transforming formal justice systems, as experience in Canada with its Civil Resolution Tribunal, and the UK, with the developing Online Civil Court and the development of Online Tribunals, shows. They are two examples of a more widespread phenomenon. It is, of course, essential that such developments do not undermine open justice in any of its facets. On the contrary, we must seize the opportunity they provide to make justice more open still. Digitization must make process more accessible. It must be used to make hearings more accessible. And it must be used to make judgments, which in turn must be clearer and simpler, more accessible. More importantly, digitization provides us with an opportunity to devise a new, under-developed, aspect of open justice. It is openness that comes from effective feedback. This has two aspects. First, it provides the opportunity to adopt one of the features of ODR that has made it so successful. As Barton and Bibas explain it, one of the inherent advantages of ODR as it has been developed by Colin Rule is the ability of the systems he designed, such as eBay, to learn.[57] Due to the amount of information the systems gather, they are able to discern patterns; to identify weaknesses; and consequently to redesign, implement change, and measure the efficacy of those changes. It is the ultimate in data-led reform. Digitization will, if we are sensible, provide us with the opportunity to gather data on the operation of our justice systems in ways that we have often been unable to before. It provides us with the opportunity to make our justice systems more adaptive, but again, only after proper scrutiny and discussion. Second, it provides us with the opportunity to reorient our justice systems so that they not only become more accessible, and thus more able to deliver justice, particularly for those who would otherwise be the digital outlaws we referred to at the outset. It also provides the opportunity to enable widespread, systemic problems in the application of the law to come to light. It enables us to put in place feedback loops between for instance the justice system and ombudsman and regulatory bodies. It will thus provide us with the opportunity to bring to light, and public scrutiny, widespread systemic problems with particular legal issues or areas. It will lay open to public scrutiny systemic weaknesses in the Rule of Law, providing an enhanced means to promote

---

[55] Plato, Apologia, s 38a.
[56] See, for instance, B Barton and S Bibas, *Rebooting Justice* (Encounter Books 2017).
[57] ibid 112.

public debate, to highlight how and where public values instantiated in law are not being developed as Parliament intended: to provide observational justice. It will thus increase the ability of courts and tribunals to promote the Rule of Law. The creation of such feedback loops is an implicit aspiration of our civil court and tribunal reforms.[58] We have an opportunity to broaden and deepen our commitment to open justice through digitization; we cannot let this unique opportunity slip through our fingers.

The purpose and principles upon which the courts and tribunals modernization programme in the UK is based reflect our commitment to the Rule of Law, access to justice, and open justice as distinct from price rationing or austerity management. They are these: **3.75**

> *The Purpose:* to give the administration of justice a new operating model with a sustainable and affordable infrastructure that delivers better services at lower cost and safeguards the rule of law by improving access to justice
>
> *The Objectives:*
>
> - Ensure justice is accessible to those who need it
> - Design systems around the people who use them—user friendly, intelligible and comprehensible justice
> - Create a system that is financially viable using a more cost-effective infrastructure (better and effective use of IT and new working practices)
> - Eliminate the most common causes of delay
> - Retain the UK's international standing as a world class provider of legal services and the judiciary as world leaders in the delivery of justice
> - Maintain the constitutional independence of the judiciary

The point about austerity is this: what is right, is right; what is fair, is fair; and what is just, is just. Justice has no second class: even in an age of austerity. Austerity, the product of the 2007–2008 financial crisis, provides a basis upon which we have had to scrutinize the ways in which we secure the Rule of Law and the individual's access to justice as a part of that. It provides the spur to re-think our approach from first principles and ask whether our systems and procedures are the best they can be. Our goal, our objective, remains constant. Austerity has no impact on that, nor could it properly do so. A properly functioning justice system to which citizens have effective access in order to determine and vindicate their rights is a mark of a liberal democracy committed to the Rule of Law. That is as true now as when Lord Diplock articulated the point in the famous *Bremer Vulcan*:[59] **3.76**

> *Every civilised system of government requires that the state should make available to all its citizens a means for the just and peaceful settlement of disputes between them as*

---

[58] Sir Terence Etherton MR, 'The Civil Court of the Future' (15 June 2017) [24] <https://www.judiciary.gov.uk/wp-content/uploads/2017/06/slynn-lecture-mr-civil-court-of-the-future-20170615.pdf>.
[59] *Bremer Vulcan Schiffbau und Machinenfabrik v South India Shipping Corp Ltd* [1981] AC 909, 979.

to their respective legal rights. The means provided are courts of justice to which every citizen has a constitutional right of access in the role of plaintiff to obtain the remedy which he claims to be entitled to in consequence of an alleged breach of his legal or equitable rights by some other citizen, the defendant.

3.77 Austerity is no more than an impetus to develop and realize a vision for a justice system that meets the needs of the twenty-first century and beyond. In 1912, a Chief Justice—of Wisconsin—not England and Wales, said this:

Equal justice ... has been the dream of the philosopher, the aim of the lawgiver, the endeavour of the judge, the ultimate test of every government and every civilisation.[60]

3.78 As judges must eschew politics rather than history or the law, it is apostate to consider on the question of reform the views of others. Richard Posner said this about the US Supreme Court:

... the Supreme Court is famously backward in utilizing technology, as backhandedly conceded in the Chief Justice's latest end-of-year report, in which he tries to excuse his Court's backwardness by asserting that 'federal judges are stewards of a judicial system that has served the Nation effectively for more than two centuries. Like other centuries-old institutions, court may have practices that are archaic and inefficient—and some are. But others rest on traditions that embody intangible wisdom.' I [that is Posner] can't find the wisdom, tangible or intangible, in the archaic and inefficient practices that persist in the Supreme Court, such as the placement of a spittoon beside each Justice's seat in the courtroom.[61]

3.79 In the UK we do not have anything comparable to such a practice. But the point is well made. If we are to ensure that our courts and tribunals fulfil their constitutional role, we—as judges—must ensure that they and their processes are not unexamined; that we lead reform in the light of evidence and through the proper use of expertise. Most importantly, we must ensure that we fulfil our duties and responsibilities as effectively as we can in order to secure open justice for all. That is the constitutional function of a leadership judge.

F. Relationship between Organizational Culture and Leadership

3.80 Leaders are both the architects and the product of organization culture. For instance, when individuals are looking for a new job, they try and work out if the organization works the way s/he likes to work. They look for symbols of the culture. When they start a new job, they look at whether their boss pays attention too, and even more so, the chief executive. Over time they find themselves talking about how things are done there.

---

[60] Chief Justice Winslow, cited in D Rhode, *Access to Justice* (OUP 2004) 185.
[61] Posner (n 50) 236.

Systems approaches see organizations as having 'identity': the enduring distinctive **3.81** character of the organization reflected in values, traditions, symbols, practices, and the way the organization translates/interprets its environment. Leaders shape identity, how the organization makes sense of its work and its environment, what relationships matter, what feedback counts, what information is available; and leaders' views and behaviours are shaped by the organization's norms and boundaries.

Organizations that enable collective adaptive identity are more likely to be suc- **3.82** cessful, and that identity is produced through collective sense-making, reflection, and language. The leadership role therefore is to focus organizational attention, create organizational space, and contribute to the process.

Namely, as observed previously Schein[62] (1992) identified that if leaders do shape **3.83** culture then they need to adhere to the following primary mechanisms:

- What leaders pay attention to—measure, control;
- Leaders' reaction to critical incidents;
- Resources allocation;
- Role modelling, teaching, coaching;
- Observed way of allocation of rewards and status;
- Observed criteria for recruitment, selecting, promotion, retirement, and excommunication.

If the starting point is organizational culture as the major determinant of organ- **3.84** izational effectiveness, then leadership effectiveness will be congruent with the impact leaders have on symbol, language, ideology, belief, ritual, and myth. Using a complex systems view of culture we see that systems leaders need to sustain processes that enable the system to make the most of its capacity and capability to adapt. In essence this approach requires persistent attention to identity, relationships, and information.

In this model, not only do leaders need to give their attention to the structure of **3.85** identity (rituals, language) but also to the way identity shapes how members make sense of their context, their impact, their work together. The leaders' task here is to question the underlying assumptions that shape decisions, interpretations and to persistently expand the 'lens' through which the organization interprets and makes sense of its environment and its own activities.

Next, we put these theories into practice within the context of judicial leadership. **3.86**

---

[62] Schein (n 14).

4

PRINCIPLES AND PRACTICE

The book now turns to examine leadership—putting theory into practice, as it **4.01** were, within the judicial leadership context.

Useem[1] stated that leadership is a method of making a variation which entails '. . . **4.02** changing an organization and making active choices among plausible alternatives, and depends on the development of others and mobilising them to get the job done'. However, Useem advocates two important capabilities connecting vision and strategy, they are: leading out and leading up. Leaders (ie managers, more generally) need the skill to lead out with more use of outsourcing. For example, if any manager thinks his job is only to send work downwards to subordinates then this will not be called a leading-out capability but it will be when he will also use his talent and creativity in delegating work to colleagues. And managers' leading-up aptitude is to guide their superiors, as managers are the decentralized authority of organizations, and they also should have the capacity to collect support from top to bottom.

A. Leadership Behaviours

Accordingly, leadership has many magnitudes and leadership style could be ex- **4.03** plained in many plausible ways, such as unitary, dictatorial, benevolent, consultative, bureaucratic, charismatic, abdicatorial, and participative. The style of

---

[1] M Useem, *Leading Up* (Penguin 2001).

managerial leadership towards subordinate staff and the focus of power can, conversely, be classified, broadly, within a simplified three-fold heading as follows (Mullins, 2007 & 2013):

> The *authoritarian* style is where the manager is the only person who makes the decision and has authority for determining policy, procedures for achieving goals, work tasks and relationships, control of rewards or punishments.

> The *democratic* style is where the manager shares the leadership functions with co-workers. Members of the group have an important role in any vital decision. Democratic managers give the full rights to agree or disagree with any judgment.

4.04   Accordingly, identifiable leader behaviours emerge, as follows:

> *Charismatic/value-based* leadership considers all the talents of charisma that a leader can use for inspiring, motivating others to high performance using all the gifts and they possess. It incorporates being creative, motivating, noble, honest, influential, and job oriented.

> *Team-oriented* leadership gives emphasis to team building and a common purpose among team members and it contains all the qualities which make leaders to be more combined, integrative, not malevolent, and organizationally skilled.

> *Participative* leadership is where leaders seek to involve other people in the process and engage them to make and apply decisions. This kind of leadership comprises being participative and not autocratic. This is similar to the democratic leadership style which is mentioned before.

> *Humane-oriented* leadership reflects being liberal, helpful, thoughtful, and sympathetic. Modesty and sensitivity to people is the main aspect of this type of leadership.

> *Autonomous* leadership put emphasis on independent and individualistic leadership, and this kind of leadership includes being sovereign and exceptional.

> *Self-protective* leadership refers behaviours that certify the leader's safety and security as well as the group. And it includes self-absorbed, egoistic, argumentative, and bureaucratic leadership.

4.05   Evidently, these leader behaviours can be applied to judicial leaders

4.06   Burns[2] also has given two fundamental forms of leadership for organizational culture: transactional or transformational leadership. The basis of transactional leadership is legal authority inside the organization's intrusive formation. It reflects the illumination of targets and aims, job assignment and results, and organizational remuneration and punishments. Transactional leadership pleads to the egotism of followers and is based on the association of shared reliance and a give and take process of 'I will give you this, if you do that.' Conversely, transformational leadership stimulates a higher level of followers' motivation and commitment. It appeals to elevated followers' principles and values, generating a sense of integrity, reliability, and belief. From the organizational point of view, this leadership form is about transforming the performance or fortunes of a business/organization.

---

[2] J Burns, *Leadership* (Harper and Row 1978).

There are therefore many variables which cause effectiveness of leadership in work **4.07** organizations which are indicated below (Mullins, 2007):

- The manager's characteristics such as personality, attitudes, abilities, value system;
- The type of the manager's authority and the basis of the leadership relationship;
- The subordinates' characteristics;
- The manager's affiliation with the group and the group members;
- The culture, the form, and the environment of the organization, and the organization's different stages in the progress;
- The nature of the assignments to be completed, the extent to which they are structured or routine;
- The organization's communication networking systems, use of technology, and technique of work;
- The administrations and formation of the organization;
- The type of problem and nature of the manager's decisions;
- The aspect of external environment and its control;
- The structure of the society and comfortable organization, and the psycho-somatic contract; and
- The national culture's influence.

As all the factors, apart from the national culture, which are mentioned above are **4.08** the elements of the culture where a manager is ensconced and the organizational culture where s/he adjusts their mindset, it is necessary to identify how leadership styles are affected by organizational culture, as discussed above. The latter will be evaluated below. However, as all of these styles and approaches, as well as theories, as discussed in Chapter 1, help us to understand the behaviours of leaders, within the judicial context this context will explain the responsibilities of judicial leaders.

B. The Responsibilities of Judicial Leaders

When considering the role of a judicial leader, it is important to recognize what **4.09** leaders can and cannot do. According to the Judicial College, three common pitfalls are faced by all judicial leaders. These are:

Perfect certainty about the future:

Managing expectations is a good leadership principle but is difficult in practice when the final outcome is unknown. Even the best plans with multiple contingencies still fall prey to unanticipated events/circumstances. All employees/workers, including JoHs crave certainty. The best method to manage this unpredictable situation is to acknowledge the situation and to recognise that there are always unknowns. Moreover, to enable a different kind of security regular updates and direct, unambiguous communications about what decisions will be made and when, should be issued.

'Yes' all the time:

Judicial leaders, like all leaders, are vital links between their colleagues/other JoHs and the wider organisation. It is imperative that leaders protect their colleagues from unnecessary intrusions, in order to enable them to focus on their work. Those not in leadership roles tend to look inward, not seeing the issues from the wider organisational perspective. Consequently, judicial leaders have to say 'No', exercising their good judgment about what is best for others and the organisation, as a whole.

The ending at the beginning:

This is an impossibility. Hindsight is a wonderful thing. However, the reality is that it is not always possible to know how things will look at the end.

4.10 Accordingly, within the context of judicial leadership (and leadership, more generally), the judicial leader has a responsibility to:

Involve JoHs and others in developing plans

Change can often feel as if it is done *to* us and it can be a disempowering process. Transformational leaders of change will be asking themselves '*What ways have I created for others to voice their views and make suggestions about the changes?*' Consulting with colleagues does not weaken a leader's position—it strengthens it and ensures others understand exactly what it is they have to do differently and why.

Allow colleagues/other JoHs the required support

In light of variable responses to change, judicial leaders should not expect others to leap to celebrate, but will allow time in their implementation of change for others to adjust.

Hold people accountable

Although change may be unpleasant, everyone is still required to continue with their judicial work. If necessary performance management should still be followed. Judicial leaders should be clear and make others clear, about what is acceptable behaviour at all times.

Reinforce desired outcomes/common goals

Use appropriate reward mechanisms for behaviour that supports the change.

Be visible and approachable

Leading by example is extremely important during change and others will take their cue from their judicial leader's response.

Give consistent messages

All judicial leaders need to communicate a very consistent message of change. Adopting language from judicial messages (in emails, Intranet and other forms of communication) increases clarity and reinforces the important messages.

4.11 Such best practice and inherent responsibilities mean that judicial leaders are change managers and as such have to be effective communicators. Therefore, good communication is essential to help manage people's reactions to change and ensure they come through the change curve to adjust to change. Many change initiatives can fail because leaders underestimate the time it takes for a change to establish and flourish—and often forget to plant the seeds of change in time for them to take root in the first place. Moreover, sometimes leaders can be reluctant to share information unless they have all the answers. This can stem from good intention: not wanting to cause anxiety in case things change from what we originally said. It can also come from less than good intentions: knowledge is power and sometimes leaders retain information just to feel one step ahead of others. For judicial leaders, good practice would suggest that you can never communicate too much. As a result, the Judicial College guides that there are some dysfunctional messages to avoid when communicating to other Judicial Office Holders (JoHs):

- **Bargaining**—'If you support me in this, I'll make sure you're OK.'
- **Cushioning**—'You'll be fine. It won't be as bad as you think.'
- **Unloading**—*'I'm really worried about my own role in all of this'*
- **Arguing**—'It's not my fault. You shouldn't ... You must ...'
- **Mechanizing**—'This is going to happen, just accept it and move on with your life.'
- **Over-empathy**—'This is awful for you. I feel bad for you.'

Therefore, some useful tips for communicating with JoHs and other colleagues **4.12** are given in Diagram 4.1:

Simplicity: everyone can understand it at all levels of the judiciary.

Vividness: people need to be able to see the future, not just hear it.

Relevance: everyone understands why it matters and sees how it affects them.

Repeatability: a consistent message across the judiciary.

Directional: change needs to have a direction of travel that is meaningful.

Diagram 4.1 A Judicial Leader Communications Checklist

Such responsibilities give rise to an ethical framework within which judicial **4.13** leaders operate.

4.14   Therefore, it is a paradigm of the judicial role in society that ethics informs and governs our own behaviour and practice. The ethical basis of decision-making is key to the governance of professionals who make life-changing decisions with individuals and that is of critical importance where the decision-maker is charged by their professional obligations to be the arbiter between individuals, other decision-makers, and, significantly, the state.[3] However, the parallels with both the private and public sectors are inherent.

C. Guiding Norms

4.15   It has from time immemorial been a constant of professional ethics that the individual practitioner should safeguard, by themselves upholding and demonstrating, the highest professional and social values and standards. The purpose is to maintain respect for the profession and its privilege, in whole or in part, to regulate the activities of its members, that is not to bring the profession into disrepute. All the more so when the profession is comprised of those who make decisions on behalf of society and whose independence is a constitutional norm. It has recently become good practice for bodies of judges to publish a statement of ethics or sometimes more narrowly a code of conduct to which, like most other professions and organizations, its members are expected to conform.[4] The principles which this monograph considers the familiar assertions in codes of conduct to those which we will contend are necessary to safeguard the Rule of Law.

Further, as this book evaluates, what marks out the leadership of the judiciary from other professions whose leadership training we share, for example, that provided by the medical Royal Colleges, the Royal Military Academy Sandhurst and the Defence Academy, the Police College, and the former School of Government at Sunningdale, are the principles which are derived from:

- Constitutional norms (including the position of the judiciary as the third limb of the state and the constitutional duties placed upon them to provide open justice and effective access to justice);
- The principles of the Rule of Law;[5] and
- Ethical standards.

---

[3] The judicial oath is to 'do right to all manner of people, after the laws and usages of this Realm, without fear or favour, affection or ill will'.

[4] The best example is the Scottish Judiciary's 'Statement of Principles of Judicial Ethics for the Scottish Judiciary' (December 2016) <https://www.scotland-judiciary.org.uk/Upload/Documents/StatementofPrinciplesofJudicialEthicsrevisedDecember2016.pdf> The judiciary of England and Wales has a 'Guide to Judicial Conduct' (March 2018) <https://www.judiciary.uk/wp-content/uploads/2016/07/judicial-conduct-v2018-final-2.pdf>, as does the United Kingdom Supreme Court (see 'Guide of Judicial Conduct 2009' <https://www.supremecourt.uk/docs/guide-to-judicial_conduct.pdf>).

[5] See Lord Bingham, *The Rule of Law* (Allen Lane 2010).

Although sometimes unhelpfully referred to as a component of the 'mystery of **4.16** the law', itself a relic of one genre of transcendental jurisprudential thinking, these principles have no one philosophical basis for investing them with validity and necessity. Or, to put it another way, it matters not what your personal jurisprudential philosophy may be, if judges are unable to describe and abide by the principles which are the basis for the continuing acceptance of their authority by society, they will eventually fail the 'observational justice' norms of trust and respect in their authority. They will cease to have the trust of those in society who need them and who expect them to demonstrate by the standards of fairness and good practice described in and by their judicial decisions the plural but common values that are held in society. They will fail to uphold and safeguard the Rule of Law which is the ultimate test of their effectiveness. And they will cease to be the glue that holds civil society together.

It matters not whether you hold office as the chief justice or head of jurisdiction **4.17** responsible for hundreds and in some cases thousands of JoHs[6] or are a junior leadership judge responsible for a handful of colleagues, the principles which govern the administration of justice by each of us are the same. They are so because, as was recently and rightly noted, principles of judicial ethics are, 'recognized as ensuring the independence, impartiality and integrity (the three big "I") of courts and judges, which have always been recognized as the core values in a democratic society, as reasonably expected from the judiciary'.[7] They are so because they underpin both the quality of procedural justice and of substantive justice that we deliver. Furthermore, as leadership judges, we are also responsible for the quality of the processes and outcomes that we, the judiciary, set for the administration of justice, the standards which are inherent in the office and our relationship with both the individuals who are affected by our decisions and the other branches of the state with whom we work. If the judiciary do not deliver those standards and rigorously enforce the principles that underpin them through our leadership then we take the risk that not only will our independent professional judgments be emasculated by pragmatic or political constraints, which is the commonplace of the encroachment of the state into the functions of other liberal professions, but also that the ultimate consequence will be damage to or even the loss of the constitutional independence of the judiciary which secures the Rule of Law in civil society.

In recent years it has become fashionable in parts of the academy to characterize the **4.18** leadership role of the judiciary as a function of a misguided liberal adventure into

---

[6] The SPT is responsible for over 5,500 judges and panel members who hold office throughout the UK in the Unified Tribunals and the Employment Tribunals.

[7] M Šimonis, 'The Role of Judicial Ethics in Court Administration: From Setting the Objectives to Practical Implementation' (2017) 10(1) Baltic Journal of Law & Politics 90, 94 <https://www. degruyter.com/downloadpdf/j/bjlp.2017.10.issue-1/bjlp-2017-0004/bjlp-2017-0004.pdf>.

the formulation and enforcement of policy, in particular social policy, which is, of course, a function more appropriately exercised by the legislature and the executive. It is not our purpose in this book to debate the extent to which, if at all, the judiciary should have been given or have arrogated to themselves the power that this function describes. There are strong arguments either way. Our purpose is to describe the entirely legitimate and, we would suggest, necessary leadership functions that the judiciary perform by reference to the constitutional norms and statutory duties and powers that inform them.

4.19 There are elements of a judge's leadership role that are tactical: the constitutional independence of the decision-maker weighing the merits of the legal and factual elements of an individual decision; clinical: the incremental development and implementation of good practice to meet judicially set outcome measures; organizational: the deployment, training, and development of that judiciary to meet changing needs; and strategic: the planning for and provision of a world class, independent judiciary and the processes it uses to meet the needs of society. For each judicial leader the component parts will have a greater or lesser importance but it is the constitutional significance of what we do that binds us all together in our pursuit of a common purpose: safeguarding the Rule of Law.

4.20 Change is inherent in our human existence and in that often misunderstood circumstance, there is a need for judicial leaders to understand their role as leaders of change, not only to safeguard the Rule of Law and maintain values and standards but also to develop and innovate practice in order to protect against institutional decline and promote the independence of the judiciary. The former is necessary to prevent the justice system being perceived to be out of touch with the needs and values that society wishes the justice system to satisfy and protect, that is to maintain trust and respect and the latter is necessary to guard against adverse encroachment both from those who hold power (including other limbs of the state and their agencies) and from those with a disproportionately powerful voice (including self-interested populist groups). This engages the concept of judicial independence. It is particularly important for the judiciary to have identifiably independent voices in the existing £1Bn courts and tribunals modernization programme which is not only the largest programme of its kind across Western justice systems but is also the most ambitious reform programme in England and Wales since the judicature acts of the 1870s.[8] The programme involves an agreement about principle and funding between the judiciary and the executive. The funding is scrutinized by Parliament, among others. The purpose of the programme is to give the administration of justice a new operating model with a sustainable and

---

[8] The LCJ, the Lord Chancellor, and the SPT have published a joint vision for the programme 'Transforming our Justice System' (September 2016) <https://www.judiciary.gov.uk/wp-content/uploads/2016/09/narrative.pdf> and the judiciary have published their own plan: 'Judiciary Matters'.

affordable infrastructure that delivers better services at lower cost. That process must safeguard the Rule of Law by improving access to justice. The context is austerity: an approach to reform which if not identified and resolved runs the risk of the price rationing of justice which is the antithesis of equal access to justice, one of the principles of the Rule of Law that the judiciary must be astute to uphold. The problem to be solved is the comparative decline in the effectiveness of the justice system as an institution as social attitudes to the means of delivery and communication of justice change and austerity impacts on the ability of the justice system to deliver and respond. The effects include: lengthy delays that are inimical to justice, process and language that are unintelligible to all but the specialist user, and a system that is so costly that the only solution so far has been the impairment of access to justice by the removal of funding for legal representation. The solution requires the involvement of the judiciary with the problem through their leadership judges to help find solutions which engage the principles which support the Rule of Law and that requires traditional judicial skills and experience but also leadership skills and abilities.

To that end, within this book we describe the model that we use by discussing **4.21** some of the principles that apply to the administration of justice and decision-making to illustrate that the leadership judiciary, by its independence in individual case decision-making and by the constitutional nature of its position in the state, are not compromised for example by other superficially attractive leadership concepts such as accountability (which for us would have the danger of political and financial control), transparency (in the sense of a fashionable coveting of populist power without responsibility), or efficiency (in the sense of price rationing). Each of these concepts has its place elsewhere, and even in the judiciary in discrete but important aspects of our role such as in the provision and form of performance and quality assurance, the improvement of user experience, and very importantly in the pursuit of open justice, but none in themselves are a substitute for the model of justice that we have. An attractive and powerful argument to this effect was made by Baroness Onora O'Neil, the leading academic ethicist, in her Reith Lectures in 2002.[9]

Moreover, in a common law tradition like ours where we do not have a codi- **4.22** fied constitution there are constitutional norms within which judges are permitted to make decisions which hold other decision-makers to account. The public trust them to do this for them, with them, and to them. Putting to one side the elaborate philosophical theories that underscore what we do, we use the principles of the Rule of Law to develop a structure that regulates itself and the decisions of other organs of the state despite having an obligation to respect

---

[9] Baroness Onora O'Neil, *A Question of Trust: The BBC Reith Lectures* (CUP 2002). <http://www.bbc.co.uk/radio4/features/the-reith-lectures/transcripts/2000/>.

the sovereignty of Parliament and the authority of government; as indeed, they have an equal obligation to respect the judiciary and its role.[10] In addition, we should not forget the way in which this theoretical basis helps us resolve lesser tensions such as those between fairness and bias, providence and capriciousness. The judiciary therefore supports the human endeavour of reconstructing nature by domesticating, organizing, and patterning in an ever-changing environment, using the value of fairness which brings together into practice the so-called five virtues: goodness, propriety, knowledge, ritual, and sagacity. If it needs to be said let us say it: '*values of this kind, even that of fairness, are not absolutes cast in stone; they are not dependent only on historic cultural norms but develop to reflect the changing norms of society and its different communities. For anyone who has not experienced it, a powerful example of the need for an understanding of values and the dangers of not being able to protect against powerful voices is given by German tutor judges to their new judges on appointment. The presenters quietly but with a strong emotional determination describe and illustrate the ethical collapse of the German judiciary during the Third Reich and comment upon the fact that the European Convention on Human Rights, drafted primarily by UK representatives, was in part a response to that*'.[11]

4.23 In any event, all professionals are in the business of curating and developing knowledge and using it for the benefit of others, that is in an ethical construct; but unlike an employer or even at times a government, the law depends upon the professions as experts in the received wisdom, good practice, and required conduct in your specialist fields. So, what is it that is different about the practice of the law itself? Ultimately it has to be the constitutional principle of the Rule of Law, the essence of which, as Lord Bingham put it, is that:

> … all persons and authorities within the state, whether public or private, should be bound by and entitled to the benefit of laws publicly made, taking effect (generally) in the future and publicly administered in the courts.[12]

4.24 The judge's role puts her/him in a unique position.

4.25 Yet, it must be remembered that constitutions are but words. It is in the actions of those who interpret them that their true worth and the values of any state are to be found and that is the role of the leader—be you a President, a Prime Minister, or a Chief Justice. The golden, ringing words of the United States Declaration of Independence, you will remember them, 'that all men are created equal, that they are endowed by their Creator with certain unalienable Rights, that among these are Life, Liberty and the Pursuit of Happiness. That to secure these rights,

---

[10] *R (Jackson & Ors) v Her Majesty's Attorney General* [2005] UKHL 56, [2006] 1 AC 262 [125].
[11] Puett M and Gross-Loh C, *The Path: What Chinese Philosophers Can Teach Us about the Good Life* (Simon & Schuster 2016).
[12] Lord Bingham (n 5) 8.

Governments are instituted among Men, deriving their just powers from the consent of the governed';[13] and yet for nearly a century after that was formally declared and after the adoption of the United States Constitution there remained slavery under the law in much of that country. By contrast in England and Wales, throughout the same period, without the benefit of such bold rhetoric, one of our judges, Lord Mansfield, had long since declared that no man could be a slave in England.[14]

Judges and lawyers are the first defences in this task. It is not always easy and it **4.26** sometimes requires moral courage and the willingness to risk criticism and unpopularity in various quarters which can make life uncomfortable, but judges must hold to what they know is right and not be deflected. Judges in particular are required to have great personal fortitude[15] and it can be a lonely task. The integrity of our judges must not be trimmed just to suit the times and we must not give away our umbrellas just because the sun is shining. Furthermore, in the international arena, the principles to which I am alluding were codified in 2001–2002 into a UN Declaration now known as the Bangalore Principles.[16] Those principles are independence, impartiality, integrity, propriety, equality of treatment before the law, competence, and diligence. Again, as the late Lord Bingham in his well-known treatise on the Rule of Law described, the following principles are fundamental to what we do:

- the law must be accessible and so far as possible intelligible, clear, and predictable;
- questions of legal right should ordinarily be resolved by application of the law and not the exercise of discretion;
- the laws of the land should apply equally to all, save to the extent that objective differences justify differentiation;
- ministers and public officers at all levels must exercise the powers conferred on them in good faith, fairly, for the purpose for which the powers were conferred, without exceeding the limits of such powers, and not unreasonably;
- the law must afford adequate protection of fundamental human rights;
- means must be provided for resolving, without prohibitive cost or inordinate delay, bona fide civil disputes which the parties themselves are unable to resolve;

---

[13] US Congress, 4 July 1776 <https://www.archives.gov/founding-docs/declaration-transcript>.

[14] *Somerset v Stewart* (1772) 98 ER 499.

[15] As Brooke LJ put it in *HM Attorney-General v Ebert* [2001] EWHC Admin 695, [2002] 2 All ER 789 [28], 'It is also not in dispute that Mr Ebert made many serious accusations against Neuberger J in many of the letters he wrote to him. Judges have to have broad shoulders, and the relevance of this evidence goes to the contention that Mr Ebert is now so completely obsessed by this litigation that he does not cavil about making allegations of corruption, high treason and crimes against humanity against the judge who has been handling the case with remarkable patience and sensitivity.'

[16] See The Bangalore Principles of Judicial Conduct (2002) <https://www.unodc.org/pdf/crime/corruption/judicial_group/Bangalore_principles.pdf>.

- adjudication procedures provided by the state should be fair; and
- the Rule of Law requires compliance by the state with its obligations in international law as in national law.[17]

4.27 In fact, the International Commission of Jurists in 1955 made the following declaration on the Rule of Law:

1 The State is subject to the law;

2 Governments should respect the rights of individuals under the Rule of Law and provide effective means for their enforcement;

3 Judges should be guided by the Rule of Law, protect and enforce it without fear of favour and resist any encroachment by governments or political parties in their independence as judges; and,

4 Lawyers of the world should preserve the independence of their profession, assert the rights of an individual under the Rule of Law and insist that every accused is afforded a fair trial.[18]

4.28 There are therefore four cornerstone constitutional norms which, among others, are those most frequently to be addressed by the senior judiciary:

- The judiciary is the third limb of the state with a duty to work, so far as that is consistent with their independence, collaboratively with the legislature and the executive (ie to have respect for and to be respected by the other two limbs);
- The judiciary are independent;
- There are duties to ensure effective access to justice and to deliver open justice; and
- The judiciary have a role as a civic, social institution (ie we are not only a role model but the public's perception of what we do, how we do it, and why we do it is important).

4.29 The judiciary's interdependence with other limbs of the state has been well described in the lectures of the former Lord Chief Justice (LCJ), which this book can gratefully adopt as an ample justification for the constitutional position of the LCJ and the Senior President of Tribunals (SPT) in the post-2005 Constitutional Reform Act settlement.[19] As this book has attested already, the ten pillars of independence described by Lord Hodge in his 2016 Denning lecture are an equally persuasive job description for a judiciary that must remain independent in order

---

[17] Lord Bingham (n 5) 8.

[18] International Commission of Jurists, Act of Athens, 18 June 1955, in N Marsh (ed), *The Rule of Law in a Free Society* (1955) 2 <https://www.icj.org/wp-content/uploads/1959/01/Rule-of-law-in-a-free-society-conference-report-1959-eng.pdf>.

[19] Lord Thomas CJ, 'The Judiciary within the State—Governance and Cohesion' (Lionel Cohen Lecture, May 2017) <https://www.judiciary.uk/wp-content/uploads/2017/05/lcj-lionel-cohen-lecture-2017515.pdf> and 'The Judiciary within the State—the Relationship between the Branches

to be able to safeguard the rule of law.[20] We have previously set out the judiciary's constitutional duties to ensure effective access to justice as an indivisible right and a key enabler for making other fundamental rights a reality and to deliver open justice, that is to ensure that the antiseptic effect of public scrutiny can be applied to what we do, providing as it does a form of accountability and the SPT [author] has described his own perception as a head of jurisdiction which is that in order to retain authority by trust and respect, the judiciary have an obligation, which can be described as 'observational justice', to be a civic role model as a social institution.

How then do these norms come to be delivered by the leadership judiciary?   **4.30**

D. Ethical Leadership

When putting theory into practice, critical to judicial leadership is ethical leadership. It goes without saying that integrity is the cornerstone of any judicial system, as the core foundation for the Rule of Law.   **4.31**

In the Western world, the definition of ethics dates back to Plato and Aristotle. Ethics comes from *ethos,* a Greek word meaning character, conduct, and/or customs. It is about what morals and values are found appropriate by members of society and individuals themselves. Ethics helps us decide what is right and good or wrong and bad in any given situation. With respect to leadership, ethics is about who leaders are—their character and what they do, their actions and behaviours.   **4.32**

Accordingly, 'ethical leadership' can be defined as the 'demonstration of normatively appropriate conduct through personal actions and interpersonal relationships, and the promotion of such conduct to followers through two-way communication, reinforcement, and decision-making'.[21] Ethical leadership is a relational concept in the sense that it is constructed in and through social interactions with followers. Furthermore, being an ethical leader is about being both a moral person as well as a moral leader. The 'moral person' part of ethical leadership can be viewed as the personal traits and characteristics of a leader, such as honesty, trustworthiness, and integrity and the moral nature of that leader's conduct (Treviño & Brown, 2005; Treviño et al, 2000).   **4.33**

---

of the State' (Ryle lecture, 15 June 2017) [15]ff https://www.judiciary.uk/wp-content/uploads/2017/06/lcj-michael-ryle-memorial-lecture-20170616.pdf.

Lord Hodge, 'Judicial Independence' (7 November 2016) <http://www.supremecourt.uk/docs/speech-161107.pdf>.

[20] Lord Hodge, 'Judicial Independence' (7 November 2016) <http://www.supremecourt.uk/docs/speech-161107.pdf>.

[21] F Brown, L K Treviño, and D A Harrison, *Ethical Leadership* (Elsevier 2005) .

4.34 When followers perceive leaders to be neither ethical nor unethical, they will most likely view them as ethically neutral. This perception limits leaders' potential to exert a positive influence on followers' moral behaviour, and it may even have counterproductive effects as 'employees will believe that the bottom line is the only value that should guide their decisions' (Treviño et al, 2000, p 129–30). Thus, while being a moral person in itself is insufficient to constitute ethical leadership, it is an important prerequisite for being a moral manager.

4.35 As leadership always entails a relationship between leaders and followers, it is important to focus on the leader as a 'moral manager'. Leadership is an essential feature of the ethical culture of an organization and it is the leader who is able to place ethics on the organizational agenda. Moral managers consciously attempt to foster their followers' moral behaviour by setting clear moral standards and expectations and creating ground rules for moral conduct. The notion of moral manager is founded on three concepts: role modelling through visible action, the use of rewards and discipline, and communicating about ethics and values. The emerging research suggests that ethical leaders are characterized as honest, caring, and principled individuals who make fair and balanced decisions. Ethical leaders also frequently communicate with their followers about ethics, set clear ethical standards, and use rewards and punishments to see that those standards are followed. Finally, ethical leaders are proactive role models for ethical conduct. Ethical theories fall into two broad categories: those theories related to leaders' behaviour and those related to leaders' character. For those theories related to conduct, there are two types: those that relate to leaders' conduct and their consequences and those that relate to the rules or duty that prescribe leaders' conduct (see Figure 4.1).

4.36 Those theories related to consequences are called *teleological theories* (*telos* being a Greek word for purposes or ends). These theories emphasize whether a leader's actions, behaviour, and/or conduct have positive outcomes. This means that the outcomes related to a person's behaviour establish whether the behaviour was

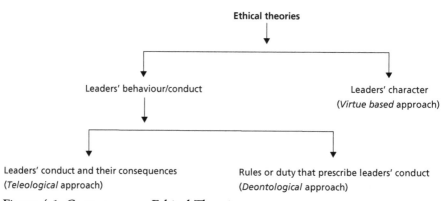

Figure 4.1 **Contemporary Ethical Theories**

ethical or unethical. Those theories related to duty or rules are called *deontological theories* (*deos* being a Greek word for duty). These theories focus on the actions that lead to consequences and whether the actions are good or bad. Those theories related to character are described as virtue-based approaches.

Teleological approaches There are three approaches to assessing outcomes and **4.37** whether they are viewed as ethical. First, *ethical egoism* describes the actions of leaders that are designed to obtain the greatest good for the leader. Second, *utilitarianism* refers to the actions of leaders that are designed to obtain the greatest good for the largest number of people. Third, *altruism* describes the actions of leaders that are designed to demonstrate concern for others' interests, even if these interests are contrary to the leader's self-interests.

Deontological approach This approach is derived from *deos,* a Greek word **4.38** meaning duty. It argues that whether or not an action is ethical depends not only on its outcome but also on whether the action, behaviour, or conduct is itself inherently good. Examples of actions and behaviours that are intrinsically good, irrespective of the outcomes, are 'telling the truth, keeping promises, being fair, and respecting others'.[22] This approach emphasizes the actions of leaders and their ethical responsibility to do what is right.

Virtue-based approach Virtue-based theories are related to leaders and who they **4.39** are and are grounded in the leader's character. In addition, these virtues can be learned and retained through experience and practice. This learning occurs in an individual's family and the various communities with which an individual interacts throughout his or her lifetime. This perspective can be traced back to Plato and Aristotle. Aristotle believed that individuals could be helped to become more virtuous and that more attention should be given to telling individuals what to be as opposed to telling them what to do. Aristotle suggested the following virtues as exemplars of an ethical person: generosity, courage, temperance, sociability, self-control, honesty, fairness, modesty, and justice. Some scholars have argued that organizational managers should learn and retain virtues 'such as perseverance, public-spiritedness, integrity, truthfulness, fidelity, benevolence, and humility'.[23]

In today's turbulent world, ethics and values are present at a number of levels for **4.40** leaders. This broader concept of ethical leadership empowers leaders to incorporate and be explicit about their own values and ethics. The following list provides a framework for developing ethical leadership. It is based on a survey and wealth of scholarly literature on the subject. Written from the perspective of the leader, these ten facets of ethical leaders offer a way to understand ethical leadership that is more complex and more useful than just a matter of 'good character and values'.

---

[22] P Northouse, *Leadership: Theory and Practice* (7th edn, Sage 2016).
[23] ibid.

4.41 Therefore, ethical leaders should have the following core characteristics:

- Articulate and embody the purpose and values of the organization;
- Focus on organizational success rather than on personal ego;
- Find the best people and develop them;
- Create a living conversation about ethics, values, and the creation of value for stakeholders;
- Create mechanisms of dissent;
- Take a charitable understanding of others' values;
- Make tough calls while being imaginative;
- Know the limits of the values and ethical principles by which they live;
- Frame actions in ethical terms;
- Connect the basic value proposition to stakeholder support and societal legitimacy.

4.42 For many years, philosophers and spiritual leaders alike have guided people on ethical ways to live and work. Even in light of the availability of this rich information and knowledge, there are untold numbers of temptations and acts of unethical and illegal behaviours within organizations, as evidenced by daily news media and governments reports. Organizations that do not participate in prevention and training programmes or ethics programmes place themselves at high risk for a substantial amount of unethical and illegal acts. To that end, it has been observed that 'individual behavior does not exist within vacuum' and emphasized the importance of each person's role to act ethically in an organization.

4.43 Five necessary elements emerge in support of ethical leadership, as follows:

- Ethical communication;
- Ethical quality;
- Ethical collaboration;
- Ethical succession planning;
- Ethical tenure.

4.44 **Ethical communication** refers to a high standard of truth set by an ethical leader. Leading by example with truthful communication is excellent, but the organization also needs to adopt truth as a primary value in a top-down approach, from board members to staff people. Leaders need to conduct investigations and review allegations of dishonesty or wrongdoing without first blaming others.

4.45 **Ethical quality** means that a leader will initiate quality throughout the organization. Three factors are important to a flourishing competitive organization: a quality product, quality customer service, and quality delivery. The organizations' leaders are responsible for implementing quality throughout every process of the organization. Leaders who are ethical know that they have an ethical obligation to the organization and community as a whole, to: (i) focus on quality of all levels; (ii) use benchmarking to denote success and failures; (iii) use innovations to heighten quality; and (iv) set standards and ways to measure every entity.

Ethical collaboration For ethical leaders to implement ethical collaboration **4.46** means that they collaborate to reduce risks at every level and ensure best practices, solve the many problems, and focus on the issues that their organization is facing. To do so, they must seek knowledgeable, trustworthy, astute, and ethical advisors within and outside their own organization as well as keep the advisors, not as a closed circle, but as an open and fluid circle. Leaders who collaborate regarding ethical practice usually make better and more ethical decisions for the good of the organization. With an ethical and wise group of advisors, ethical leaders will usually decide upon implementing plausible solutions with worthwhile and practical actions and procedures.

Ethical succession planning is a way for leaders to allow and enable other leaders **4.47** to surface within an organization so that successors have an opportunity to develop their leadership skills and exercise them. Once these leaders emerge, the existing leaders need to mentor them for future succession without fear of territorial loss. Ethical leaders realize the critical nature of having prospective leaders; that is, to have a strong leadership succession programme for the overall long-term success of the organization.

Ethical tenure Effective ethical leaders are hard to find, but when an organization **4.48** finds that leader, it must invest in that leader for the sake of the organization. The ethical tenure translates to the 'shelf life' of a leader and the length of time of success in relationship to the person's leadership, which will depend on the ethical conduct of that leader. People sometimes rate leaders more on their trustworthiness than on their talents and skills at leadership, and on their level of commitment to serve the institution and not themselves. Leaders who can subdue their ego in order to build a successful organization will have a longer tenure within that organization.

Such characteristics should not be alien to any JoHs and in particular, all judicial **4.49** leaders.

E. The Importance of Ethical Leadership to the Judiciary

More generally, ethical leadership is considered in the modern age to be im- **4.50** portant because of the outcomes it is thought to influence. Consistent with a social learning perspective, followers emulate ethical leaders' behaviour because such leaders are attractive and credible models who model normatively appropriate behaviour. In addition, ethical leaders communicate the importance of ethical standards and use the performance management system to hold employees accountable for their conduct. As a result, it is anticipated that ethical leaders will influence ethics-related conduct, such as employee decision-making and pro-social and counterproductive behaviours primarily through modelling and vicarious learning processes. In addition, ethical leaders should influence employees' positive and negative behaviour because employees will view their relationships with ethical leaders in terms of social exchange.

4.51 Accordingly, variant follower patterns emerge through the application of ethical leadership, such as:

4.52 **Follower ethical decision-making** It is important to consider whether ethical leadership can influence the ethical quality of follower decisions, particularly when the leader is not physically present. First, as attractive role models, ethical leaders are going to be an important source of ethical guidance for their employees. Ethical leaders set ethical standards and communicate them to followers. They also make decisions that take account of stakeholders' needs and that are considered to be fair and principled. The followers of ethical leaders therefore have the opportunity to observe and learn ethically appropriate decision-making. These opportunities should challenge followers' thinking, and support and encourage their own ethical decision-making. Second, prior research indicates that leader moral reasoning can influence moral reasoning in work groups. Given that ethical leaders are higher in moral reasoning they should also influence the moral reasoning of work group members, thus producing more ethical decisions. Finally, followers of an ethical leader know that the leader will be holding them accountable for their decisions and will use rewards and discipline to do so. Thus, the followers of ethical leaders should be more likely to focus on the ethical implications of their decisions and make more ethical decisions as a result.

4.53 **Employee pro-social behaviour** Ethical leadership should influence employees' pro-social or citizenship behaviour through social learning, as well as social exchange processes. Again, ethical leaders are attractive and legitimate role models who focus followers' attention on their ethical standards and their normatively appropriate behaviour. Thus, followers of ethical leaders should identify with these leaders and emulate their behaviour. Further, going beyond social learning theory, relationships between ethical leaders and their followers are likely to be characterized by social exchange rather than simple economic exchange. Transactional exchanges are contract-like and are characterized by a 'quid pro quo' logic. Social exchange relationships are less well specified and depend upon trust and norms of reciprocity. Accordingly, social exchange tends to engender feelings of personal obligation, gratitude, and trust. Therefore, the followers of ethical leaders are more likely to perceive themselves as being in social exchange relationships with their leaders because of the fair and caring treatment they receive and because of the trust they feel. As a result, they should be inclined to go above and beyond the call of duty for these leaders.

Employee counterproductive behaviour A number of terms, such as deviance, anti-   **4.54**
social behaviour, counterproductive behaviour, organizational misbehaviour, have been used to describe negative employee behaviour that is harmful to the organization or other employees. Research has shown that ethical leadership should be associated with reduced counterproductive behaviour because followers look to ethical leaders as models and emulate their ethical behaviour. Further, ethical leaders make the standards of appropriate conduct as well as the outcomes of rule violation clear. Because ethical leaders are legitimate models of ethical standards and conduct, employees should learn what is expected and be inclined to comply. Finally, given the social exchange relationship, employees are more likely to have more productive relationships with ethical leaders, as followers should wish to reciprocate the caring and fair treatment they receive and the trust in the relationship, making counterproductive behaviour less likely. Employees who have a high-quality exchange relationship with their managers are less likely to engage in negative behaviour(s).

Follower work attitudes Finally, ethical leadership should be associated with a   **4.55**
number of positive follower attitudes. A review of transformational leadership research found that leaders' high ratings on transformational leadership are associated with followers' satisfaction, commitment, and motivation. These relationships have been attributed largely to shared values[24] and the extent to which followers identify with these leaders. Transformational leaders also take care of followers through their consideration leadership style (Bass, 1985).[25] Ethical leadership therefore, it is postulated, is directly related to positive follower attitudes because of ethical leaders' honesty, trustworthiness, caring and concern for employees and other people, and their fair and principled decision-making. In support of this assertion, ethical leadership can be associated with satisfaction with the leader and with job dedication.

Given such ethical frameworks, arguably there are three leadership theories that   **4.56**
overlap the ethical leadership domain. Notably, transformational, spiritual, and authentic theories of leadership all address the moral potential of leadership in some way. Next, we delineate the connections and distinctions between these and the ethical leadership construct. Also, the relationship between authentic, transformational, and spiritual leadership has already been well documented and is beyond the scope of this monograph. Yet, below, we summarize some of the key similarities and differences between ethical leadership and these related constructs. See Diagram 4.2.

---

[24] J Burns, *Leadership* (Harper and Row 1978).
[25] B Bass, *Leadership and Performance Beyond Expectations* (Free Press 1985).

	Similarities	Differences
Authentic	Key similarities:	Key differences:
	Concern for others (Altruism)	Ethical leaders emphasize moral management (more transactional)
	Ethical decision-making	
	Integrity	Authentic leaders emphasize authenticity and self-awareness
	Role modeling	
Spiritual		
	Concern for others (Altruism)	Ethical leaders emphasize moral management
	Integrity	Spiritual leaders emphasize visioning, hope/faith; work as vocation
	Role modeling	
Transformational		
	Concern for others (Altruism)	Ethical leaders emphasize ethical
		standards, and moral management (more transactional)
	Ethical decision-making	
	Integrity	Transformational leaders
		emphasize vision, values, and
		intellectual stimulation
	Role modeling	

Diagram 4.2 Similarities and Differences between Theories of Leadership

4.57 Burns[26] proposed that transformational leadership is moral leadership because transformational leaders inspire their followers to look beyond self-interest and work together for a collective purpose. However, this seminal work sparked a debate about the ethics of transformational and charismatic leadership with scholars weighing in on both sides of the issue. Some scholars have argued that transformational leadership involved an ethical influence process, while transactional

---

[26] Burns (n 2).

leadership did not. But Bass[27] argued that transformational leaders could be ethical or unethical depending upon their motivation. Such documented research claimed that authentic transformational leaders are moral leaders because of the legitimacy of the leader's moral values (eg honesty, fairness), the leader's social motivation, and the avoidance of coercion and manipulative influence. On the other hand, pseudo-transformational leaders are more selfishly and politically motivated. Accordingly, questions about the relationship between ethics and transformational and charismatic leadership remains. However, empirical research tends to support the view that transformational leadership, at least as conceptualized and measured by Bass and Avolio (1994) describe a leader with an ethical orientation.

Authentic leaders are 'individuals who are deeply aware of how they think and behave and are perceived by others as being aware of their own and others' values/moral perspective, knowledge, and strengths; aware of the context in which they operate; and who are confident, hopeful, optimistic, resilient, and high on moral character.   **4.58**

Self-awareness, openness, transparency, and consistency are at the core of authentic leadership. In addition, being motivated by positive end values and concern for others (rather than by self-interest) is essential to authentic leadership. Authentic leaders model positive attributes such as hope, optimism, and resiliency. Finally, authentic leaders are capable of judging ambiguous ethical issues, viewing them from multiple perspectives, and aligning decisions with their own moral values. Like transformational leadership, authentic leadership appears to overlap with ethical leadership, particularly in terms of individual characteristics. Both authentic and ethical leaders share a social motivation and a consideration leadership style. Both are ethically principled leaders who consider the ethical consequences of their decisions. However, authentic leadership also contains content that is unrelated to the ethical leadership construct. Ethical leaders' care and concern for others was paramount. Whereas, spiritual leadership is comprised of 'the values, attitudes, and behaviors that are necessary to intrinsically motivate one's self and others so that they have a sense of spiritual survival through calling and membership' and is inclusive of the religious-and ethics and values-based approaches to leadership. Alternatively, spiritual leadership has also been described as: **4.59**

> *occurring when a person in a leadership position embodies spiritual values such as integrity, honesty, and humility, creating the self as an example of someone who can be trusted, relied upon, and admired. Spiritual leadership is also demonstrated through behavior, whether in individual reflective practice or in the ethical, compassionate, and respectful treatment of others.*[28]

Overall, Diagram 4.2 demonstrates that all of these types of leaders (including ethical leaders) are altruistically motivated, demonstrating a genuine caring and   **4.60**

---

[27] Bass (n 25).
[28] Reave, 2005, p. 663.

concern for people. All of them also are thought to be individuals of integrity who make ethical decisions and who become models for others. Employees are more likely to admire such leaders, identify with their vision and values, and wish to be like them. However, except for ethical leadership, none of these approaches focuses on leaders' proactive influence on the ethical/unethical conduct of followers in the context of work organizations. Ethical leaders explicitly focus attention on ethical standards through communication and accountability processes. This more 'transactional' aspect of ethical leadership is a key differentiator between ethical leadership and these related constructs. In addition, these other constructs include characteristics that are not part of the ethical leadership construct (ie visionary orientation, religious orientation, self-awareness). Thus, ethical leadership is clearly related to, but distinct from, these other leadership theories. Therefore, demonstrably ethical leadership is at the centre of judicial leadership, as observed earlier in Chapter 2.

F. The Ethics of the Judiciary

4.61   The essence of the way the common law judiciary work is of course to safeguard protections that are necessary to the Rule of Law by applying them from first principle to new factual circumstances but in a coherent, consistent way derived out of settled law. Like all declarations of right, ethical codes are commitments of principle which are vision statements combining both prospective intent and retrospective justification. Their interpretation and use must accordingly be approached with caution by any judge who is a decision-maker, whether in an individual case or as a leadership judge (and for that reason there are those who criticize Lord Bingham's summaries as going too far). For those who are not Heads of Jurisdiction, members of judicial executive boards, or sitting in the Supreme or Divisional Courts on issues of high principle, there is fortunately a clear and unarguable structure within which leadership decisions are to be made—a structure which helps preserve the separation of functions, supports the independence of the judiciary, and provides not only a legal basis for decision-making about the administration of justice but a defence to accusations of inappropriate, that is non-judicial behaviour. For the rest of the senior leadership judiciary, the same structure applies to business as usual but there is a superimposed obligation to ensure that the exercise of our obligations and responsibilities is within a system whose governance conforms to first principles, that is the leadership and administrative structures are appropriate.

4.62   The system has at its heart and at the level below broad constitutional principles a collection of statutory duties that are both bold and seminal. They now arise out of the constitutional settlement that gave rise to the Concordat in 2004 and the Constitutional Reform Act 2005. The Lord Chancellor must make the necessary arrangements for an effective and efficient system to support the carrying on of business in the courts and tribunals (by section 1 of the Courts Act 2003 and section 39(1) of the Tribunals Courts and Enforcement Act 2007). This includes the provision of staff, services, and accommodation. For the LCJ of England and Wales, section 7(2) of the Constitutional Reform Act 2005 vests responsibility in him for representing the views of his judiciary to Parliament and the executive; for maintaining arrangements for welfare, training, and guidance; and for the deployment of his judiciary and the allocation of work within courts. Section 5 of that Act empowers him to make written representations to Parliament on matters of importance relating to the judiciary and the administration of justice. For the SPT, the obligations in respect of the Tribunals' judiciary and the administration of justice are more interesting in that in addition to the duties placed on the LCJ (which are replicated for the SPT in the 2007 Act) there are duties to have regard to accessibility, fairness, speed and efficiency, the expertise of the judiciary in respect of the subject matter of their decisions, and the development of innovative dispute resolution which are described in section 2 of that Act. These duties are reflective of the user-focussed managed service that has been a hallmark of the tribunals since their inception. In addition, there are very important powers and duties relating to diversity, discipline, and appointments.

Furthermore, the obligation on the senior judiciary to make 'appropriate arrange- **4.63** ments . . . ' is an organizational function of leadership to provide effective and efficient governance that facilitates the delivery of justice in each jurisdiction through rules, practice directions, and guidance. That is the unfinished business of the 2005 constitutional settlement. The senior judiciary will have to lead and manage our functional and formal separation of powers through its own process of reform if we are to be fit for the purpose of providing the governance of the judiciary during and after the courts and tribunals modernization programme.

It is in that context that the administration of justice at the local level is governed **4.64** by the imperatives that stem from the delegation of the statutory powers and duties to which I have referred and the Rules of Court and Practice Directions. Each jurisdiction has an overriding objective in Rules of Court or their equivalent in the tribunals. There are important differences that reflect procedural fairness in the particular jurisdiction and the impact, for example, of the justice in acquitting the innocent and convicting the guilty in crime, the proportionality of costs and sanctions for non-compliance in civil, and the prescription of informality and flexibility in the tribunals where there is a duty to use the specialist expertise of the tribunal effectively. The Civil and Family Procedure Rules and the Court of Protection Rules make provision for the court to allot resources to the individual case which take account of the need to allot resources to other cases and the Criminal Procedure Rules require that cases are dealt with in ways that take into account the needs of other cases. They all require that cases are dealt with expeditiously, fairly, and in ways that are proportionate to specified criteria. Proportionality is a concept that runs through the provisions.

4.65 Further, Practice Directions and guidance build upon the powers and duties I have identified to set out how, and by reference to what, decisions are to be made. It is perhaps unsurprising that given the way in which the court's inherent power to regulate its process and decision-making has been developed over time, the requirement of judges to make decisions by reference to proportionality which will implicitly involve considerations of resource allocation reflect the present constitutional arrangement where the Lord Chancellor shares responsibility with the LCJ and the SPT under a Framework Agreement developed out of the new constitutional settlement. That necessitates the use of the rules and practice-based framework that has been developed and which must inform the leadership judge as much as the judge in the individual case. That is not to say that the rules-based leadership process is well developed, it is arguably inconsistent as between jurisdictions where the rulers differ without explanation and superficial in its attention to detail but that is where the leadership training of judges comes to the fore bringing to life the very real decisions that they have to make about resources, allocation, priorities, guidance, and HR/welfare questions, among others.

4.66 Consequently, ten principles which underpin judicial leadership have been developed and which are derived from the principles described within this text. They are intended to inform leadership training and development and help judicial leaders make decisions about policy and practice that are in accordance with principle. They are:

- Open justice
- Accountability
- Accessible justice
- Democratic participation and civic engagement
- Localism
- Proportionality, speed, and efficiency
- Diversity and inclusivity
- Specialism and expertise
- Innovation that is evidence based and tested
- Coherent governance

4.67 It is perhaps worth stressing that the judiciary is a collegiate structure derived in part from the history of our association together as professionals bound by a firm constitutional rule that no judge interferes with or comments upon the decision of another judge or the published reasoning for the decision in a case unless s/he is sitting on appeal. That engenders a collective reputation and confidence, the corollary of which is trust. Among the leadership judiciary there is an overwhelming public service ethic which is a corporate imperative to do right by all manner of people in accordance with the law. It is also right to emphasize that the role of the liberal profession of the law in supporting what the judiciary does. Almost all judges are lawyers by training and profession[29] and that informs our expectations as judges of the way represented parties will behave, but the landscape in which we work is changing. Traditional adversarial litigation where parties are legally represented remains a strong component of our tradition but the significant increase in litigants in person, less formal quasi-inquisitorial or investigative processes where the judge is far more than a referee on a playing field and has to facilitate access to justice for those without any relevant skills or abilities and digital tools that are increasingly available to parties and the court, place the individual judge in increasingly complex situations. Those situations will cause a judge to dig deep into his or her skills and abilities and that includes experience as an advocate or litigator with the benefit of the ethics of the legal professions that have been honed over the centuries. With an increasingly diverse judiciary, some of whom will not have had the benefit of sitting in a particular jurisdiction or even at all before appointment, the collegiate support of colleagues and most particularly leadership judges is acutely important. They can help a judge to navigate problems so that they are solved without interference in the independence of the judge's decision-making in the individual case, for example in the support they will give to colleagues in identifying and promoting good practice, that is the behaviours and rituals that are the practical observance of professional ethics and advanced skills that include the equality and diversity issues arising out of providing reasonable adjustments to process within hearings, guarding against unconscious bias, and understanding heuristics. Frameworks of good practice exist within every jurisdiction to give effect to statutory protections, for example, in relation to children, the vulnerable, and those who lack legal capacity or to promote active case management and proportionate dispute resolution in accordance with the overriding objective described in the Rules for each jurisdiction,[30] and leadership judges can be expected to be experts in relation to both good practice and how it should be developed.

4.68 It is helpful to say a little more about lawyers. They are members of ancient professions. Lawyers have been working in the Royal Courts since the late thirteenth century, but it was about 650 years ago that barristers first came together in four learned societies for the learning, teaching, and practice of the law. Ever since that time the 'Inns of Court' have been training those who wished to learn the law and practise as advocates in the higher courts. The four Inns of Court still retain the right to admit students to the Bar and thereby to confer on them the right to present and argue cases in the higher courts. In more recent times solicitors with higher advocacy rights have joined them. Solicitors have to much extent an equally long tradition pre-dating both the Attorneys and Solicitors Act of 1728

---

[29] The SPT is entitled to appoint judges who are not lawyers and has done so: there are surveyors who are entitled to conduct hearings without a legally qualified judge or as the chair of a panel.

[30] As discussed in E Ryder, 'The Role of the Justice System in Decision-Making For Children' (9 April 2018) [28]ff <https://www.judiciary.uk/wp-content/uploads/2018/04/spt-ryder-bapscan-april2018.pdf>.

and the incorporation of the Law Society in 1823. In Scotland the College of Justice and the Writers of the Signet hold an exclusive constitutional position derived from article 19 of the Treaty of Union 1706.

4.69   All of these bodies have governing members who are senior practitioners or judges providing a great deal of their time to the business of each learned society, particularly its role in the education and training of new lawyers, continuing education, and the development and maintenance of standards not just for the collegiate body as a whole but most particularly for their members who are thereby entitled to practise as part of a modern-day profession. Yet, the expectation of the Court and of fellow professionals sets the tone and the benchmark by which we are all judged by the public and the public's perception of the Rule of Law is fundamental to its integrity. There can be all manner of pressures on judges to do what they see as the right thing, for the wrong reason, pressures which will seek to divert them from doing right according to the law. The opinion of others not involved with the case, their family and friends, colleagues, the press and public, and government opinion. These must be resisted. It is worth remembering that in some places in the world government or administrations seek to interfere. We are fortunate that that is not a problem for us.

4.70   We ensure that the principles which underpin the rule of law are reflected in our individual cases and in the way in which we administer the justice system by articulating rules of fair procedure, consistency of practice by process, good practice by innovative change based on rational and empirical approaches to problem solving. Our process and behaviours should be empathetic to those who come voluntarily or otherwise to justice. The rules and practices contain a recognition that an aspect, some would say, a fundamental or even dominant aspect of humankind is its potential to do violence. Our adversarial process with all its protections to try and ensure fairness is a stylized contest that is ultimately violent. The winner may well be harmed but not as much or in the same way that the loser wished him to be harmed. Our inquisitorial process is a reflection on the collective will of people to protect themselves, collectively and individually—it is a security blanket—balancing the difficult issues of protection in mental health, terrorism, the protection of children, asylum seekers, the elderly, and those who are unwell, that is those who are more vulnerable than the majority in society. Our administrative process seeks to provide equality of arms in unequal situations, where the state makes a decision that affects a citizen, for example on taxation or benefits, where an employer makes a decision about an employee, or a developer seeks to influence the property rights of the individual. Like our decision-making in sensitive cases, it is an intuitive approach, the human empathy that must help resolve emotional, irrational, perverse, chaotic, or complex problems but structured by governance and informed by the principles that tend to uphold the Rule of Law. Judges take risks in solving problems but do so in a context that is informed by much more than a code of conduct.

To that extent, judicial leadership is all about maintenance of the Rule of Law. **4.71** The reliance on law as opposed to arbitrary power is the substitution of settlement by law for settlement by force—the law furthers the promotion of a civic society and the citizen's place within it. The Rule of Law is the sum total of the principles, rules, procedures, and institutions that adds up to order and stability, equality, liberty, and individual freedom. The judiciary have been given an unenviable role to be part of the leadership of society. Their role is in part dependent on the strength of other professions who jealously guard some or all of the same principles but ultimately it is our role to guard the guardians and protect our communities. The latter is an ethical imperative.

G. Corporate Social Responsibility and Leadership

In 1953, the idea of corporate social responsibility began. The reason was that **4.72** in the oil industry one shareholder asserted that humanitarian activities decrease shareholders' profits. The Supreme Court in New Jersey, in this unique situation, permitted the oil industry to donate money to Princeton University as a charitable activity. The organization cannot exist without the support of its stakeholders. These stakeholders have an effect on corporate activities and can be affected by the organization.

Groups of each of these stakeholders have their own requirements and effects **4.73** on the businesses. Every organization implements and expresses a certain set of response policies to meet these stakeholders' needs. Stakeholders play a significant role in organizational performance. For example, employees of any organization serve and provide their intellectual capabilities, skills, and knowledge for increasing sales of the organization's goods and services. Therefore, the corporate social responsibility of any organization is liable to keep a strong association with the society and environment in which it is operating. There are several theories of corporate social responsibility to follow, they are; *institutional theory, resource based view of the firm, theory of the firm, agency theory*, and *the stakeholder theory*.

For example, corporate social responsibility can be described as an idea which in- **4.74** cludes all the actions of value chain process and its impact on the society, economy, and natural environment and which cares for its stakeholders. In the business world corporate social responsibility has no generally accepted definition, however different researchers have conducted research on its multiple characteristics stated that corporate social responsibility is the organizations' constant arrangement to provide morally and sustainable effort towards economy and society for the improvement of their employees and their families and local connection.

Three characteristics of corporate social responsibility have been described by **4.75** Sethi (1975) they are; 'social obligation, responsibility and responsiveness'. Social obligation includes legitimate and market-focused behaviour and refers to the execution of legal obligations. It is also a marketing instrument whilst the organization is making profit. Social responsibility indicates the organizational behaviour for the social benefit to fulfil society's anticipations and requirements. Social responsiveness indicates organizational active and protective actions to meet the demands of the society. Carroll (1991) proposed a model which includes four dimensions of corporate social responsibility to reflect the society's expectations.

4.76 These dimensions are, *economic responsibility, ethical responsibility, social responsibility*, and *philanthropic responsibility*. Economic responsibility involves revenue and profits of the organization, while ethical responsibility includes fairness, justice, decent and ethical activities of the organization. Social responsibility describes the organization's respect for the social rules and regulations. Also, philanthropic responsibility involves charity and voluntarily performances of the businesses. Carroll also opined that organizations may not have enough resources or there might be a lack of awareness on the part of organizations to perform these responsibilities properly. For that reason, Carroll later suggested a pyramid model to describe the four responsibilities and prioritized them according to the fundamental needs of the organization. Therefore, as Carroll asserted 'economic responsibility' is also indicated as key element of the pyramid because it is recognized as the organization's primary, need followed by ethical, legal, and philanthropic respectively (Carroll, 1991). Corporate social responsibility however can be subject to principles, processes, and outcomes of the organization. In particular, Wood describes principles in three sub forms—social legitimacy refers to institutional principle, public responsibility refers to organizational principle, and managerial responsibility as an individual principle. The main focus of processes is on the organizational behaviour, that is how it behaves when the organization experiences social pressure to consider environmental issues. Further, there can be two dimensions to corporate social responsibility, in terms of the span—narrow to wide—and the varieties of outcome of corporate social responsibility. Like Carroll (1991), corporate social responsibility can be categorized as three types: as economic, social, and environmental where economic responsibility involves the financial efficiency and profitability of the organization.

4.77 Environment responsibility is related to resource management, preservation of biological variety, environmental protection such as climate change, avoiding pollution and so on. Social responsibility takes account of the whole liabilities of society. Among all these three responsibilities, economic responsibility is considered as essential for the other two. Thus, it is apparent that corporate social responsibility identifies the moral conduct of organizations. For instance, organizations with social responsibility perform good activities which benefit society even if they are beyond the firm's interests. Similarly, organizations with corporate social responsibility show respect for law and order and refrain from unlawful activities. Organizations have a positive and strong relationship with their stakeholders, mainly employees, which generate competitive advantage as well as performing reliable and honest corporate activities.

So it can be concluded that organizations which exercise proper corporate social **4.78** responsibility should be considered as ethical organizations, especially when they treat their employees, their surroundings, and the environment in a decent and moral way.

Having therefore defined leadership and ethical leadership and articulated how it **4.79** overlaps within the judicial context, we must now evaluate alternative leadership approaches in the next Chapter, before assessing the current UK judicial leadership approach and reappraising a new strategic judicial leadership approach.

5

APPROACHES TO LEADERSHIP

5.01 This chapter analyses the variant pre-existing and alternative models of leadership within higher education, healthcare, and the military. These three alternative models were selected as they bore the most relevance to judicial leadership in terms of their collaborative, values-based, and hierarchical leadership styles.

5.02 When evaluating the alternative models of leadership, it ought to be reaffirmed at the outset that as Scouller (2011) identified, each leadership model operationalizes itself at three distinct levels—the '3 Ps model'. That is, it attempts to combine the strengths of well-established leadership theories (such as traits, behavioural, situational, and functional—as previously discussed in Chapter 3). The three levels referred to in the model's name are: Public, Private, and Personal leadership. Essentially, the first two levels—public and private leadership—are outer/behavioural levels. The third level—personal leadership—is an inner level and concerns a person's leadership presence, knowhow, skills, beliefs, emotions, and unconscious habits. Overall, the idea is that if leaders want to be effective they must work on all three levels in parallel. The two outer levels—public and private leadership—are what the leader must do behaviourally with individuals or groups to address the 'four dimensions of leadership'. These are: a shared, motivating group purpose/vision; action, progress, and results; collective unity; and individual motivation, whilst, the inner level—personal leadership—refers to what leaders should do to grow their leadership presence, knowhow, and skill. It has three aspects: developing one's technical knowhow and skill; cultivating the right attitude towards other people; and, working on psychological self-mastery. Notably, Scouller (2011) argued that self-mastery is the key to growing one's leadership presence, building trusting relationships with followers, and enabling behavioural flexibility as circumstances change while remaining authentic, that is true to the cause one is connected with.

A. Academic Leadership

5.03 Leadership in the context of higher education is regarded as an emerging research area with leadership models having been largely developed in the corporate context. Academic leadership is commonly viewed from a leader perspective with its focus on the leadership of academics and/or by academics. It is recognized as being relevant to all educational sectors, that is schools, colleges, as well as higher education institutions (HEIs) (ie universities).

5.04 Notably, Lumby[1] asserts that academic leadership in higher education has a number of distinctive features, not least because of its operating context. Leaders must motivate teams in particularly uncertain conditions, with changes in government policy often altering key priorities. Furthermore, there is a requirement to balance what may be seen as conflicting goals, including meeting the needs of students/consumers, research expectations, and commercial outcomes. Such an approach clashes with the more considered traditional approaches (ie goal theory) to leadership.

5.05 Furthermore, according to Evans et al[2] there is no agreed definition of an academic leader. They further argue that at its broadest, the term could be applied to any person working in an academic institution. This assertion may be regarded as simplistic however, in that not all those working in educational organizations are academics and not all engage with followers, a prerequisite for leadership.[3] From the myriad of definitions in the literature, it is however possible to identify three principal stances in relation to the meaning of academic leader; a *role perspective*, whereby academic leaders are viewed as those placed in formal leadership roles, a *behaviour perspective* whereby academic leaders are viewed as those who influence other academics, and an *expertise perspective* whereby academic leaders are viewed as those who are experts in their field.

5.06 Leadership is manifested by academics in many ways, including, but not limited to: contributions to the intellectual life of their discipline(s); developing novel lines of enquiry; taking responsibility for educational programmes; professing the knowledge of a field to the wider community; supporting and nurturing those

---

[1] J Lumby, Review Paper: *What do we know about Leadership in Higher Education?* (Leadership Foundation for Higher Education 2012).
[2] L Evans, M Homer, and S Rayner, 'Professors as Academic Leaders: The Perspectives of "the Led"' (2013) 41(5) Educational Management, Administration and Leadership 674.
[3] G Yukl, *Leadership in Organizations* (8th edn, Pearson 2013).

learning or establishing themselves within the academic community; and being open to engagement with cross-disciplinary collaboration.

According to a recent report by Lumby[4] commissioned by the Leadership Foundation for Higher Education (LFHE), many academics have come into higher education because of their 'passion for their subject' rather than the thought of becoming a manager. However, in recent years as the management of universities (ie across the HE sector) grows ever more complex, what can we do to encourage those academics who have leadership aspirations? What's more, how can the sector help challenge the notional divide between academia and administration that often characterizes debate and development in this area? Consequently, an academic leadership model has emerged, where a university leader needs to be an academic to gain the respect of the faculty s/he leads and to fully understand at the ground level the nature of the HEI's core intellectual functions. At the same time, an academic leader needs to be an entrepreneur, able to make the bold business decisions demanded and to seize the initiative where required, given the inception of HEI key performance indicators (KPIs) and national metrics, such as prescribed by HEFCE/Office for Students and/or the National Student Survey. **5.07**

According to the Higher Education Academy (HEA), with higher education being redefined in many ways, it is becoming increasingly important for HEIs to find multifaceted leaders to meet the diverse challenges of a changing sector. Consequently, in order to remain viable and competitive, universities must continually invest in their faculty leaders and staff. **5.08**

1. Academic Leadership Programmes

One of the most successful academic alliance leadership initiatives is the Academic Leadership Programme (ALP). It was established in 1989 and the aim of this intensive professional development experience was to develop the leadership and managerial skills of faculty who have demonstrated exceptional ability and academic promise. Many of the programme's nearly 1000 fellows have gone on to serve with distinction as college presidents, provosts, and deans. **5.09**

Historically, the LFHE[5] was established in 2004 by Universities UK and Guild HE (formerly the Standing Conference of Principals). In fact, it took over the function of the Higher Education Staff Development Agency. The LFHE Foundation delivers it work through programmes and events; institutional advice and consultancy; and providing research on leadership, management, and governance for HEIs. It cooperates with a wide range of organizations and associations in order **5.10**

---

[4] Lumby (n 1).
[5] <https://www.lfhe.ac.uk/>.

to do this. It has programmes for: new leaders, senior leaders, and executive senior leaders in HE.[6]

5.11   In addition, the HEA[7] is a British professional institution promoting excellence in higher education. The HEA advocates evidence-based teaching methods and awards fellowships as a method of professional recognition for university teachers. The HEA is responsible for the UK Professional Standards Framework (UKPSF)[8] for teaching and supporting learning in HE. The UKPSF is a voluntary scheme for describing the core values and competences expected of UK university staff. The scheme consists of four 'descriptors', corresponding to different roles in higher education, and defines the areas of activity, core knowledge, and professional values expected at each level. The introduction of national professional standards for university teachers was first canvassed in 2003. The framework has two elements: the 'descriptors' which describe higher education roles and the associated competences, and the 'dimensions of practice' which describe the activities, core knowledge, and professional values expected of practitioners. There are four descriptors corresponding to support staff with minor teaching duties, full academics (eg lecturers), senior academics with teaching specialisms, and senior management with strategic responsibility for teaching.

5.12   The HEA operates a professional recognition scheme for university teachers who have demonstrated that their teaching practices are well aligned with UKPSF. This is intended both to encourage excellence in teaching and to provide academics with a portable qualification transferable between institutions. There are four grades:

- AFHEA—Associate Fellow of the Higher Education Academy
- FHEA—Fellow of the Higher Education Academy
- SFHEA—Senior Fellow of the Higher Education Academy
- PFHEA—Principal Fellow of the Higher Education Academy

5.13   Such recognition provides a nationally recognized framework for benchmarking success within HE teaching and learning support.

5.14   It is generally accepted that an academic leader is an individual who heads an academic unit. Usually this means that the individual leader recruits faculty staff and identifies/determines faculty roles and priorities, as well as developing and updating the curriculum. They will also foster and promote scholarly activity, as well as develop/mentor/coach faculty staff; they will create a supportive, productive work environment/culture, alongside creating a shared vision, setting goals, developing plans, and administering academic/human resources/legal

---

6   <https://www.lfhe.ac.uk/en/programmes-events/index.cfm>.
7   <https://www.heacademy.ac.uk/>.
8   <https://www.heacademy.ac.uk/ukpsf>.

policies. In addition, the academic leader will typically serve as an advocate for the faculty's/department's interests. This the academic leader does, as well as performing roles of a faculty member by teaching classes, advising and mentoring students, participating on examination boards and other committees, and conducting their own research and scholarly activities.

Such a multifaceted role ensures that the academic leader remains in touch with what is taking place within their HEI and academia more widely. In fact, this was affirmed by Bolden's Report in 2012[9] which showed that academic leadership relates directly to the core academic functions of teaching, research, and service (including academic administration and outreach), as distinct from managerial aspects of leading HEIs such as financial and strategic planning, marketing, and human resource management (HRM). Accordingly, the complexity of managing and moving HEIs towards change and transformation within a dynamic business environment is overwhelming and calls for effective leadership approaches as highlighted by Timiyo (2017).[10] This research discovered that whilst some HEIs are advocating to be governed by relational leadership models, others remain sceptical and contend that the bureaucratic nature of HEIs poses a threat to this change in leadership model. The study further identified three leadership taxonomies—*blended leadership, collegial leadership,* and *contextual leadership*—considered suitable for managing HEIs. That is, given the multifaceted nature of higher education across the UK, then academic leadership required a blend of styles and approaches, as discussed in Chapters 3 and 4.   **5.15**

However, in 2018, the Advance HE[11] was created by the merger of the Equality Challenge Unit (ECU), the HEA, and the LFHE.   **5.16**

B. Healthcare Leadership

Traditionally, the healthcare sector, namely the NHS, has had recognized management training for decades. The NHS philosophy since its inception has been simple—great leadership development improves leadership behaviours and skills. Better leadership leads to better patient care, experience, and outcomes. As a result, the NHS's purpose is to work with healthcare practitioners to deliver excellent leadership across the NHS to have a direct impact in patient care. Accordingly, there is a range of tools, models, programmes, and bank of expertise to support individuals, organizations, and local academies to develop leaders, celebrating and sharing where outstanding leadership makes a real difference.   **5.17**

---

[9] <https://ore.exeter.ac.uk/repository/handle/10871/15098>.
[10] <https://www.researchgate.net/publication/318744946_Leadership_Models_for_Higher_Education_Institutions_An_Empirical_Investigation>.
[11] <https://www.heacademy.ac.uk/about-us/advance-he>.

5.18 In order to develop outstanding leadership in health, in order to improve people's health, and their experiences of the NHS, the healthcare sector leadership programme[12] aims to:

- Broaden, and where necessary change, the range of leadership behaviours people in the health system use;
- Professionalize leadership: raising the profile, performance, and impact of health system leaders; requiring and supporting them to demonstrate their fit and proper readiness to carry out their leadership role and defining what we expect from them;
- Work in partnership to make leadership in the health system more inclusive and representative of the communities it serves; and
- Develop leaders who are more innovative and can create a climate where innovation can flourish.

As a result, the new NHS Leadership Academy has been created to galvanize this national leadership initiative in health.

1. NHS Leadership Academy

5.19 Recent reports in health (Francis, Berwick, and Keogh[13]) all highlight that failure in leadership leads to failures in patient care. The NHS Leadership Academy therefore sets out the leadership development principles as:

- For leaders to be at their most effective they need confidence in their role.
- To secure confidence they need competence, skills, expertise, experience, and support. This comes from expert development and training as well as on the job learning.
- Leaders need to have a breadth of behaviours to draw on to exercise their role in a multi-agency, complex system such as healthcare. Lack of development tends to result in leaders having a very narrow range of styles to draw on.
- Leaders need the right behaviours to build alliances with a wide range of professionals and across organizational boundaries to serve the needs of diverse communities with enduringly complex needs. The success of the NHS over the next decade or so will rely heavily on the behaviours adopted by healthcare leaders at all levels being able to work with leaders in other parts of the public and private system.
- Leaders need to be able to engage and empower those working with them and rely less on old-style command and control approaches that inhibit innovation.

---

[12] <https://www.leadershipacademy.nhs.uk/programmes/>.
[13] <https://www.gov.uk/government/publications/report-of-the-mid-staffordshire-nhs-foundation-trust-public-inquiry; https://www.gov.uk/government/publications/berwick-review-into-patient-safety; https://www.nhs.uk/nhsengland/bruce-keogh-review/documents/outcomes/keogh-review-final-report.pdf>.

And, apply such, discretionary effort, and a more caring and considerate climate, in order to generate both greater employee engagement and compassion in care.

These key principles have developed a new model for Leadership in Healthcare.[14] **5.20** Further, this newly devised Healthcare Leadership Model assesses leadership behaviours to more fully understand leadership development with a 360 degree feedback tool. Such insights into other people's perceptions of leadership abilities and behaviours frames a reflective approach. The Healthcare Leadership Model seeks to help healthcare managers become better leaders in their day-to-day role. In fact, the Healthcare Leadership Model is useful for everyone because it describes the things you can see leaders doing at work and demonstrates how you can develop as a leader. The model is made up of nine leadership dimensions.[15] Once the healthcare leader has explored the dimensions, s/he undertakes a self-assessment tool which assesses their leadership behaviours to more fully understand their leadership development.

Similarly, the Kings Fund Leadership scheme provides programmes for chief ex- **5.21** ecutives of NHS providers, chairs and chief operating officers of clinical commissioning groups, and experienced senior directors involved in planning and securing transformational change locally.[16] Furthermore, this pioneering work of Sir David Dalton at Salford on performance management of healthcare specialists has enabled intensive programmes which provide experienced leaders with protected spaces to develop the skills and behaviours associated with a more collaborative style of leadership. It also explores the style, culture, and behaviour that participants are setting within their organization—as staff at all levels will need to work more collaboratively across organizational boundaries if new health and care models are to succeed. Such a programme run over nine months comprises of four modules—one two-day module (module one) and three one-and-a-half-day modules (modules two, three, and four); and, telephone conversations between the programme participants and programme director, which will be held four to six weeks before the programme starts to identify personal goals and ambitions. This information will be used to design the content of the modules.

Such programmes enable healthcare leadership to focus upon collaborative leader- **5.22** ship within multi-professional/disciplinary teams. In fact, in December 2016 NHS England had been working with the other health Arms-Length Bodies to develop the new evidence-based national framework on improvement skill-building, leadership

---

[14] <http://www.leadershipacademy.nhs.uk/about/>.

[15] <https://www.leadershipacademy.nhs.uk/wp-content/uploads/2014/10/NHSLeadership-LeadershipModel-colour.pdf>.

[16] <https://www.nhsconfed.org/-/media/Confederation/Files/Events/ACE14/Sir-David-Dalton-Chief-Executive-Salford-Royal-NHS-FT.pdf?la=en&hash=BC4CE3F41957BD3F1B0AC65F51C0C75EE0CA0AA9tps://www.kingsfund.org.uk/courses/building-collaborative-leadership>.

development, and talent management for people in NHS-funded roles. This is an evidence-based national framework to guide action on improvement skill-building, leadership development, and talent management for people in NHS-funded roles. The framework[17] applies to everyone in NHS-funded roles in all professions and skill areas, clinical and otherwise. Primarily its purpose is to equip and encourage people in NHS-funded roles to deliver continuous improvement in local health and care systems and gain pride and joy from their work. To that end, the framework aims to guide team leaders at every level of the NHS to develop a critical set of improvement and leadership capabilities among their staff and themselves.

5.23 Overall, it aims to develop capabilities; and giving people the time and support required to see them bear fruit is a reliable strategy for closing the three gaps identified in the NHS Five Year Forward View. The critical capabilities to be developed include: systems leadership skills for leaders improving local health and care systems, whether through sustainability and transformation plans, vanguards, or other new care models. These skills help healthcare leaders to build trusting relationships, agree shared system goals, and collaborate across organizational and professional boundaries. It also seeks to encourage compassionate, inclusive leadership skills for leaders at all levels. Compassionate leadership means paying close attention to all the people you lead, understanding the situations they face, responding empathetically, and taking thoughtful and appropriate action to help. Inclusive leadership means progressing equality, valuing diversity, and challenging power imbalances.[18]

5.24 According to the Kings Fund:

> . . . the framework presents a critical set of improvement and leadership capabilities for staff, including: systems leadership skills for those managing the integration of local health and care systems; quality improvement skills for staff at all levels; compassionate, inclusive leadership skills for leaders at all levels; and, talent management to fill senior and leadership vacancies appropriately.[19]

Henceforth, a new healthcare leadership project exists within the NHS. Health Education England described this new national initiative as 'an evidence-based model that reflects the values of the NHS'.[20] In any event, given that the NHS is one of the UK's largest employers nationwide, it defines fifteen qualities required by its healthcare leaders, sorted into three sections:

- Personal qualities
- Setting direction
- Delivering the service

---

[17] <https://improvement.nhs.uk/documents/542/Developing_People-Improving_Care-010216.pdf>.
[18] <https://improvement.nhs.uk/uploads/documents/Developing_People-Improving_Care-010216.pdf>.
[19] <https://www.kingsfund.org.uk/projects/national-improvement-leadership-framework>.
[20] <https://eoeleadership.hee.nhs.uk/nhs_hlm>.

This set of competences—a combination of applied skills put into action—rather **5.25** than qualities, describes five core personal qualities, or characteristics, expected of NHS leaders:

Self-belief: a 'can do' approach, standing up for what they believe in, determination, sense of confidence, requires success and learning over time.

Self-awareness: recognising one's own strengths and limitations, learning from failure, understanding the impact they have on others.

Self-management: regulating their own behaviour, tenacious, resilient, coping with a complex environment.

Drive for improvement: wanting to make a real difference to people's health, a focus on *goals to achieve improvements, investing energy to do so.*

Personal integrity: working in a way consistent with public service values, acting as a role model.

Evidently, a new style of leadership is being piloted in the NHS in which leaders en- **5.26** gage staff, patients, and partner organizations to improve patient care and health outcomes. The question, however, is whether they mean it, and even more important, can they deliver it, nationwide.

C. Military Leadership

Military leadership in its most fundamental form is the process of influencing others **5.27** to accomplish the mission by providing purpose, direction, and motivation.

Since the fifth century BC, Sun Tzu in the treatise 'The Art of War', in thirteen **5.28** chapters, set out the key 'estimates', that is the tenets of military leadership. Most notably, it was recognized that 'War is a matter of vital importance to the State'. Therefore, five fundamental factors—the 'essentials'—needed to be appraised, these were identified as: moral influence, weather, terrain, command, and doctrine. Of these, 'command' was depicted as having five virtues: wisdom, sincerity, humanity, courage, and strictness. Such five virtues vested in generals would enable organization, control, assignment of ranks, regulation of routes, and the provision of defence.

Expectantly, from ancient times to now, command is the authority a person in **5.29** the military service lawfully exercises over subordinates by virtue of his rank and assignment or position. The basic responsibilities of a military leader are: the accomplishment of the mission and the welfare of the soldiers. In fact, the most fundamental and important organizational technique used by the military is the chain of command.[21]

---

[21] <https://www.army.mod.uk/documents/general/rmas_ADR002383-developingLeaders.pdf>.

5.30 The chain of command is the sequence of commanders in an organization who have direct authority and primary responsibility for accomplishing the assigned unit mission while caring for personnel and property in their charge.

5.31 A military leader therefore has three types of duties:

- Specified duties
- Directed duties
- Implied duties

5.32 The Professional Military Ethic is underwritten by loyalty to the nation, the military, and the unit; duty; and selfless service. Selfless service is defined as putting the needs and goals of the nation, the military, your unit, and your soldier ahead of your personal needs and interest.[22]

5.33 Professionalism is important in the military for two significant reasons. First, the military leader is a public servant responsible for the defence of the nation. Second, the military organization is often responsible for the life of its soldiers.

5.34 The four leadership indicators are: *morale, esprit de corps, discipline, and proficiency*. The three different styles of leadership are *directing, participating*, and *delegating*. Actions that good military leaders avoid are: violation of dignity to individuals, mass punishment or ridicule of the troops, hurry-up and wait formations and similar drills that waste time, resting before his men, shirking the responsibility of checking his men's position, blaming the next higher in command for a rough and unsuccessful mission, blaming subordinates for a squad's failure in satisfactorily completing a specific mission, eating before his men have eaten, favouritism, and moral weakness.

5.35 A good military leader must also have a thorough knowledge of command essentials. The command essentials are: command policies, authority, responsibility, chain of command and other channels, military rank, military discipline and conduct, and the enlisted aspects of command. One of the essentials of military leadership is to seek responsibility and take responsibility for those actions. Defined, this means to take the initiative in the absence of orders and accept the responsibility for your actions.

5.36 Furthermore, integrity is utter sincerity, honesty, and candour. It is the avoidance of any kind of deceptive, shallow, or expedient behaviour. Justice is the fair treatment of all people regardless of race, religion, colour, sex, age, or national origin. Tact is a sensitive perception of people, their values, feelings, and views which allows positive interaction. An unselfish leader is one who avoids providing for her/his own comfort and advancement at the expense of others.

---

[22] <https://mwi.usma.edu/state-military-leadership-21st-century/>.

Within the context of military leadership, the relationship between the con- **5.37** cepts of command, leadership, and management are often blurred. To that extent, command has a legal status as the authority vested in an individual for the direction, coordination, and control of military forces. Thus, leadership is requisite for those who exercise the function of command, but it also operates where there is no command authority. Unlike command, the power of leadership is not established through military law and vested authority. Rather, leadership achieves ends by 'persuasion, compulsion and example'. It is dynamic and inspirational. For example, in the Army, management and leadership are important and are inter-dependent. Some military leaders perceive management as the business of resources, efficiency, and certainty and leadership as the source of vision, support, and challenge. It can be useful to consider management as taking people in a direction that they would follow naturally in an organized manner and leadership as inspiring people to take a journey against their instincts. Further, where management exists without leadership, the organization is generally dependable, but resistant to change and lacking inspiration and vision.

1. The Military Covenant

Most notably, the Military Covenant[23] reflects the unique responsibilities, roles, **5.38** and requirements of the Armed Forces. The Armed Forces are the only organizations that have the right to bear arms in deliberate offensive action. All members of the Armed Forces swear an Oath of Allegiance that recognizes a contract of unlimited liability. This liability to both risk and take life is no small matter and places the most demanding pressures on leadership.

The essence of this ethos is duty—to subordinates, peers, superiors, the mis- **5.39** sion and the Crown. For a military leader, training might seem less challenging than operations, but there are subtle complexities. Training must be well resourced, demanding, and realistic, yet if troops/sailors, submariners, and air personnel are worked too hard then they will lose sight of the objective and resent authority. High standards need to be set for subordinates, but also mistakes tolerated, otherwise the leader smothers initiative and stifles a 'learning environment'.[24]

Furthermore, as military leadership continues to remodify itself, there emerges an **5.40** overarching leadership aim to produce the strategic and people leaders of the future, when cadets and officers alike are learning command and control.

---

[23] <https://www.gov.uk/government/collections/armed-forces-covenant-supporting-information>.
[24] <http://www.army.mod.uk/training_education/24475.aspx?t=/sandhurst>.

D. Civil Service Leadership

5.41 The UK Civil Service has been established since the nineteenth century. However, Her Majesty's Civil Service is the permanent secretariat of Crown employees that supports and advises the government of the day. To that end, the Civil Service, as it is more commonly known, ensures that executive decisions of government ministers are implemented. Civil servants also have some traditional and statutory responsibilities which to some extent protect them from being used for the political advantage of the party in power. Senior civil servants may be called to account to Parliament.

5.42 All civil servants are subject to Civil Service Codes. The current Civil Service Code was introduced on 6 June 2006 to outline the core values and standards expected of civil servants. The core values are defined as *integrity, honesty, objectivity,* and *impartiality.* A key change from previous values is the removal of *anonymity* within the core values. The Code includes an independent line of appeal to the Civil Service Commissioners on alleged breaches of the Code. The Civil Service Management Code (CSMC) also sets out the regulations and instructions to departments and agencies regarding the terms and conditions of service of civil servants. It is the guiding document which gives delegation to civil service organizations, from the Minister for the Civil Service, in order for them to make internal personnel policies. Furthermore, the Civil Service Commissioners' Recruitment Code is maintained by the Civil Service Commissioners and is based on the *principle of selection on merit on the basis of fair and open competition.*

5.43 As part of Civil Service reform, the government aims to ensure that all civil servants:

- have the tools and skills they need to provide public services more effectively;
- can be deployed across departments.

5.44 The 'Meeting the Challenge of Change: A Capabilities Plan for the Civil Service' outlines plans to improve skills and performance across the Civil Service. The capability plan includes a strategy for building individuals' skills and competencies, and it examines how the Civil Service can use structures and management processes to harness these skills. For example:

- all civil servants are entitled to five days of learning and development each year, targeted to help them perform better in their work;
- there is a wide range of opportunities such as job shadowing and on-the-job learning, as well as formal training courses.

5.45 The plan also encourages more secondments into (and from) the private and voluntary sectors. Competencies are the skills, knowledge, and behaviours that lead to successful performance. Moreover, the Civil Service Competency Framework[25]

---

[25] <https://assets.publishing.service.gov.uk/government/uploads/system/uploads/attachment_data/file/436073/cscf_fulla4potrait_2013-2017_v2d.pdf>.

set out how civil servants should work. In addition, Civil Service Learning provides e-learning, online resources, and classroom courses to support a Civil Service career. There are also twenty-five professional networks, each led by a head of profession:

- Corporate Finance Profession
- Government Communication Service
- Government Economic Service
- Government Finance Profession
- Government IT Profession
- Government Knowledge and Information Management Profession
- Government Legal Service
- Government Occupational Psychology Profession
- Government Operational Research Service
- Government Planning Inspectors
- Government Planning Profession
- Government Property Profession
- Government Science and Engineering Profession
- Government Social Research Profession
- Government Statistical Service Profession
- Government Tax Profession
- Government Veterinary Profession
- Human Resources Profession
- Intelligence Analysis
- Internal Audit Profession
- Medical Profession
- Operational Delivery Profession
- Policy Profession
- Procurement Profession
- Project Delivery Profession

In general terms, the professional networks: **5.46**

- provide a governance structure
- raise standards
- provide career development opportunities
- encourage collaboration

Further, the Civil Fast Stream has the following schemes: **5.47**

- Generalist
- Diplomatic Service
- Houses of Parliament
- Science and Engineering
- Diplomatic Economic Scheme

- Finance
- Commercial
- Government Communication Service
- Human Resources
- Project Delivery

1. Civil Service College

5.48 However, the Civil Service College (CSC)[26] since 2012, following the closure of the National School of Government in 2010, has become the beacon and centre point for training programmes that were previously offered by the school and since then has increased the number of programmes on offer, ensuring that the available training reflects the current needs of those working in the public sector.

5.49 CSC therefore offers innovative training courses across subjects, from accountability and governance to leadership training, finance management, project management, and personal development. All courses can be customized to fit specific training needs. The CSC is therefore a leading provider of high quality, bespoke training for those working in the public sector and Civil Service, here in the UK and abroad. The CSC's values guide their strategy and day-to-day activities:

- provide excellent and professional training provided by the most knowledgeable people in their field;
- are resilient, committed to delivering the best service to clients whatever the obstacles;
- tailor their courses based on really listening to the clients' individual needs;
- have a team who work together to provide excellent customer experience.

5.50 In terms of leadership, the CSC provides leadership training. In fact, its programme provides:

Leadership & Management

Being an effective leader is essential in order to make an impact within your organisation. However, we are aware that one leadership style does not fit all and that in today's turbulent back-drop against which the Civil Service and Public Sector operates different challenges call for different leadership techniques.

Whether you need to keep your team motivated in these uncertain times, to give your employees a boost of vitality after a slump in productivity, or to streamline your systems and implement a more positive organisational culture, Civil Service College offers numerous courses that are tailored to address a variety of leadership challenges.

Source: CSC

---

[26] <https://www.civilservicecollege.org.uk/training-courses>.

Within this programme some twenty-one courses/modules are offered, in- **5.51**
cluding digital leadership. Civil Service leadership is therefore like all other
sectors, crucial to the process of influencing others and delivery of government. However, it is transformational and collaborative in style. Accordingly,
civil service leadership is:

Most significantly, this statement on Civil Service leadership takes as its starting
point the responsibility that the Civil Service has for the effective delivery of the
government's programme and ministers' priorities, living its values, and serving
the public. It also highlights the three key characteristics that civil servants have
indicated they expect from their leaders, and that we expect Civil Service leaders
to live up to. They are:

Inspiring—about our work and its future

- We will show our pride in and passion for public service, communicating purpose
  and direction with clarity and enthusiasm
- We will value and model professional excellence and expertise
- We will reward innovation and initiative, ensuring we learn from what has not
  worked as well as what has

Confident—in our engagement

- We will be straightforward, truthful and candid in our communications, surfacing
  tensions and resolving ambiguities
- We will give clear, honest feedback, supporting our teams to succeed
- We will be team players, and will not tolerate uncollaborative behaviour which
  protects silos and departmentalism

Empowering—our teams to deliver

- We will give our teams the space and authority to deliver their clearly set
  objectives
- We will be visible, approachable, and welcome challenge, however uncomfortable
- We will champion both difference and external experience, recognising the value
  they bring
- We will invest in the capabilities of our people, to be effective now and in the future

Sir Michael Bichard, a former Permanent Secretary, draws a clear distinction be- **5.52**
tween managers and leaders:

*Managers who control their organisations effectively may enable them to survive. But it is
the leaders who create a sense of purpose and direction, and who analyse, anticipate and
inspire.*[27]

Strong leadership is therefore essential if a Civil Service team is to be innova- **5.53**
tive, efficient, and successful. And yet one of the minor mysteries of the modern
world is why there are so few effective leaders—in both the public and private

---

[27] <https://www.civilservant.org.uk/l&m-leadership.html>.

sectors—when there is so much advice available. Effective Civil Service leaders are therefore trained to be able to answer the following questions from anyone at any time:

- Where are we going?
- Why are we going there?
- How will we get there?

5.54 It has been observed by Martin Stanley, a former Senior Civil Servant and now CEO, that effective Civil Service leaders also have a good number if not all of the following attributes. For instance, they:

- have a remorseless iron determination to make things happen;
- have an unshakeable inner conviction;
- lead decisively and confidently;
- constantly promote the same message;
- are different;
- have at least one weakness;
- provide a role model and set an example;
- keep things simple;
- are a little theatrical;
- are authoritative and respected;
- are committed to their team;
- accept blame;
- are honest;
- are physically strong; and
- take risks.

5.55 More importantly, a good Civil Service leader knows exactly when to be straight, when to be economical with the truth, when to lay it on with a trowel, and when to dissemble. This is absolutely right, but most of us spend too much time dissembling and too little time being honest with our staff. In particular, we have to be honest in making it clear to staff that they are employed for no other reason than to help the leader achieve his or her objectives. However much they like working together, the team must be directed to achieving a common goal. Everyone is then much better directed and motivated. Those who skirt round this fundamental truth simply waste time and create confused expectations. Effective leaders also give clear and honest feedback to their staff—not all the time, but frequently enough to be effective. Any sustained failure to give honest feedback to colleagues—and of course we have all failed to some extent, and regretted it—can only end in disappointment, confusion and demoralisation. Honest appraisal is also a necessary companion to empowerment.

5.56 All of the above comparative approaches canvass the variant styles of leadership.

E. Judicial Leadership Styles

Accordingly, from the above evaluation, the tenets of judicial leadership are clearly **5.57** a combination of the variant leadership styles. Such a hybrid judicial leadership focuses upon the ethical framework, whilst utilizing the leadership styles which encompass how leaders relate to others within and outside the organization, how they view themselves and their position.

Factors that also influence the style to be used include: how much time is avail- **5.58** able; whether relationships are based on respect and trust or on disrespect; who has the information, you, your employees, or both; how well your employees are trained and how well you know the task, internal conflicts, stress levels, type of task, whether it is structured, unstructured, complicated, or simple; and laws or established procedures and training plans.

Within judicial leadership is a classic/tactical model of 'military' style of leader- **5.59** ship termed, 'commanding', probably the most often used because the objective is very clear, such as to complete the task by making a decision. Such autocratic management style operates with the manager in control who issues orders because she/he feels more knowledgeable. Subordinates are given some level of flexibility in carrying out their work, but within specific limits and procedure (Bass, 2008). The communication in groups led by autocratic leaders is top down. Since it rarely involves praise and frequently employs criticism, it undercuts morale, job satisfaction, and leads to absenteeism of employees.

Further, according to Bass (2008), the bureaucrat knows the rules of the insti- **5.60** tution and has the team abide by them. Such rings true of judicial leadership. Therefore, bureaucratic leadership applies when there are rigid policies and guidelines in place, the bureaucrat makes sure that they are maintained and used to the best of their ability. As Northouse[28] contends, leaders in organizations that use coercive/directing and bureaucratic styles of leadership have low productivity. This seems to be in line with what the authors are asserting in terms of judicial routine responsibilities. Yet, transformational leadership applies where judicial leaders are required to enhance the motivation, morale, and performance of followers through a variety of mechanisms. These include connecting the follower's sense of identity and self to the mission and the collective identity of the organization; being a role model who inspires followers; challenging followers to take greater ownership for their work; and understanding the strengths and weaknesses of followers, so the leader can align followers with tasks that optimize their performance (Bass, 2008).

---

[28] P Northouse, *Leadership: Theory and Practice* (7th edn, Sage 2016).

5.61   Notably, Burns[29] first introduced the concept of transforming leadership in his descriptive research on political leaders, but this term is now used in other organizational systems as well. Burns related to the difficulty in differentiation between management and leadership and claimed that the differences are in characteristics and behaviours. He established two concepts; 'transforming leadership' and 'transactional leadership'. These are inherently part of what modern judges do. According to Burns, the transforming approach creates significant change in the life of people and organizations. That, of course, is what judges do, collectively, daily. Yet, unlike the transactional approach, it is not based on a 'give and take' leadership, but on the leaders' personality, traits and ability to make a change through example, articulation of an energizing vision, and challenging goals. Transforming judicial leaders are therefore idealized in the sense that they are a moral exemplar of working towards the benefit of the team, organization, or community and can change organizational culture.

5.62   Whilst other scholars are quick to observe that in complex organizations with different tasks, like the judiciary, there is a need for more professionalism and characteristics of collaborative leadership styles. They add that most leadership styles used only focus on one organization, maybe with different departments or sections. They suggest, therefore, that all leadership styles should culminate into collaborative leadership which would include various skills and working with different organizations and stakeholders. The latter is certainly true of the modern judiciary.

5.63   Plainly from this survey of alternative leadership models, we evidence how variant leadership approaches are. Further, we also observe the commonalties which the judiciary share with other spheres of life. For instance, judicial leaders engage in multifaceted and inter-disciplinary work, like academic leaders. Moreover, judicial leaders are subject to goal-driven and collaborative working, such as healthcare leaders. More typically, judicial leaders having sworn allegiance to the Crown, also work within a command chain and hierarchical structure, such as military leaders. Yet, whatever the context, it is incontrovertibly clear that leaders share personal integrity within their variant frameworks.

In the next chapter, we identify and evaluate current thinking on judicial leadership.

---

[29]   J Burns, *Leadership* (Harper and Row 1978).

6

DEVELOPING A NEW STRATEGIC
APPROACH FOR THE JUDICIARY

Sir Peter Gross in his 2006 Gresham Lecture observed that 'the range and extent of judicial leadership activity is striking'.[1] He described the hallmarks of judicial leadership as: **6.01**

> developing the law; developing procedure; reforming the justice system; and, domestic security.

Judges can no longer avoid the increasing demands of administration, their function is now beyond that. The 'modern judge' is likely to do a lot more out of court than his predecessors, whether at a local, regional, or national level and the tasks now extend beyond 'mere' administration. **6.02**

In recent times, observers of the legal system have witnessed a proliferation in judicial leadership roles among the senior first instance judiciary across the UK. As identified by this book, the demands of the modern judge require leadership qualities alongside other judicial skills, knowledge, and attributes. **6.03**

The former Lord Chief Justice, Lord Thomas of Cwmgiedd, in a speech on judicial leadership, in 2015 observed that: **6.04**

> ... the way in which the judiciary now can lead can be seen in the development of the plans for the overhaul of the machinery of justice. As I have mentioned, part of the evolution after 2005 involved the creation of a new model of governance for Her Majesty's Courts and Tribunals Service. In 2008 with the adoption of the current model of governance of court administration which placed the court administration in the joint control

---

[1] <https://www.gresham.ac.uk/professors-and-speakers/the-rt-hon-sir-peter-gross/>.

of the Executive and the judiciary. The judiciary could now itself formulate proposals for reform, but it could also encourage others to come forward with ideas ....[2]

6.05 Similarly, the Chancellor of the High Court, Sir Geoffrey Vos, reaffirmed that

Judges and the judiciary must be individually and systemically independent from the State, because judges have routinely to decide cases between the State and the citizen. Both the State and the citizen must be able to have absolute confidence that such cases will be decided free from inappropriate interference from either the executive or the legislature. You do not have to spend long to identify the growing number of areas in which issues need to be decided between the citizen and the state: all criminal cases, public law children cases between local authorities and parents, any number of administrative law challenges to government decisions in relation to every aspect of our lives, to name but a few.[3]

6.06 As aptly summarized by Beatson LJ as:

The meaning and significance of judicial independence in our constitution is a huge topic, and there are many international articulations of the principles.[4]

6.07 That independence is the touchstone of judicial leadership and the part played by judicial leadership in reform, was affirmed by Gross LJ when he commented: '*An inevitable consequence of these reforms, which cannot be underestimated, is the massive expansion of judicial leadership, management and administration roles: the "day job" in court is now just the tip of an extremely deep iceberg.*'[5]

6.08 As Lord Judge CJ noted,

... the modern Judge is increasingly involved in ... administration. The days are over when the judicial function was performed by the judge turning up at court at 9 o' clock, reading the papers for the day's work, going into court at 10 or 10.30, sitting the court hours, adjourning at 4.30 or thereabouts, working on the day's work in preparation for the summing up or the judgment and then going home ... the modern judge is likely to be involved directly or indirectly with many responsibilities out of court, which have nothing whatever to do with his or her judicial judgments. All this is new, but the burdens are likely to increase rather than diminish. Do not get me wrong: they add greatly to the interest of the job, but the time in which to do it does not increase ....It is therefore clear that the Judiciary now has a significant leadership structure, with (for better or worse) a proliferation of judicial leadership roles. A huge amount of work is done by leadership Judges of every description.[6]

---

[2] The Right Hon. The Lord Thomas of CWMGIEDD Lord Chief Justice of England and Wales Judicial Leadership Conference on the Paradox of Judicial Independence UCL Constitution Unit, 22 June 2015 <https://www.judiciary.uk/wp-content/uploads/2015/06/ucl-judicial-independence-speech-june-2015.pdf>.

[3] (20 June 2017) <https://www.judiciary.gov.uk/wp-content/uploads/2017/06/chc-speech-faculty-of-advocates.pdf>.

[4] (14 November 2017) <https://www.judiciary.gov.uk/wp-content/uploads/2017/12/beatson-lj-atkin-lecture-20171201.pdf>.

[5] See (n 1), p. 1

[6] (February 2017, Bahrain) <https://www.judiciary.gov.uk/wp-content/uploads/2017/03/bahrain-speechby-sir-gross.pdf>.

Clearly to enable such change the face of judicial leadership must be adaptable, **6.09** flexible, and enabled to change—to become 'fit for purpose' in an ever-changing justice system. To meet these changes and challenges, the Judicial Colleges have become engaged.

A. The Judicial College(s)

The Lord Chief Justice (LCJ) is responsible for arrangements for training the **6.10** courts' judiciary in England and Wales under the Constitutional Reform Act 2005. Similarly, the Senior President of Tribunals (SPT) has an equivalent responsibility in relation to judges and members of the tribunals under the Tribunals, Courts and Enforcement Act 2007. These responsibilities are exercised through the Judicial College in England and Wales and the Judicial Institute in Scotland.

The Judicial College was established in 2011, replacing the Judicial Studies Board **6.11** which had been in existence since 1979. The LCJ and SPT have oversight of the College through the Judicial Office, of which it is a part and which supports them in their leadership, organization, and management roles. The Chairman of the College is a member of the Judicial Executive Board (JEB) and through that body advises and supports the senior judiciary on training issues. From April 2013, the training of coroners has become part of the Judicial College's responsibilities.

The Board of the Judicial College is the governing body of the College. It sets the **6.12** overall strategy for the College, agrees business plans, and oversees the delivery of training within the budget allocated to the College. A Court of Appeal Judge is appointed as Chairman of the Board of the Judicial College for a three-year term (presently Lady Justice Rafferty). The College Board's membership consists of courts' and tribunals' judiciary who can represent the training interests of each college of the judiciary, magistrates, the senior leadership judiciary, and the judiciary who sit in Wales. The Board is supported by a series of second tier committees responsible for the various detailed training programmes as follows:

- The Tribunals Committee

  It considers the common training needs across the tribunals' judiciary and works together with the Courts Committee and the College Faculty to implement the College strategy.

- The Courts' Committee

  It discusses plans and priorities for training across the entire courts' system and works together with the Tribunals Committee and the College Faculty to implement the College strategy.

- The Wales Training Committee

  It monitors judicial obligations under the Welsh Language Act 1993, and considers the training implications regarding any devolved legislation passed by the Welsh

Government. Wherever possible, it will provide advice and solutions on how to integrate these additional needs within the existing College programmes or alternatively make the case for dedicated training.

• The International Committee

It implements the College's international strategy to participate in international training projects that strengthen judicial independence, the rule of law and judicial skills.

6.13 In 2016, the Judicial College 'Faculty' came into being. It seeks to provide a significant rationalization of the College's current academic and pedagogic profile which will further enhance the reputation of the Judicial College as a world leader in judicial education. The Faculty sits within the Judicial College and is a central resource to assist in developing best practice for pervasive work themes and in the delivery and design of the governing principles set by the Judicial College in a five-year strategy.[7] That strategy incorporates judicial training which has three elements: (1) substantive law, evidence, and procedure and, where appropriate, expertise in other subjects; (2) the acquisition and improvement of judicial skills including, where appropriate, *leadership* and management skills; (3) the social context within which judging occurs.

6.14 Consequently, *all* Judicial Office Holders (JoHs) in England and Wales are trained by one body—the Judicial College. Its training courses cover civil, criminal, family, tribunals, magistrates, senior judiciary, cross-jurisdictional, and international legal knowledge and skills. All of the judiciary receive full induction and continuation training throughout their judicial careers. The Judicial College is headed by two Directors of Training—one for courts (His Honour Judge Andrew Hatton) and one for tribunals (Employment Judge Crista Christensen) who are also Joint Deans of the Faculty of the Judicial College.

6.15 The Lord President of the Court of Session became Head of the Scottish Judiciary on 1 April 2010 and that legislation placed upon the Lord President responsibility for 'making and maintaining appropriate arrangements for the welfare, training and guidance of judicial office holders'. This involves the making and maintaining of arrangements which are sufficient for the needs of an independent judiciary in a modern Scotland. The Lord President delegates responsibility for judicial training to the Judicial Institute, of which he is President. The governing body of the Judicial Institute, founded in 2013, is comprised of JoHs from all levels of the judiciary and lay members, one from an educational background. The Judicial Institute for Scotland implements the training objectives agreed by the governing

---

[7] <https://www.judiciary.gov.uk/wp-content/uploads/2015/01/judicial-college-strategy-2015-2017.pdf>.

body under the overall supervision of the Lord President. The Lord President has agreed the terms of the Judicial Institute Governance Framework, which came into effect on 29 June 2018. Lady Stacey is the Chair of the governing body of the Judicial Institute and Lord Armstrong is Vice-Chair. Operational responsibility for the delivery of training rests with the Director of the Judicial Institute. The Judicial Institute is based in Parliament House and virtually all training and education takes place there in a modern learning suite. The guiding philosophy of the Judicial Institute is that judicial training is judge-led, judge-devised, and judge-delivered. Training covers a variety of relevant, topical courses on specific subjects, including topics such as sentencing, criminal law, family law, and private law. An emphasis is also placed on bench-specific skills, including court and case management. The Judicial Institute has developed specific training modules in relation to domestic abuse; diversity awareness; equal treatment; and judicial ethics in public life. The Judicial Institute is also involved in outreach work commenced and developed by the Judicial Studies Committee in order that the Scottish judiciary have access to modern, relevant, practical training and education.

B. The 'LMD' Programme

The Judicial College's first 'LMD' (ie Leadership Management Development) **6.16** Programme was launched in 2014 and was specifically designed to be cross-jurisdictional in order to promote the sharing of experiences and expertise among courts judges, tribunal judges, and coroners alike, in terms of judicial leadership. In fact, in June 2013 the Judicial College decided to prioritize judicial leadership. Notably, the Judicial College determined that this area of learning and development was crucial to the modernization of the judiciary. In particular it was noted that 'Understanding the organisation, communicating and working with others, people management, managing oneself as a leader' was essential for all judicial leaders.

Subsequently, the first Judicial College LMD Programme was launched in **6.17** March 2014. The programme was designed to develop the skills and attributes essential for a JoH with leadership responsibilities, based on the Judicial Skills and Abilities Framework (see Appendix 4). Such an innovation demonstrated foresight, given the climate of constant change and reduced resources, where the judiciary has to respond to legislative and process changes as well as political decision-making in order to enhance its effectiveness. The LMD Programme aims to ensure that judicial leaders have the necessary practical skills and knowledge to lead these changes.

The LMD Programme consists of three modules, the content of which was de- **6.18** signed with the support and involvement of a cross-jurisdictional group of existing senior judicial leaders. It developed out of pilots initiated by Sir Brian Leveson when he was Senior Presiding Judge. The present Course Director and judicial tutors worked tirelessly with a dedicated team of educational advisors to incorporate appropriate leadership concepts and procedural examples from across the professions. Each module begins with a face-to-face workshop and is followed by a number of work-based activities linked to the role of judicial leader. It is intended that the workplace activities will overlap with each subsequent module's workshop, as illustrated below in Diagram 6.1:

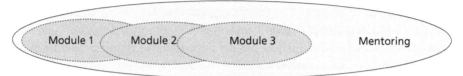

Diagram 6.1 Judicial College LMD Model

However, the workshops cover three modules (see Appendices 1–3). Each module has been designed to support the following learning process as set out in Diagram 6.2:

The three specific Judicial College Leadership modules are:

Diagram 6.2 Judicial College Learning Process (2015)

Module 1: Understanding your Organisation, Communicating and Working with other Organisations

The workshop provides opportunities for the attendee to develop their ideas and skills in the following areas:

- The principles of leadership and management
- Their role as a judicial leader and manager
- Managing and leading change
- Developing the priorities and strategies for their areas of responsibility

Understanding the Organisation, Communicating and Working with Others

Workshop	Work based application
Introduction to the Leadership and Management Programme	Prepare a plan to continue your application of skills from the workshop
Your role as a leadership and management judge	Meet with your leadership and management mentor
• Whom do you lead and whom do you influence?	
• What does your role look like?	Discuss your budget and management information systems with those who can support you
• Establishing and clarifying your environment	
Leading and managing change	Hold meetings with relevant contacts across your environment.
• Understanding the process of change	Create your plan to deliver your priorities for your area of responsibility
Communication skills	
• The principles of influencing	Develop a communication plan to ensure that others understand your priorities.
• Control, Influence, Concerns	
Strategic planning	Continue to develop relationships with other leadership and management judges. Use this net work to support your development.
• Creating your priorities to improve the service for colleagues and users	
• Implementing your plans	

Module 2: People Management

Whereas this workshop provides for the development of the attendee's ideas and skills in the following areas:

- The management and leadership of people
- The people side of change
- Managing well-being and stress in others
- Effective one to one conversations

People Management

Workshop	Work based application
Review of Module 1	Prepare a plan to continue your application of skills from the workshop
• Reviewing your workplace activities.	
• Identifying any further learning required to support the skills from module 1	Read the change management guidance
Building effective and collaborative groups of judges	Complete stress management self-assessment
• Getting the best from others	Hold the difficult conversation that you have been putting off
Managing welfare issues and stress in others	
• Recognising issues and responding appropriately	Conduct a development focused conversation with someone for whom you are responsible
• Knowing where to find the resources to help you	
Holding one to one conversations	Hold a meeting with staff for whom you are responsible to discuss your expectations of each other
• Understanding the scope of your responsibility and sources of support	
• Increasing your confidence and skills in having difficult conversations	Meet with other leadership and management judges to discuss issues in people management
Developing others	
• Motivating others	
• Preparing others for future roles	

Module 3: Managing Yourself as Leader

The final workshop provides opportunities for the attendee to further develop their skills in:

- Their approach to leadership and management
- Managing their time and delegating to others
- Developing their personal resilience

Managing Yourself as Leader

Workshop	Work based application
Review of Module 2	Prepare a plan to continue your application of skills from the workshop
• Reviewing workplace activities	
• Identifying further learning required to support the skills from module 2	Delegate one piece of work (where appropriate) and review time priorities
Time management and delegation	Ask others for feedback on your leadership style
• Clarifying priorities and dealing with competing demands	Complete emotional intelligence self-assessment
• Managing seasonal activities	
• Overcoming the challenges in delegating to others	Meet with other leadership and management judges to discuss the challenges of being a leadership and management judge
Understanding your personal effectiveness	
• Enhancing your emotional intelligence	
• Understanding your personal leadership style	Undertake one activity to enhance your resilience
• Appreciating your strengths and weaknesses as a leader	
Increasing your resilience	
• Reviewing current resilience levels	
• Planning to strengthen resilience levels	

6.19 As part of the LMD Programme each participant is allocated a mentor from a group of trained leadership mentors nominated by Chamber/Pillar Presidents and Presiding Judges or the Chief Coroner. The mentor will support the participant in their leadership role. The Programme takes four months to complete; however, the mentoring element is available for up to twelve months. As can be seen, the Judicial College has adopted a behavioural and skills approach to its leadership training using these three core modules to emphasize the skills required of the judicial leader.

C. Judicial Skills and Abilities Framework

6.20 As stated by the then SPT in 2014 'The Judicial Skills and Abilities Framework brings together all the work undertaken in recent years to identify and describe the skills and abilities required by judicial office-holders (both judges and tribunal members) in courts and tribunals including those in leadership and management roles.'

Subsequently, and since April 2015, this Framework has replaced all the existing competence frameworks for recruitment, appraisal schemes, and training purposes.

The Framework brings together a single set of skills and abilities which provide a **6.21** clear set of expectations common to all jurisdictions against which JoHs will be selected, trained, encouraged, and appraised. A single standard is used by all individual JoHs to identify their strengths, assess their personal development needs, and consider their career aspirations against a clear statement of expectations. In fact, the Framework describes the skills and abilities required by JoHs and those in judicial leadership roles. See Figure 6.1.

1. How to use the Framework

The left-hand column shows the statements that apply to all JoHs. Next to this are **6.22** the elements that define the statements. Each element does not need to be demonstrated for the overarching statement to be fulfilled. The right-hand column shows the extra statements which apply to those in judicial leadership and management roles. Next to this are the supporting elements that define the statements. *Level 1* is designed to apply to senior leadership and management roles (eg Presiding Judges, Family Division Liaison Judges, Chancery Supervising Judges, Chamber Presidents, and similar roles). *Level 2* is designed to apply to all other leadership and management roles (eg Resident Judges, Designated Family Judges, Designated Civil Judges, Presidents of the Regional Tribunal Judges, and similar roles).

While the Framework clearly sets out the qualities required of all JoHs, it also in- **6.23** directly establishes what judicial leaders should expect from the judicial colleagues they lead. It also serves to remind judicial leaders that their role is distinct from being simply another JoH. Leadership is a process that is related to management in many ways. It is an intrinsic component of management because leadership involves influencing and entails working with people. Yet, leadership is primarily concerned with effective goal accomplishment. While the primary functions of management are planning, organizing, staffing, and controlling, leadership is concerned with seeking and bringing about adaptive and constructive change (ie a reinforcement of the path-goal theory).

D. Roles of the Modern Judicial Leader

Katz[8] established three definitive basic leadership skills: **6.24**

technical, the *human*, and the *conceptual*.

The technical clearly applies to *knowledge* and proficiency/competency in a specific **6.25** type of work or activity. Given the discussion above, the Judicial Skills Framework

---

[8] RL Katz, 'Skills of an Effective Administrator' [1955] 1(33) Harvard Business Review 33.

Judicial Office-holder Skills & Abilities	Judicial Office-holder Elements	Leadership & Management Elements	Leadership & Management Skills
Assimilating and Clarifying Information: **Quickly assimilates information to identify essential issues, develops a clear understanding and clarifies uncertainty through eliciting and exploring information.**	• Possesses the ability to quickly absorb, recall and analyse information, facts and legal argument. • Identifies and focuses on the real issues; is not lost in irrelevant detail. • Properly applies appropriate legal rules and principles to the relevant facts. • Is able to weigh evidence in order to decide the facts of a case.	**Level 1** - Establishes, and communicates the evolving strategic direction in their jurisdiction, chamber or region. **Level 2** - Communicates priorities and leads their court/tribunal through personal example.	**Leading the way**
Working with Others: **Conducts proceedings appropriately, values diversity and shows empathy and sensitivity in building relationships.**	• Manages hearings through fair and objective direction and intervention. • Has an awareness of the diversity of the communities which the courts and tribunals serve. • Works constructively with others to encourage co-operation and collaboration when needed. • Treats people with respect, sensitivity and in a fair manner without discrimination; ensuring the requirements of those with differing needs are properly met. • Maintains effective relationships, demonstrating the appropriate balance between formality and informality in hearings and with all contacts. • Is able to recognise and deal appropriately with actual or potential conflicts of interest.	**Level 1** - Acts as the judicial figurehead and builds effective relationships with the centre, agencies and key policy areas across their jurisdiction/chamber or region. **Level 2** - Uses an inclusive approach to develop and maintain the reputation of the court/tribunal within the community.	**Working with others**
Exercising Judgement: **Demonstrates integrity and applies independence of mind to make incisive, fair and legally sound decisions.**	• Makes timely and appropriate decisions. • Exercises sound judgement and common sense. • Reaches clear, reasoned decisions objectively, based on relevant law and findings of fact. • Demonstrates integrity and independence of mind. • Does not exercise bias or prejudice.	**Level 1** - Works to improve judicial performance across the wider justice system and within the region to ensure it can meet existing and future needs. **Level 2** - Provides support to maintain and improve the performance of the judiciary and the court/tribunal to meet existing and future needs.	**Supporting and encouraging performance**

Figure 6.1 The Judicial Skills Framework
Source: Judicial College (2017)

Possessing and Building Knowledge: Possesses a detailed knowledge of a relevant jurisdiction, law and practice and demonstrates an ability and willingness to learn and develop professionally.	• Possesses a high level of expertise in chosen area or profession. • Possesses an appropriate and up to date knowledge of the relevant law and its underlying principles and procedure. • Shows an ability and willingness to learn and develop.	**Level 1** - Keeps approaches and knowledge up to date to meet evolving requirements within the jurisdiction, chamber or region. **Level 2** - Encourages learning, keeps knowledge up to date and communicates developments within the court/tribunal.	**Building knowledge and learning**
Managing Work Efficiently: Works effectively and plans to make the best use of resources available.	• Runs trials/hearings effectively to facilitate a fair and efficient conclusion. • Prioritises effectively and minimises delays and irrelevancies. • Shows ability to work at speed and under pressure. • Deals effectively with case management. • Undertakes necessary preparatory work.	**Level 1** - Maintains and improves efficiency within the jurisdiction/chamber or region. **Level 2** - Takes personal accountability for the efficient and effective use of judicial and court/tribunal time and resources.	**Delivering an efficient judicial system**
Communicating Effectively: Demonstrates good oral and written communication skills and authority.	• Establishes authority and inspires respect and confidence. • Remains calm and authoritative even when challenged. • Explains relevant legal or procedural information in language that is succinct, clear and readily understood by all. • Asks clear, concise, relevant and understandable questions. • Willing to listen with patience and courtesy	**Level 1** - Drives change across their Jurisdiction, chamber or region. **Level 2** - Supports and delivers change within the court/tribunal centre.	**Facilitating change**

Figure 6.1 Continued

embodies the 'technical' (knowledge) skill required. Further, Katz's human skills is about the ability to work with *people*. The latter skill is important for all JoHs, but as seen in earlier chapters of this book, the judicial leader's ability to communicate and effectively manage judicial colleagues places people management at the centre of judicial leadership skills. Finally, the hallmark of the judicial leader is the conceptual skill, as Katz described it '… the ability to work with ideas and concepts'. Such conceptual skills are central to creating a vision and *strategic* thinking.

Such a skills matrix, and/or model, as exemplified in Mumford's (2000) work, engages competencies as well as embraces individual's attributes, career experiences, **6.26** and environmental/organizational culture influences and goals/outcomes. Such a model when applied to judicial leaders identifies: *knowledge*, *people*, and *strategic* thinking skills which are core to the judicial skills model fit for the twenty-first century. Furthermore, such a judicial skills model enables path-goal theory in order to motivate followers (ie all JoHs) so as to accomplish designated goals/ outcomes. Such a model might even be deemed to be a 'transformational' leadership model, given the charismatic change management involved, as Antonakis[9] propounded.

6.27 In any event, what Katz identified long ago remains relevant as a core framework for judicial leaders today. Namely, no JoH could undertake the business of judging without an appreciation of basic skills. However, notwithstanding what labels and/or theories are attached to modern judicial leadership, it is evident that numerous roles prevail, such as:

- **Welfare role**—each judicial leader has supervision of the welfare of each JoH under their control;
- **Delegation role**—each judicial leader must delegate responsibilities to other JoHs;
- **Role model**—each judicial leader must act as role model for their respective JoHs;
- **Good governance role**—each judicial leader has to demonstrate good governance in order to evidence their effective leadership of their JoHs.

6.28 The 'leadership judges' undertake three tasks: (i) the effective management of workload and performance in their jurisdiction; (ii) the leadership of the judiciary in their respective courts/tribunals; and (iii) liaison with Her Majesty's Courts and Tribunals Service (HMCTS) and other operational managers in relation to IT, estates, and support services that are necessary for the effective and efficient administration of justice. Applying Scouller's '3Ps' model to such a framework for judicial leadership, given its multifaceted roles, it is plain that judicial leaders/ leadership judges operate at all three levels (as discussed previously in Chapter 3 of this book).

6.29 Adopting the Scouller (2011) '3Ps model', judicial leaders must operate at all three levels in order to ensure that the business of judging, as Bingham put it, is multi-dimensional so as to be fair. Justice is done and seen to be done. Therefore, the role of 'leadership judges/judicial leaders is key to the overall success of the business of judging, that is the administration of justice. While the courts and tribunals are managed and led in different jurisdictional and regional structures, 'leadership judges' are needed as the glue which keeps the machinery of justice moving. Stronger judicial leadership, underpinned by the Judicial College's LMD Programme and more continuing professional development leadership training

---

[9] J Antonakis, 'Transformational and Charismatic Leadership' in D Day and J Antonakis (eds), *The Nature of Leadership* (Sage 2012) 119.

will undoubtedly be needed as the pace of change and the demands of effective and efficient administration increase.

E. Future Judicial Leaders

As 2022 approaches and the completion of the *'Judiciary Matters'* Reform **6.30** Programme gathers pace, it is clear that new ways of working are emerging. Those changes consolidate the need for:

> … new ideas and … the challenge of matching the needs of justice in the 21st Century.[10]

Such a new vision requires more judicial engagement with the digital economy; **6.31** better use of judicial time, being flexible about when and where JoHs work; increased diversity; and stronger leadership, including more training for leadership judges. Evidently, from the comparative research undertaken for this book, it is plain that *six key characteristics* emerge in judicial leaders:

Ambition A desire to achieve something visible and noteworthy propels indi- **6.32** vidual leaders and their companies to strive to reach their potential. Leaders need a healthy dose of it to push themselves and others.

Drive and tenacity Some leaders have an inner motor that pushes them to get to **6.33** the heart of an issue and find solutions. They drill for specific answers and don't give up until they get them. Their *high energy* is infectious. They consistently drive their priorities through the organization. They search tenaciously for information they are missing and keep tweaking their mental models until they arrive at a positioning that works.

Self-confidence The ability to listen to your own inner voice and endure the **6.34** lonely moments when an important decision falls on your shoulders. The ability to be able to speak your mind and act decisively knowing that you can withstand the consequences. It is having a tough inner core, or what some refer to as 'emotional fortitude'. Underlying fears and insecurities can be just as detrimental to your know-hows as can excessive self-confidence in the form of narcissism or arrogance.

Psychological openness The willingness to allow yourself to be influenced by **6.35** other people and to share your ideas openly enhances the know-hows, while being psychologically closed can cause problems. Leaders who are psychologically open seek diverse opinions, so they see and hear more and factor a wider range of information into their decisions. Their openness permeates the social system, enhancing candour and communication.

---

[10] LCJ Briefing, 'Judiciary Matters: Our part in reforming the Courts and Tribunals' (July 2017).

6.36 **Realism** Realism is the mid-point between optimism and pessimism, and the degree to which you tend towards one or the other has a particularly powerful effect on your use of the know-hows.

6.37 **Appetite for learning** Know-hows improve with exposure to diverse situations with increasing levels of complexity, so an eagerness for new challenges is essential. Leaders who seek out new experiences and learn from them will build their know-hows faster than those who act to the contrary.

6.38 It should be plain that where steps are taken to transform a justice system, one of the key principles that underpins this is the need to build stronger judicial leadership. Appendix 5—The Judicial Leadership Toolkit—is intended to be a reflective guide to the skills that are required.

F. Justice, Dignity, and Humanity Model

6.39 A new framework for judicial leadership prevails from what we can learn from styles, theories, and other leadership models. Yet, given that the sanctity of safeguarding the Rule of Law which is at the centre of what all JoHs and judicial leaders do, then we have to invest in our judicial leaders to ensure that justice is accessible to those who need it and that 'leadership judges' design systems around the people who use them (ie they are user friendly). Furthermore, effective judicial leaders must ensure that they create systems that are financially viable using a more cost-effective infrastructure (ie better and effective use of IT and new working practices).

6.40 They must strive to eliminate the most common causes of delay. Overall, effective judicial leaders retain the UK's international standing as a world class provider of legal services and the judiciary as world leaders in the delivery of justice, as well as maintaining the constitutional independence of the judiciary.

6.41 To that end, judicial leaders engage with:

6.42 **Problem solving** Managed decline that is not sustainable: lengthy delays that are inimical to justice, process and language that is unintelligible to all but the specialist user and a system that is so costly that access to justice is impaired by the lack of affordable legal representation. Judicial leaders therefore manage the issues daily. Judicial leaders also maintain quality by retaining the formality and expense of judicial face-to-face determinations for the more complex and sensitive cases, whilst providing more proportionate, simpler, and more accessible process for less complex cases, judicially managing workload by innovative process, better quality outcomes, and new ways of working.

6.43 **Innovation** Remove paper save where there is no alternative by using digital process from evidence through charge/application to courtroom presentation using the common platform and alternate dispute resolution. Judicial leaders, by the deployment of registrar(s) and/or case officer support for judicially controlled and delegated functions in all jurisdictions (for example, triage, case progression and standard case management), reduce the need for and frequency of face-to-face hearings and digitize and simplify HMCTS administrative services for the user and judges alike.

Better quality Reduced delay, improved and new processes—causing affordable **6.44** access to justice in fewer, better buildings with refurbished/new facilities—improve judicial working conditions and user experience. Improved IT and service support for the judiciary and the user create improved judicial leadership of jurisdictions and geographic centres and workload.

New ways of working Judicial leaders who embrace: ejudiciary and access to docu- **6.45** ments and cloud-based case management software from anywhere; virtual hearing facilities including new video and telephone conferencing and web-based services, including online presentation facilities for all documents and virtual hearing of submissions on new screens and online scheduling/listing facilities. Also, alternative courts/hearing venues in local facilities (eg local authority committee rooms and more peripatetic use of existing facilities) and alternative working hours in some jurisdictions where that meets the needs of users.

People and policy engagement Judicial leaders liaise with: the main Boards, such **6.46** as JEB, Tribunals Judiciary Executive Board (TJEB), Judges Council, Tribunals Judges Council, HMCTS Board, HMCTS Portfolio (reform) Board; as well as specialist reform boards, Jurisdictional Engagement Groups (*JEGs*) and Local and Regional Leadership Groups (*LLGs* and *RLGs*), Judicial Associations and Litigant in Person and Professional Engagement Groups

These key responsibilities of judicial leaders evidence the importance of judicial **6.47** leadership to the administration of justice. We suggest that a Judicial Leadership toolkit, whereby judicial leaders can evidence their skills (Appendix 5) and attainment, as well as record their training needs will help promote the LMD skills and Framework skills that will form the basis of how judicial leaders work.

This collection of variant roles, not only emphasizes the multifaceted nature of **6.48** judicial leadership, but also seeks to illuminate that the skills framework is embedded in the work that all JoHs and judicial leaders undertake.

In the next and final chapter, we conclude with what leadership skills and training **6.49** modern judicial leaders in the twenty-first century require.

7

CONCLUSIONS

Judicial Independence is the hallmark of every/any democracy. But with independence comes responsibilities.[1] Yet as Pollock so aptly puts is: 'The behaviour which is expected of a judge in different ages and by different systems of law seems to fluctuate . . . .'.[2] **7.01**

Accordingly to Ryder (author) as Senior President of Tribunals (SPT) '*Access to justice has been described as the most fundamental of rights that we have*'.[3] Without it our other rights—whether they are rights to property, rights under contract, public law rights or human rights—are chimerical. Access to justice is 'not just a right in itself. It is [the] key enabler for making other fundamental rights a reality.'[4] It is incumbent on all of us—whether judges, lawyers, law teachers, law students, just as it is of wider society—to do all we can to ensure that access to justice is such a reality. We are all called on to assist access to justice. There are a number of necessarily related ideas: **7.02**

- a principled basis for access to justice;
- the judiciary's responsibility for securing effective access in order to promote the effective administration of justice and the rule of law; and
- civic responsibility for securing effective access.

---

[1] See Lord Judge, *The Safest Shield* (Hart Publishing 2015) 276.
[2] F Pollock and FW Maitland, *The History of English Law* (CUP 1967).
[3] Sir Ernest Ryder SPT, *Assisting Access to Justice* (Keele University, March 2018).
[4] Michael O'Flaherty, Director of the Fundamental Rights Agency, <http://www.equineteurope. org/New-practical-guide-on-access-to-justice-in-European-law>.

7.03 The usual starting point for explaining the importance of access to justice is to highlight how effective access is to the courts as an essential feature of a liberal democracy, one committed to the Rule of law. Support for this idea would, for instance, be Lord Diplock's imprecation from the *Bremer Vulcan* case,[5] that:

> Every civilised system of government requires that the state should make available to all its citizens a means for the just and peaceful settlement of disputes between them as to their respective legal rights. The means provided are courts of justice to which every citizen has a constitutional right of access in the role of plaintiff to obtain the remedy which he claims to be entitled to in consequence of an alleged breach of his legal or equitable rights by some other citizen, the defendant.

7.04 More recent support—and as clear an explanation of the importance of access to justice as you will find—is that of Lord Reed in the Supreme Court's decision in the *Unison* case. In his judgment, he emphasized how the constitutional right of access was 'inherent in the Rule of Law'.[6] He went further than that, however, and went on to explain:

> *At the heart of the concept of the rule of law is the idea that society is governed by law. Parliament exists primarily in order to make laws for society in this country. Democratic procedures exist primarily in order to ensure that the Parliament which makes those laws includes Members of Parliament who are chosen by the people of this country and are accountable to them. Courts exist in order to ensure that the laws made by Parliament, and the common law created by the courts themselves, are applied and enforced. That role includes ensuring that the executive branch of government carries out its functions in accordance with the law. In order for the courts to perform that role, people must in principle have unimpeded access to them. Without such access, laws are liable to become a dead letter, the work done by Parliament may be rendered nugatory, and the democratic election of Members of Parliament may become a meaningless charade. That is why the courts do not merely provide a public service like any other.*
>
> *… the value to society of the right of access to the courts is not confined to cases in which the courts decide questions of general importance. People and businesses need to know, on the one hand, that they will be able to enforce their rights if they have to do so, and, on the other hand, that if they fail to meet their obligations, there is likely to be a remedy against them. It is that knowledge which underpins everyday economic and social relations. That is so, notwithstanding that judicial enforcement of the law is not usually necessary, and notwithstanding that the resolution of disputes by other methods is often desirable.*[7]

7.05 Lord Reed's judgment is particularly important as a caution to anyone who wrongly thinks that the courts exist as service providers. It is an antidote to the fallacious consumer service view of the justice system. It is also important because it highlights aspects of justice that go beyond, but yet are necessary

---

[5] *Bremer Vulcan Schiffbau und Maschinenfabrik v South India Shipping Corp Ltd* [1981] AC 909, 979.

[6] *R (UNISON) v Lord Chancellor* [2017] UKSC 51, [2017] 3 WLR 409 [66]ff.

[7] ibid [68] and [71].

for, the courts to be the effective means to secure rights enforcement. In particular, it highlights how effective access is necessary for there to be a properly functioning democracy. It does so in two ways: first, most obviously, by emphasizing how individuals need access in order to enforce their rights; and, second, through a broader public access to the courts and their decisions. What does this mean?

Broader public access rests on an understanding of constitutional government **7.06** that has been remarked upon a number of times in the United States. It is the idea articulated by James Madison that a constitution, in and of itself, is nothing more than a '*parchment barrier*' protecting individual liberty. He was, of course, referring to the nascent US Constitution. We have no equivalent codified constitution here. Our constitution is far more of a living instrument contained within a number of Acts of Parliament, constitutional conventions and practices. His point is and will remain valid here. It was that unless the Constitution and the values it articulated was one that lived in the hearts and minds of citizens, it would be of little practical utility as a defence of liberty, of rights.[8]

There are many ways in which a state can ensure that its constitutional values **7.07** are lived values. Education. Citizen engagement in wider, civic, society. Active participation in democratic government. And through effective access to justice. Through participation in our justice system. We can, and do, secure such participation in a number of ways.

First, and most obviously, we secure it through our courts and tribunals, their **7.08** processes, and their judgments being open to all. The constitutional right to open justice, to public justice, is the foundation of effective public participation.[9] It is through this that the courts can play their part, although that is with the government and Parliament, in explaining the laws, and the constitutional and legal values they embody. It is an example of the interdependence between the three branches of the State; of how they work together even if independently to help secure our democratic constitution. It is through doing this that we are able to ensure that the public, not least through the media reporting what goes on in the courts accurately and fairly, are able to engage with those values and our laws. It enables them to debate and consider them. It helps maintain their vibrancy, while also helping to ensure that those values can develop over time as society develops. And so, it helps ensure that our constitution and laws evolve as society evolves.

---

[8] A point underscored by Justice Learned Hand in *The Spirit of Liberty* in 1944, 'I often wonder whether we do not rest our hopes too much upon constitutions, upon laws and upon courts. These are false hopes; believe me, these are false hopes. Liberty lies in the hearts of men and women; when it dies there, no constitution, no law, no court can even do much to help it.' <http://www.digitalhistory.uh.edu/disp_textbook_print.cfm?smtid=3&psid=1199>.
[9] *Scott v Scott* [1913] AC 417.

7.09 Second, this has a further, and wider, democratic role. Access to our courts helps to ensure that our courts, as institutions of the state, do not become estranged from society. Access is a means to ensure that our courts as social institutions remain inclusive ones. There are, of course, many different ways in which we achieve this. Democratic participation through the lay jury in the Crown Court and through lay justices in the Magistrates' courts are two such ways to secure direct participation. Lay panel members in the specialist tribunals is another. Scrutiny of our open justice in the civil courts and tribunals is another, less direct, but equally important way. When we consider both this, and access through judgments and open proceedings, we need to be astute to take appropriate steps to ensure that we secure them effectively.

7.10 Third, and this links to the previous two points, we secure participation through court judgments providing the framework within which socio-economic activity takes place. As Lord Reed rightly pointed out, judgments developing the common law, articulating and enforcing statutory law, provide the underpinning of our daily lives. In the shadow of *Donoghue v Stevenson*, as he noted, we buy drinks from cafes.[10] In the shadow of *Entick v Carrington*, we rely on our property rights and the limits of state power.[11] And so on. We rely on them without being aware of that fact. We give life to them and the values they give life to, whether we end up involved in a dispute that ends up in court. For very many, if not the vast majority of society, we do so notwithstanding the fact that we never become involved in litigation.

7.11 Importantly, it is through effective access to courts and tribunals that we test those decisions and the values they articulate. And it is through effective access to judgments that we can test them in public, democratic debate. Again, the framework and access to it and the means to test it, to develop—and correct it in the light of social evolution. This aspect of *'observational justice'* should not be underestimated, particularly at a time when there is something of a growing tendency otherwise to irrational populism or at least populist propositions that are incapable of empirical validation.[12]

7.12 Access to justice is therefore more than access to courts in order to enable claims and the rights and obligations they engage to be adjudicated. It is the means through which we uphold and articulate the law and ensure that our laws and constitution remain living instruments of our democracy. It is on this understanding that we consider the judiciary's and civic society's role and responsibility for ensuring access is effective access.

---

[10] [1932] AC 562.

[11] (1765) 19 Howell's State Trials 1030.

[12] Sir Ernest Ryder SPT, *Open Justice* (Max Planck Institute Luxembourg for Procedural Law & Saarland University, Luxembourg, 1 February 2018) <https://www.judiciary.gov.uk/wp-content/uploads/2018/02/ryder-spt-open-justice-luxembourg-feb-2018.pdf>.

A. The Judiciary's Responsibility for Securing Effective Access

The starting point is that it is beyond doubt that the judiciary has a responsibility **7.13** for securing effective access to justice. This arises in a number of ways, some well understood, others perhaps not so well understood.

Most obviously, and most well understood, is the responsibility a judge has to **7.14** ensure that justice is done in the courtroom. It is the responsibility to ensure that proceedings and trials are carried out consistently with procedural principle. This is given effect through long-established common law principles such as: the right to due notice of the case put against you; the right to evidentiary disclosure; the right to challenge the case and evidence against you; the right to equality of arms; and, of course, the right to open justice and judgment in its many facets.

Throughout this book we have described how such principles are now supple- **7.15** mented by more modern developments, such as the now fundamentally im- portant principle of proportionality. Although, one might suggest, it is not as new as some commentators believe and we can trace that principle back into the past. We can see it in the creation of our County Courts, which provided a simpler, less expensive, and more effective form of justice than provided by the great common law and equity courts and then the High Court. We can see it in Magna Carta's requirement that the punishment must fit the crime.[13] It now underpins the op- eration of all our civil, family, and tribunals justice systems. Modern case manage- ment techniques also ensure that judges are able to ensure that effective access is secured for all claims, through ensuring—as we are required to do in for instance civil proceedings—that when we manage claims we do so taking account of the effect of our decisions on other claims. We do not manage claims in isolation from each other. We manage a whole system of claims, and do so holistically.[14] And it underscores the responsibility we have to ensure that where individual litigants are unable to afford or do not wish to have legal representation we take such steps as are necessary to ensure they receive a fair trial.[15]

Some commentators still observe, and quite wrongly we would suggest, that the **7.16** judicial role extends to no more than ensuring that justice is done in that way. The judiciary as an institution, and as one of the three institutions of the state, requires judges—and particularly those in what are now known as leadership roles—to

---

[13] Magna Carta (1215) chapters 20 and 21.
[14] A point emphasized by Lord Dyson MR, 'The Application of the Amendments to the Civil Procedure Rules (2014) 33 CJQ 124 and underscored by *Mitchell v News Group Newspapers Ltd* [2013] EWCA Civ 1537, [2014] 1 WLR 795 and *Denton v White* [2014] EWCA Civ 906, [2014] 1 WLR 3926.
[15] See, for instance, CPR r 3.1A.

take a wider role. The SPT has—by way of example—a statutory responsibility to have regard to the need to ensure that the tribunals are accessible and to develop innovative means to resolve disputes.[16] It is difficult to conceive of how this duty could be carried out if the SPT were not to play such a leadership role. This role is in addition to the fundamental role that the Lord Chief Justice (LCJ) and the SPT have in the administration of Her Majesty's Courts and Tribunals Service (HMCTS). That is a constitutional partnership between the judiciary and the executive, which is encapsulated within the HMCTS Framework Agreement.[17] The Lord Chancellor represents the latter, and does so through discharging his statutory role in providing the resources, buildings, and staff to run the courts and tribunals. The LCJ and the SPT represent the former, to ensure, through their leadership of the courts and tribunals' judiciary, that HMCTS can support the courts and tribunals in exercising the judicial power of the state. The idea that we could not or should not properly be engaged in developing and leading the HMCTS reform programme is one that stands no scrutiny; it rests on the misconception that the judiciary should not be involved in leading the reform of the means through which they discharge their functions. More than that it rests on a conception of the judiciary that was rejected in this country in 2005, when the Concordat between the Lord Chancellor and LCJ, and the partnership model for the delivery of justice it contained, was given effect through the Constitutional Reform Act 2005.

7.17 Within the UK, the courts and tribunals modernization programme is reshaping our system. As a formal, constitutional partnership between the government and the judiciary, reform cannot but be carried out in partnership. It is not a question of the judiciary involving itself in reform impermissibly. On the contrary, for one partner in a constitutional settlement to absent themselves from the reform of a joint venture would be an impermissible abdication of responsibility. We cannot but, we must, take a leading role. And our guiding principle in doing so is that we seek to ensure that our justice system is one that can better deliver effective access to justice. We are not in the business of reducing access or of producing a second-class system of justice. If that were our aim or intention we would be complicit in a series of reforms that would undermine the Rule of Law. No judge can or could properly do that.

7.18 It might be objected that the HMCTS reform programme was born of austerity following the 2007–2008 financial crisis. That, as such, it is a belt-tightening exercise but austerity must not be permitted to harm the principles underpinning our justice system and in particular our commitment to ensuring that each individual can have effective access to justice. Austerity was the spur to fundamental

---

[16] Tribunals, Courts and Enforcement Act 2007, s 2.
[17] See <https://www.gov.uk/government/uploads/system/uploads/attachment_data/file/384922/hmcts-framework-document-2014.pdf>.

reform, not its objective.[18] For economists, this is a point that they would know well from Milton Friedman. He famously noted that '*... only a crisis—actual or perceived—produces real change. When the crisis occurs, the actions that are taken depend on the ideas lying around.*'[19] That crisis for us was the financial crisis. It forced us to consider exactly how we delivered justice. It did so at a time of fundamental societal change. It did so because 2007 was also the year that the smartphone revolution took off, with the launch of the first iPhone. The idea that just happened to be lying around was that provided by the technological revolution—the fourth industrial revolution. This is not to say that we ran headlong, and without due consideration, into embracing the use of technology as a means to reform the courts and tribunals. Detailed consideration was given to how and in what ways the use of digital technology could be used in this way by reform bodies such as Justice and the Civil Justice Council.[20] Consideration was given to how other jurisdictions, such as British Columbia and the Netherlands were putting technology to innovative use through the development of online dispute resolution (ODR) systems.[21] And, of course, serious consideration was given to the issue by Lord Briggs in his Civil Courts Structure Review.[22]

The upshot of all this work was the development of the HMCTS reform pro- **7.19** gramme on principled lines agreed by the Lord Chancellor, LCJ, and the SPT in 2016.[23] Those reform principles were, and remain that our justice system must be: Just; Proportionate; and Accessible.[24] By this we meant that,

> *... the procedures and remedies should be available and intelligible to non-lawyers. People with disabilities should never feel excluded because they cannot attend a physical courtroom or handle documents or traditional procedures. Likewise, people who are not comfortable with new technology must always be supported.*[25]

However, from a practical perspective, this has meant, for instance, that we have **7.20** been developing digitization of our processes through pilot schemes, such as the

---

[18] Sir Ernest Ryder SPT, 'The Modernization of Access to Justice' in J Copper (ed), *Being a Judge in the Modern World* (OUP 2017) 136.

[19] M Friedman cited in M Blyth, *Austerity—The History of a Dangerous Idea* (Oxford University Press 2013) 103.

[20] JUSTICE, *Delivering Justice in an Age of Austerity* (2015) <http://2bquk8cdew6192tsu41lay8t. wpengine.netdna-cdn.com/wp-content/uploads/2015/04/JUSTICE-working-party-report-Delivering-Justice-in-an-Age-of-Austerity.pdf>; Civil Justice Council, *Online Dispute Resolution for Low Value Claims* (2015) <https://www.judiciary.gov.uk/wp-content/uploads/2015/02/Online-Dispute-Resolution-Final-Web-Version1.pdf>.

[21] ibid 13–29.

[22] M Briggs, 'Civil Courts Structure Review—Interim Report' (December 2015) <https://www. judiciary.gov.uk/wp-content/uploads/2016/01/CCSR-interim-report-dec-15-final-31.pdf>; M Briggs, 'Civil Courts Structure Review—Final Report' (July 2016) <https://www.judiciary.gov.uk/ wp-content/uploads/2016/07/civil-courts-structure-review-final-report-jul-16.pdf>.

[23] Lord Chief Justice, Senior President of Tribunals, 'Transforming our Justice System' (September 2016) <https://www.judiciary.gov.uk/wp-content/uploads/2016/09/narrative.pdf>.

[24] ibid.

[25] ibid.

civil money claims online (court) pilot in the County Court, and through various pilot schemes in the tribunals. At all times, it must however be remembered that these pilots, and the reform programme, are taking place within the context of the HMCTS Framework Agreement. They are a partnership, one in which the judiciary has a duty to lead. Our aim here is not reform for reform's sake. Our aim is, on the contrary, specific and targeted. It is to create a better and more accessible justice system. One with better buildings. One with a better, and less daunting, environment within those court buildings. One with new, simpler, more accessible processes. And one which facilitates better use and deployment of our expert judges.

7.21 Our destination, for civil, family, and tribunals is for the creation of a single web-based system, leading to e-filing and management. The aim is a system where there are fewer complex rules or rule books to master, but rather easy-to-use webpages which guide litigants through the litigation process, especially those who either choose to or cannot but litigate in person. Our traditional approach has tended to the daunting; a brief look through the various procedural rules for our various justice systems shows that. They are unintelligible to all but the specialist professional. Greater use of the internet and well-designed courts and tribunals platforms should enable us to ensure that access truly is accessible. It is not only our court and tribunal rules and procedures that can be daunting. We sometimes talk about the majesty of the law and of our law courts. I do not underestimate that our buildings are part of an institution that needs to command confidence, trust, and legitimacy, that is respect, in order to function, but 'majesty' can sometimes be used when what we mean to say is that something is daunting. A court building and a courtroom can be, and perhaps often are, daunting to a litigant, particularly one who does not have a lawyer to represent them. Where this is the case we can, unless we are careful, fail—by omission—to secure effective access. The daunting all too often translates into inaction, into rights not being vindicated, into abuse of private and public rights remaining unchallenged and effectively unchallengeable. Access is more than simply being able to navigate court procedure and ensure your claim comes before a judge. Access requires you to take part in the proceeding effectively. If litigants are intimidated it is unlikely that they will properly secure effective access without assistance.

7.22 We already take a number of steps to ensure that they can do so, whether that is through active case management or whether it is through the very good work carried out by the volunteers who work in Personal Support Units throughout the country. We can go further. Our reform programme through focusing on greater use of digital processes, and digitally accessible hearings, aims to utilize what the vast majority of society is now familiar with: the internet. With so much of our lives now being online, whether buying through Amazon or direct from businesses, selling via eBay or similar web platforms, blogging or tweeting, we are at home on the net. That we are suggests that an internet-based process to initiate and manage and conduct proceedings will be something with which individuals will be familiar, and to a far greater extent than the previous paper and court-building process. Greater use of the internet can thus be harnessed to increase access to justice, to genuinely equal access. This is not to say that all process will take place online. We are not moving to an entirely online process. It will remain essential for many claims and procedures that they take place in the established way, that is face to face and, for some users, on paper. For those claims and hearings that should take place in court buildings, the reform programme and its focus on increasing our use of technology should enable us to ensure that litigants, judges, and the courts and tribunals' administration have an improved environment. Reform enables us to move away from our post-Victorian, and in some cases, Victorian court estate. We can design our courts for today's environment, one where court bundles need not be on paper, but can be on a memory stick—already an option in the UK Supreme Court. It also enables us make better use of available space: as back-offices can reduce in size through less use of paper filing, we can better use it for litigants and lawyers when they need to attend court. It should go without saying that reducing the amount of times an individual is required to attend court reduces the cost and inconvenience of litigation. As Jeremy Bentham might have said, '*we increase access to justice by reducing justice's vexations*'.

7.23 Better access has another meaning. We are not just concerned with creating a better and more accessible system for those individuals who would litigate under the unreformed system. The reform programme's vision—and this can be seen from Lord Briggs' original vision in the Civil Courts Structure Review—is an expansive one. It seeks to make our justice system accessible to those who would not otherwise bring their disputes to court. As such it seeks to expand justice's reach to those who at the present time sit outside the law's protection because they do not perceive the courts and tribunals to be presently open to them or cannot afford the risk of access—an expansive vision of an accessible reality.

7.24 The current reform programme therefore is expansive in another sense. It seeks to remake our courts and tribunals in the light of modern technology so that we are looking to expand our concept of justice. Historically, justice dispensed in the courts stood in parallel to justice secured via mediation, negotiation, and other forms of consensual settlement or Alternative Dispute Resolution (ADR). Reform in the shadow of online developments in ADR—that is in ODR, has given rise to a broader vision of justice. We must not shrink from the fact that we must maintain the incremental development of the common law through precedent if the Rule of Law is to remain strong and enforceable but an appropriate and compatible aim in the civil courts and tribunals is to incorporate negotiation, mediation, and forms of preventative or preventive justice into the formal process: there will be 'just dispute resolution', or as it has been described, a problem-solving approach to justice.[26] An expansive vision is one that sees accessible justice as access to a wider variety of forms of dispute resolution. It seeks to provide the right one for the right dispute, rather than one or two sizes fit all.

7.25 Just as one size does not fit all, as this book has attested at several points throughout, a further practical effect of the reform programme, and one that was clearly stated in the statement of the reform principles set out earlier, is the benefit that the development of assisted digital can bring. This was foreshadowed by Sir Brian Leveson when he referred to the development of what he described as '*digital navigators*'.[27] By this he meant 'individuals who could help the public "navigate" the system'. They would do so through telephone or secure live web chat platforms or face to face. From this earlier expression of the idea we have been developing, as part of the reform programme, systems known as 'Assisted Digital' to help individuals who are unable to access the internet effectively. We are testing these systems and, particularly through the online court and tribunals pilots, we are learning from the feedback we are receiving to tailor the system. And here we see a lesson that justice reform has learnt from developments in private ODR systems, such as those used by eBay. Those systems learn from their users. And they put that learning into practice through changing the way their system operates. In this way they can easily and quickly resolve problems in the system. They can understand where there are gaps in the system, and they can plug those gaps.

7.26 'Assisted digital' is not just a means to improve access for those who would otherwise be excluded. It is a means by which the system itself can learn. It can assist the system as it assists the users. We have to ensure that this ability to learn from its own operation is something that we hardwire into our digitized courts and tribunals. If we do so it will mark a quantum leap forward in terms of our ability to understand how our justice systems work, where and how they do not work, and crucially the extent to which they deliver access to justice. Whether it is through the use of embedded data that is harvested for analysis and research or the use of artificial intelligence to capture good practice, it is my hope that we can ensure that through the reform programme we are able to fully realize this vision.

7.27 Finally, there is another form of accessibility; one which the judiciary also have a duty to secure. That is the duty to bring about a more diverse judiciary, one reflective of the society we live in. We see this duty, particularly in the obligation placed on the LCJ to act to encourage diversity in section 137A of the Constitutional Reform Act 2005. It is a duty that the SPT has strongly endorsed

---

[26] Sir Terence Etherton MR, 'The Civil Court of the Future' [29] (14 June 2017) <https://www.judiciary.gov.uk/wp-content/uploads/2017/06/slynn-lecture-mr-civil-court-of-the-future-20170615.pdf>.
[27] Sir Brian Leveson PQBD, 'Justice for the 21st Century' (Isle of Man, 9 October 2015) [46] <https://www.judiciary.gov.uk/wp-content/uploads/2015/10/pqbd-caroline-weatherill-lecture-2.pdf>.

through, for instance, the emphasis on new generic recruitment principles for the tribunals judiciary and work on the judicial mentoring scheme.[28]

There are many reasons why increasing judicial diversity is of central importance. **7.28** A more diverse judiciary means that the long web of the common law can draw upon the experience, knowledge, and values of society as it is today. It helps to ensure that our law draws its strength from all of society and not a thin strand. It supports constitutional norms to draw their strength, their value from civic engagement. Engagement occurs when people are part of something; when they can and do take part. If our courts and tribunals are to properly engage society, they need to be part of society and society in its breadth and diversity must be part of our courts.

Moreover, our society is an open society. Our courts are open courts. And our **7.29** judiciary must be an open judiciary. We ought to do all we properly can; we say properly because we must of course act consistently with what the law permits, to reach out to society and in particular those in education to improve their understanding of what we do. We must also encourage applications to the judiciary from all parts of society including those who are presently underrepresented. None must be left behind in this. We must focus on all and not just some. And in this we must tailor our approach. What works for gender diversity may not work for BAME diversity, which in turn may not work for socioeconomic diversity. It is often said that justice must not only be done, it must be seen to be done. That is equally true of improving judicial diversity. We must do and be seen to do: if we do not, then it will become difficult for the courts and tribunals to maintain public confidence. All parts of society must see they have a stake in the delivery of justice. We show that by what we do. And what we do—what we must continue to do—is ensure that the judiciary as an institution is open to all with talent, ability, and experience. If—as we rightly do—we recruit the judiciary on merit, as a society we need to ensure that we nurture and develop that talent.

Therefore, there remains also a civic responsibility for assisting access to justice. **7.30** The starting point here again is the idea that justice is not something that is done to you. A just society is one where the delivery of justice, the commitment to do justice, is inherent in all our institutions, in all of civic society. There are many examples of excellent work being done in this respect across the country. And it takes many shapes and forms.

On the one hand, our universities demonstrate real leadership. Law and its study **7.31** is, of course, very often as practical as it is theoretical. This is particularly true of our common law system. Oliver Wendell Holmes was quite right when he

---

[28] See, for instance, *The Judicial Mentoring Scheme* (21 February 2015) <https://www.judiciary. gov.uk/about-the-judiciary/judges-career-paths/judicial-mentoring-scheme/>.

emphasized the fact that the life of the law was not logic but experience.[29] Our laws have grown from cases; from practical problems. Our universities now embody this truth in the work they do through their legal advice clinics and their clinic legal education programmes. The work done by the universities across the country is inspiring and the assistance they get from courts and tribunals and in particular community liaison judges is vital. There are fine examples in Keele where the CLOCK programme was ground-breaking[30] and services such as Kent University's law clinic[31] or University College London's Access to Justice Centre[32] or Coventry University's representation before tribunals through its partnership with the Central England Law Centre. The work they do for the disadvantaged in society is vitally important. It is civic engagement in the pursuit of a more accessible justice system at its best. With the ever-increasing growth in litigants-in-person, their work with the Litigants in Person Network cannot be underestimated. Their programmes should serve as a template for others to emulate. These examples show engagement by our civic institutions at its finest. Just as the courts and tribunals are subject to a reform programme, the aim of which is to create better access to justice, we can go further than we have already. There is always room to innovate. Such a challenge was laid down approximately fifteen months ago by the Master of the Rolls, Sir Terence Etherton. In a lecture to LawWorks, he suggested that 'universities, pro bono advice centres and organisations, and law firms [should collaborate] to create an expanded advice scheme'.[33]

7.32 The idea was that, along with the legal professional regulators and the courts and government, there was scope to expand the nature of such pro bono assistance to litigants-in-person by law students. He did not suggest this would be unsupervised assistance. On the contrary, he suggested that there should be greater access to appropriate supervision, they would be insured and they would be subject to professional regulation. The benefit to society is obvious: greater assistance for those who need it most. It draws more of society within the protection of the law. The benefit to the student is the ability to use that experience to enter the profession. He called for detailed consideration of the idea, which deserves repetition and support from leadership judges. Our universities have shown they have the will and the experience to innovate here, to develop programmes that are both socially responsible and of benefit to their students. In the spirit of assisting further

---

[29] OW Holmes, 'The Common Law, Lecture I, Early Forms of Liability' [1] 'The life of the law has not been logic; it has been experience. The law embodies the story of a nation's development... it cannot be dealt with as if it contained the axioms and corollaries of a book of mathematics ... In order to know what it is, we must know what it has been, and what it tends to become.'

[30] See <https://www.keele.ac.uk/law/legaloutreachcollaboration/>.

[31] See <https://www.kent.ac.uk/law/clinic/>.

[32] See <https://www.ucl.ac.uk/access-to-justice/>.

[33] Sir Terence Etherton MR, 'LawWorks Annual Pro Bono Awards Lecture' (15 December 2015) [24]ff <https://www.judiciary.gov.uk/wp-content/uploads/2016/12/law-works-lecture-mr-20161205.pdf>.

civic engagement could they not take the lead in helping to develop the Master of the Rolls' idea? It is to be hoped that other parts of civic society will join them in doing so.

The universities are not alone. The legal profession through the development of its **7.33** own pro bono schemes, such as the Bar litigants-in-person support scheme or the long-established Free Representation Unit, and the important work done by the Law Society under its Pro Bono Charter, exemplify their civic engagement. Again, this shows the breadth of what is being done. It is not just pro bono work though. The Legal Education Foundation has through its Justice First Fellowship Scheme funded training contracts and pupillages and CILEx qualifying placements for law graduates who intend to work in the field of social welfare law. It not only provides training, it helps its Fellows—as they are called—gain the necessary broader skills to develop successful careers.[34]

If all these schemes and those behind them came together and collaborated we **7.34** could not only achieve a significant increase in civic engagement by our universities, legal professions, and those charities that work in this area. We would also provide a clear template for wider civic engagement.

If leadership judges are to lead by example they must be seen to support those who **7.35** help to secure access to justice for all—that is the heart of a living constitution.

B. The Way Forward—A New Strategic Approach to Judicial Leadership

A new strategic approach to judicial leadership requires, as the great US scholar **7.36** Professor Lon Fuller once described: '*law as a shared enterprise*'. It was, and is, one where individual conduct is made subject to the 'governance of law'.[35] In a recent, and excellent book, Professor Gillian Hadfield has examined that idea in the context of the IT and digital revolution and the effect it is having, could, and ought to have, on our justice systems.[36] That she has, has a particular resonance with the authors of this book.

As judges we manage daily our engagement in the Courts and Tribunals **7.37** Modernization Programme (the so-called, more commonly known as, the 're-form programme'). Both sets of reforms, and particularly the latter, centre on the effective application of improved process and digital technology to our courts and tribunals. The reform programme is a shared endeavour. It, like HMCTS itself, is

---

[34] See <https://jff.thelegaleducationfoundation.org/about/about-the-fellowship/>.
[35] L Fuller, *The Morality of Law* (Yale 1964).
[36] G Hadfield, *Rules for a Flat World* (OUP 2016).

a partnership between the judiciary and the government. It is one that is underpinned by statutory reform;[37] as such it is also a partnership with Parliament. All three branches of state are thus working together to improve our justice system. As with any shared endeavour, for it to succeed there must be effective leadership. If considered unreflectively, the question who should lead the reform programme would suggest one answer: the government. In this case that would mean the Lord Chancellor and the Ministry of Justice. They would be responsible, as they are generally, for justice policy and for preparing and introducing necessary legislation to Parliament. It might appear that the judiciary would have no leadership role to play.

7.38 Since 2005, however, the landscape has changed fundamentally. The reform was foreshadowed by the 2004 Concordat: the agreement between Lord Falconer LC and Lord Woolf CJ that set out how their respective roles would change to better reflect the separation of powers. Under that agreement, the Lord Chancellor's role as head of the judiciary, which had been in place since the Judicature Act 1873,[38] was to be transferred to the LCJ.[39] It also delineated the responsibilities that were to fall to both the Lord Chancellor and LCJ under the new constitutional settlement. Importantly, it stated that the latter would become responsible for: representing the judiciary's views to Parliament and the government; putting in place structures to secure the well-being, training, and guidance of the judiciary; and for putting in place structures for the effective deployment of judges and the allocation of work in the courts.[40]

7.39 The Concordat is a document of constitutional importance. It reflects an agreement between two branches of the state concerning the governance of the judiciary. It formed the basis of what became the Constitutional Reform Act 2005, which effected the statutory changes necessary to transform the LCJ into the President of all the courts in England and Wales, into the Head of the courts' judiciary.[41] It also gave statutory force to the responsibilities we outlined a moment ago.[42] The new

---

[37] See for instance, The Courts and Tribunals (Judiciary and Functions of Staff) Bill 2018. <https://publications.parliament.uk/pa/bills/lbill/2017-2019/0108/18108.pdf>, and previously the Prisons and Courts Bill 2017 <https://publications.parliament.uk/pa/bills/cbill/2016-2017/0170/17170.pdf>, which was originally intended to provide the statutory underpinning to the reform programme but which fell with the 2017 General Election.

[38] See Judicature Act 1873, ss 5 and 6, which made the Lord Chancellor both the President of the Court of Appeal and High Court.

[39] *'Constitutional Reform—The Lord Chancellor's judiciary-related functions:* Proposals' (January 2004), known as The Concordat, para 11. It is reprinted in Report from the Select Committee on the Constitutional Bill, vol 1, HL Paper No 125-I (24 June 2004), Appendix 6. For an overview, see S Shetreet and S Turenne, *Judges on Trial* (CUP 2013) chs 1–3.

[40] The Concordat, para 4.

[41] Constitutional Reform Act 2005, s 7(1).

[42] Constitutional Reform Act 2005, s 7(2); Crime and Courts Act 2013, s 21.

constitutional settlement placed these, and other, duties upon the LCJ: duties of leadership.[43]

In fact, the relationship between the courts and the government was not alone in **7.40** undergoing fundamental reform in the first decade of the century. The tribunals underwent arguably more wide-reaching reform. Following the Leggatt Review of 2001,[44] the many and varied tribunals were unified via the Tribunals, Courts and Enforcement Act 2007. It created the First-tier and Upper Tribunal, the latter being a superior court of record with all the powers and duties of the High Court and the office of SPT as Head of the Tribunals judiciary.[45] As with the LCJ, the SPT was to be responsible for representing the views of tribunal judges to the government and Parliament; for making effective arrangements for their welfare, training, and guidance; and for their deployment.[46] Additionally, and reflecting the inherent nature of the tribunals, the SPT is also required to ensure they are accessible, fair, handle disputes quickly and efficiently, for tribunal members to be experts in their fields, and to develop innovative dispute resolution methods.[47] The duties of leadership do not stop there. Both the LCJ and the SPT have the responsibility for issuing Practice Directions, that is to exercise the common law power (in respect of the courts) and statutory power (in respect of the tribunals) to provide rules of practice and procedure for the courts and tribunals.[48] Additionally, the LCJ has a duty, held jointly with the Lord Chancellor, to encourage diversity among the judiciary.[49] Since the Crime and Courts Act 2013, both the LCJ and the SPT are responsible for making judicial appointments, in my case of almost all my judicial office holders (JoHs).[50] As a result they come under a number of duties imposed by the Equality Act 2010 concerning such appointments. And equally, the LCJ, again jointly with the Lord Chancellor, is responsible for judicial discipline;[51] a duty which I share.[52] In these last set of duties, we can see a further feature of the new constitutional settlement: partnership. Leadership is not required of the judiciary alone. It is carried out with the government. This is most clearly seen through the administration of the courts and tribunals. Since 2007,

---

[43] A flavour of the extent of the duties can be seen by those that have been variously delegated since 2006: see Lord Chief Justice's Statutory Delegations No 1 of 2018 <https://www.judiciary.uk/wp-content/uploads/2015/12/lcj-delegations-schedule-no-1-of-2018.pdf>.

[44] A Leggatt, *Review of the Tribunals, Tribunals for Users, One System, One Service* (HMSO 2001) <http://webarchive.nationalarchives.gov.uk/+/http://www.tribunals-review.org.uk/leggatthtm/leg-00.htm>.

[45] Tribunals, Courts and Enforcement Act 2007, s 2.

[46] Tribunals, Courts and Enforcement Act 2007, sch 1, part 4, paras 13 and 14; sch 2, para 8; and sch 3, para 9; sch 4, part 2.

[47] Tribunals, Courts and Enforcement Act 2007, s 2(3).

[48] Constitutional Reform Act 2005, sch 2; Tribunals, Courts and Enforcement Act 2007, s 23.

[49] Constitutional Reform Act 2005, s 137A.

[50] Crime and Courts Act 2013, sch 13, part 4.

[51] Constitutional Reform Act 2005, s 108.

[52] Lord Chief Justice's Statutory Delegations No 1 of 2018 at 157–66.

HMCTS has operated as a formal partnership between the Lord Chancellor, the LCJ, and the SPT.[53] In strict constitutional theory, HMCTS is an aspect of the executive; it is part of the Ministry of Justice. Acknowledging the post-2005 and post-2007 settlements, the Lord Chancellor has, however, agreed that it should operate under a board which, uniquely, is responsible to both the executive and judiciary. Both of these branches of the state are thus under a duty to provide leadership to the administrative means by which the courts and tribunals deliver justice.

7.41 Having outlined the nature of the leadership duties now placed upon the judiciary throughout this text, we now focus on and explore two salient issues:

- First, the manner in which we give effect to those duties; and
- Second, the principles which guide their application.

C. Implementing the Principles

7.42 It is one thing to have duties and responsibilities, it is another to be able to carry them out effectively and then to do so. When the Lord Chancellor was head of the judiciary, discharging the various duties relating to the judiciary that went with that office, it was something that could be carried out through the Lord Chancellor's Department. As is well known, ministers can act through their senior civil servants under what is known as the *Carltona* doctrine.[54] The Lord Chancellor thus had the necessary means to effectively carry out his duty of leadership.

7.43 Prior to the 2005 Act, the LCJ and the other Heads of Division had small private offices. Very often these consisted of their clerk, a private secretary, and, for some, a diary secretary. There was no dedicated civil service for the senior judiciary; no department for the judiciary. The first thing that was needed therefore was an administration akin to, what is now, the Ministry of Justice. That administration was created by way of what is known as the 'mini-Concordat'; the agreement between the government and judiciary which made provision for the creation of what is now the Judicial Office of England and Wales.[55] It provides the cadre of civil servants who work for the LCJ, other Heads of Division, and, since 2007, for the SPT. Their primary duty, consistent with the constitutional principle of judicial independence, is to the judiciary.[56] There is however one particular and

---

[53] HMCTS Framework Document (July 2014) <https://assets.publishing.service.gov.uk/government/uploads/system/uploads/attachment_data/file/384922/hmcts-framework-document-2014.pdf>.

[54] *Carltona v Commissioner of Works* [1943] 2 ALL ER 560.

[55] See Shetreet and Turenne (n 39) 66.

[56] The SPT also has access to and obtains considerable independent advice from the Scottish Judicial Office and the office of the LCJ in Northern Ireland.

fundamental difference between the Judicial Office and the Ministry of Justice. It relates to the *Carltona* doctrine. While the matter has not been before a court for determination, it is believed that that doctrine does not apply to the Judicial Office. There are two difficulties.

The first is applying *Carltona* to civil servants working for and to the judiciary, **7.44** rather than those who work for ministers in central government. A distinction can be drawn between members of the executive—civil servants—carrying out acts for the executive—ministers, and members of the executive carrying out acts, albeit executive acts, for judges who are not themselves members of the executive. On the other hand it could be said that as the powers transferred to the judiciary by the 2005 Act, and provided for the SPT through the 2007 Act, are executive ones, then *Carltona* should apply now as it did when the Lord Chancellor exercised them.

The second difficulty, and one which also points away from reliance on *Carltona*, **7.45** is the fact that the 2005 Act introduced a baroque scheme of express delegation for the various functions.[57] A similar, albeit wider, delegation power exists for the SPT under the 2007 Act.[58] The provision of such an express power would seem to point away from the application of *Carltona*.

Whatever the ultimate answer to this question, the approach which has been taken **7.46** is that where functions can be delegated they are delegated to specific judges— those with expertise and those with a specific interest.[59] Hence, functions relating to civil justice are delegated to the Master of the Rolls as Head of Civil Justice; disciplinary functions concerning tribunals judges are delegated to the SPT and so on. They are then exercised by the delegate personally, although members of the Judicial Office provide expert advice and assistance. The structure thus created, the extent of which can be seen from a 351-page document called the *Lord Chief Justice's—Statutory Delegations*, is complex. One important difference between the manner in which the SPT exercises his functions and the way the LCJ exercises his, is that the 2007 Act provides the SPT with an express power to exercise any function which can be delegated while the delegation is in force. The 2005 Act does not make similar provision for the LCJ. There is a therefore a certain degree of additional flexibility in the tribunals' approach:

Formal delegation is further supplemented by organizational arrangements. Both **7.47** the 2005 and 2007 Acts provide for some functions, those relating to training,

---

[57] See Lord Chief Justice's Statutory Delegations No 1 of 2018.

[58] Tribunals, Courts and Enforcement Act 2007, s 8.

[59] As was noted during the passage of the Constitutional Reform Act, by Shetreet and Turenne, 'It was not intended that the Lord Chief Justice should exercise all these powers and functions personally … '; see Shetreet and Turenne (n 39) 47.

guidance, and welfare, to be carried out by way of 'appropriate arrangements' put in place by or on behalf of the LCJ and SPT.[60] These do not require formal delegation; the statutory language provides the basis for a more informal approach. It also permits decisions to be taken by Judicial Office staff members. And, equally it provides a basis for the senior judiciary to develop, refine, and then implement policy decisions. Such arrangements encompass the carrying out of local leadership and welfare functions by Presiding Judges and Tribunal Chamber Presidents, the development and implementation of programmes to facilitate diversity in the judiciary, and the most recent, the establishment of the Judicial Data Protection Panel. At the apex of these arrangements sits the Judicial Executive Board (JEB) and the Tribunals Judiciary Executive Board (TJEB), both of which act as a form of advisory Cabinet for the LCJ and SPT.[61]

7.48 The means by which we give effect to our leadership duties can thus be summarized as follows:

- The Judicial Office provides executive, management, human resources, policy, and legal support for the senior judiciary to help enable them carry out their duties effectively;
- The various duties and leadership functions are carried out by a wide range of members of the judiciary either under express delegation or via arrangements put in place by the LCJ and SPT;
- High level policy decisions are considered by the JEB and TJEB, with decisions then taken in the light of such consideration and advice, by the LCJ or SPT.[62]

7.49 It should be apparent that the wide variety of leadership functions impose very significant time and management pressures on the senior judiciary, many of whom already have very significant administrative responsibilities. And of course, this is all on top of their primary role: managing proceedings and trying cases.

D. The Guiding Principles

7.50 Having outlined the architecture of leadership throughout this book, the pertinent question remaining is: how should it operate? Here I want to stress a point which is in my view beyond argument: the senior judiciary have no option but to exercise these duties and powers. The common law has imposed them and Parliament has entrusted them to the judiciary following the 2005 and 2007 constitutional settlements. Accordingly, all judges have a duty to lead. That is

---

[60] Constitutional Reform Act 2005, s 7(2)(b) and (c); Tribunals, Courts and Enforcement Act 2007, 2007, sch 1, part 4, paras 13 and 14; sch 2, para 8 and sch 3, para 9; sch 4, part 2.

[61] For a short discussion see Shetreet and Turenne (n 39) 67.

[62] See, Sales LJ in *R (Richardson) v Judicial Executive Board* [2018] EWHC 1825 (Admin).

the system which Parliament gave effect to, following the agreement reached between the executive and judiciary in the Concordat, in the 2005 and 2007 Acts. The question is not should we lead, but how do we lead? What are the principles that guide the exercise of the various leadership duties and responsibilities? It is this question to which this book now turns to explore. In doing so we will evaluate three broad themes: accessibility and accountability; efficacy; and finally, evidence-led proportionality.

E. Accessibility and Accountability

The first group of principles come under the theme of accessibility and account- **7.51** ability. They are: open justice and accountability; democratic participation and civic engagement; diversity and inclusion; and the coherence of our governance.

The first principle to guide the exercise of our leadership duty is that of open **7.52** justice and accountability. This has a number of elements. First, justice must be open to litigants. Not only in the sense that our citizens must be able to exercise their right of access to a court. But also in the sense that their disputes must be capable of being adjudicated effectively by courts. Openness is not just a function of the cost of access. It is also a function of the nature of access. Most clearly we see this second issue in the growth in e-commerce disputes, significant numbers of which are resolved consensually through ODR mechanisms. Our courts and tribunals need to be able to adjudicate such disputes. If our justice system is to be open, and not to place certain types of digital disputes beyond the reach of the law, it needs to be reformed so as to facilitate the bringing of such claims. Claims must be within the ambit of justice, not outside of it.

Equally, openness requires us to ensure that our courts and tribunals remain open **7.53** to public and in particular, media scrutiny. We cannot accept a position where they fall outside the view of the public. A judge, a court, or tribunal observed is, as Lord Neuberger MR observed in the case of *Al-Rawi*, democratically accountable.[63] Publicity is the means to ensure justice does not become arbitrary: it ensures justice is done, the law is applied properly. It ensures that the decisions judges make can be scrutinized and debated by civic society. If, as they do, courts and tribunals articulate the values instantiated in our laws,[64] their decisions must be capable of robust public debate so that Parliament and ultimately the electorate can, if they think proper, revise, restate, or develop the law through the democratic process. Hence open justice and democratic accountability go hand in hand.

---

[63] *Al-Rawi v Security Services* [2010] EWCA 482, [2012] 1 AC 531, 543.
[64] O Fiss, 'Against Settlement' (1984) 93 Yale LJ 1073, 1085.

7.54   Democratic accountability is itself linked to the next principle: democratic participation and civic engagement. Justice is not something which can or should be done to people. A just society is one where the delivery of justice, the commitment to do justice, is inherent in all our institutions, in all of civic society.[65] Courts and tribunals, and for that matter the judiciary as a whole, need to be open to society more broadly than through access to proceedings. There needs to be broader engagement with civic society. This can and is being achieved in a number of ways. Both the LCJ and the SPT, as part of their leadership role, inform Parliament about the operation of the justice system. Senior judges appear regularly now, within proper constitutional limits, before Parliamentary Select Committees, notably the Justice Select and the Constitution Committees.

7.55   More broadly than these forms of democratic accountability, the LCJ engages through an annual press conference. And most recently, the LCJ and I have added to the work already being done across the country to engage with schools and colleges as part of public legal education. Both the Master and the Rolls and the SPT have also both led calls for greater collaborative work by universities, the professions, and wider society to develop means to promote effective access to the courts.[66] And, most recently, the LCJ has very persuasively argued that civic engagement, properly done, is one of the means by which the judiciary can help explain the role of the courts and tribunals, their role in upholding the rule of law. As he put it,

> *The judiciary invites misunderstanding or incomprehension if it stands completely apart and aloof from society. Engagement within proper constitutional bounds will benefit society and the judiciary.*[67]

7.56   Engagement, as observed in Chapter 2, is therefore necessary if we are to properly fulfil our duty of leadership.

7.57   Accessibility is also given expression by the need to ensure that the judiciary is properly diverse and inclusive. Two points arise here. If the judiciary is not to stand apart from society it must be, and must be seen to be, part of society. It must be seen to be open to all within society. If the law is to develop, drawing on the wisdom of all parts of society, just as it draws on the wisdom of the past though the winnowing of the common law method, the judiciary must be able to draw upon the experience, knowledge, and values of the society of today. Our law, and society, is impoverished to the extent that it cannot and does not do so. Appointment on merit is a *sine qua non*. But equally, appointment must be from a diverse pool of merit, drawn from across society. Judges must do all we can to

---

[65]   Ryder (n 3). <https://www.judiciary.uk/wp-content/uploads/2018/03/speech-ryder-spt-keele-uni-march2018.pdf>.

[66]   Etherton (n 33); Ryder (n 3).

[67]   Lord Burnett CJ, 'Becoming Stronger Together' (Brisbane, September 2018) <https://www.judiciary.uk/wp-content/uploads/2018/09/lcj-speech-brisbane-lecture-20180910.pdf>.

ensure that is and cannot but be the case. Securing a properly diverse judiciary is not simply a public good in terms of the judiciary itself. It is a public good in another, and perhaps more important way. Successful societies are ones which, in addition to the Rule of Law, have stable governance, free and fair elections and, among other things, are societies which are open and inclusive. They are ones where everyone has, and sees that they have, a proper stake in that society. Securing a diverse—an inclusive—judiciary is one of the means by which our society can ensure that this aspect of the health of the nation is continually built upon in the future.[68]

Therefore, the final principle under this theme turns inward. It is the need for there to be a coherent, modern, and effective governance structure for the judiciary. This is a theme which Lord Thomas CJ considered in detail.[69] It is one on which I have argued that we need to look to how we organize the structure of judicial management of the courts and tribunals.[70] Do we need to consider the approach to training judges who exercise leadership roles in modern management techniques? Do we need a management structure which reflects the nature and size of the judiciary today? What might we learn from other jurisdictions, both common law and civilian ones, in terms of how they structure the internal management of their courts and judiciary? The duty of leadership requires us to consider the possible answers, and to take what appropriate steps we can to put them in place. **7.58**

F. Efficacy

The second group of principles can be grouped under the theme of efficacy. They are: specialism and expertise; localism; and innovation. **7.59**

First, specialism. Historically, there has always been a tension between specialism and uniformity in our approach to the delivery of justice. Prior to the nineteenth century reforms, there were numerous courts with specialist procedures, differing jurisdictions and judiciaries. It was a form of specialism which benefited few. It was specialism as a barrier to effective access to justice. Since then the courts have moved towards uniform processes. A movement which culminated in the merger **7.60**

---

[68] For a discussion of the features of healthy societies, and the necessity of inclusiveness, see D Acemoglu and J Robinson, *Why Nations Fail—The Origins of Power, Prosperity and Poverty* (Profile Books 2012).

[69] Lord Thomas CJ, 'The Judiciary within the State – Governance and Cohesion' (Lionel Cohen Lecture, May 2017) <https://www.judiciary.uk/wp-content/uploads/2017/05/lcj-lionel-cohen-lecture-20170515.pdf>.

[70] See Sir Ernest Ryder SPT, 'Securing Open Justice' (MPI Luxembourg, February 2018) <https://www.judiciary.uk/wp-content/uploads/2018/02/ryder-spt-open-justice-luxembourg-feb-2018.pdf>.

of the Rules of the Supreme Court and the County Court Rules in the Civil Procedure Rules (CPR) in 1999.

7.61 To a certain extent the division between specialism and uniformity is a false one. Both are needed. Both have their place. The one-size-fits all approach of the CPR was in reality never that. There were common processes at a general level: for issue and service of claims for instance. And then there were specialist procedures for specific types of claims, whether they be small claims or commercial claims. A common set of high-level rules governs the approach in the tribunals. And the original HMCTS reform concept—and the right one—was to develop a common set of high-level procedures for civil, family, and tribunal proceedings. And those high-level rules could then be properly complemented by specialist rules for specialist processes as necessary. However, specialism does not end with procedure. Its focus is also decision-making, or rather the decision-maker. The original idea behind the tribunals was to draw on specialist knowledge; hence many of them were mixed tribunals drawing on legal and expert practical knowledge. That remains the case. We go further now, and can go further still. Since the reform of the tribunals in 2007, and the increase in the ability to deploy judges across the courts and tribunals since 2013, via the Crime and Courts Act, our ability to ensure that we can develop greater judicial expertise has increased. Equally, we are better able to deploy specialist judges to deal with all manner of cases which fall within their field of expertise. For instance, the UK judiciary has been able to develop and utilize specialist expertise in administrative law across the Upper Tribunal and the Administrative Court. Further, the UK judiciary is developing what is becoming known as 'double-hatting' where a specialist judge sits to hear proceedings simultaneously in both the courts and tribunals where cases engage their overlapping jurisdictions.[71] Well-developed judicial specialism, properly deployed, cannot but be necessary for the future development of our justice system. If we are to secure better access to proportionate dispute resolution through expert decision-making, this is a principle that must inform how we exercise leadership of the judiciary.

7.62 Specialism is not sufficient. It must equally go hand in hand with localism. Local justice has been a feature of our justice system since its earliest development. Its link to democratic participation is patent: justice must be something you can experience within your immediate community, town, or city. It cannot be remote, cloistered only in London or other large cities across the country. If it were or were to become remote, it would cease to be something we share as a society. Localism thus has an intrinsic link back to civic engagement. It is also, and fundamentally, an issue of accessibility. Local justice is accessible justice. Throughout Great Britain the First-tier Tribunal sits at local hearing centres. The Upper Tribunal

---

[71] See for instance the scheme operative in the County Court at Central London and the First-tier Tribunal Property Chamber <http://41todw2i37w9c74zg3ndz7xp-wpengine.netdna-ssl.com/wp-content/uploads/2018/08/Guidance-unopposed-business-lease-renewals.pdf>.

Administrative Appeals Chamber and the Employment Appeal Tribunal (EAT) sit in national geographic centres. The Upper Tribunal Immigration and Asylum sits regionally, and Lands and Tax and Chancery Chambers sit where cases require. On the courts side, the Business and Property Courts have centres throughout England and Wales. Administrative justice is as much a matter for hearing in Manchester and Birmingham as it is in London. As Lord Thomas CJ said, no case is too big to be heard outside London.[72]

Modernization must therefore ensure that local justice in these forms is main- **7.63**
tained. It must enhance it. This can be achieved in a number of ways. First, by the active leadership of judges in advisory councils, such as the Civil and Family Justice Councils, or in the recently established Administrative Justice Council. Second, through ensuring that modernization reforms, which utilize technology, enable greater local accessibility of the justice system. Technology should, for instance, be considered as a means of bringing justice to local town halls and other civic spaces. Third, by facilitating greater cross-jurisdictional use of local and regional hearing centres. Fourth, by developing greater use of continuous and asynchronous hearings, which enable court and tribunal users to access live hearings in a manner which best suits their lives, which best facilitates their active participation. By way of example here, there is to be a pilot digital evidence sharing with the Department for Work and Pensions (DWP) and asynchronous conversations so that we can conduct some live hearings without the need for a disabled user to face a difficult journey to a hearing room which many say they find threatening. Local justice need not stop at the town square.

Finally, in terms of innovation, it is Gillian Hadfield's theme; and that which **7.64**
has underpinned the very valuable work done by Richard Susskind on court and tribunal reform. It focuses on the question of what should we be doing to re-shape justice and its delivery in ways that can properly engage today's society? It asks us to focus modernization on what society needs given our data-driven, technology-based lives. To that end we need to focus far more than we have in the recent past on the nature of disputes, on the nature of evidence, and on what our justice system should deliver and how it should do so. The post-War world saw a need to develop administrative law and human rights law in ways that pre-War society had not done. Just as it had seen the need to develop new types of procedure and causes of action to deal with a world of mass production, we are now facing a world where the digital economy, whether it be smart contracts, or e-commerce, requires us to reconsider how we configure our justice systems. In that regard Lord Briggs' vision of an online civil court embodying ODR and adjudication was a signal step forward. It was an example of clear-sighted innovation.

---

[72] Lord Thomas CJ, 'Justice in One Fixed Place or Several?' (Lord Birkenhead lecture, October 2013) <https://www.judiciary.uk/wp-content/uploads/JCO/Documents/Speeches/lcj-birkenhead-lecture-21102013.pdf>.

We need to build on such a vision and develop it further. To do so it will be essential for the judiciary to engage constructively with the academy, with individuals who are expert in the new economy, with ombudsmen, with approaches being taken overseas such as the Civil Resolution Tribunal in British Columbia, Canada. Leadership requires the judiciary to learn from those with expertise, with those who themselves innovate. Leadership requires innovation. And innovation depends on engagement. We cannot shy away from it. And after innovation and engagement there is the additional task of effective implementation.

G. Evidence-led Proportionality

7.65 Finally, we turn to evidence-led proportionality. In 1995, Lord Woolf in his Interim Access to Justice report, noted that civil procedure and its cost should be 'proportionate to the nature of the issues involved'.[73] This was not, as some might believe, the first time that proportionality was a guiding principle in the development or delivery of justice in England and Wales. Proportionality was inherent in the dual development of the County Courts and their relatively simpler forms of process and the High Court and its more detailed procedures. It was inherent in the development of the tribunals, their procedures, and the fact that they were intended and designed to be accessed by litigants rather than primarily by lawyers.

7.66 Since the late 1990s proportionality has moved from being one principle that has guided the operation of our justice system to centre stage. Just as it underpins modern case management, it underpins increasingly flexibility deployment of the judiciary across the courts and tribunals, and the development of innovative approaches to dual sittings of the courts and tribunals where they have overlapping jurisdiction, referred to earlier. It also informs our approach to leadership. It does not do so in an esoteric way. It is a practical principle, as can readily be seen by the broad use of the statutory delegation powers by the LCJ and myself. If it is to guide our approach to leading the modernization of the justice system how ought it to do so? This book advocates however that a four-stage approach should be taken.[74]

7.67 First, when considering reform or reforms we must ask ourselves if the policy objective we are pursuing furthers the achievement of accessible, accountable, open justice. An example of this practical focus can be seen in something Lord Dyson said whilst he was Master of the Rolls. Considering the current reform

---

[73] Lord Woolf, *Access to Justice: Interim Report to the Lord Chancellor on the Civil Justice System in England and Wales* (HMSO 1995) ch 1, para 3.

[74] The approach is articulated in *Huang v Secretary of State for the Home Department* [2007] 2 AC 167 [19] and *(R) Quila v Secretary of State for the Home Department* [2012] 1 AC 621 [45]. See Ryder (n 70) [30]–[33.

programme, he paused over the role technology was to play. He cautioned against reform for technology's sake; against a 'because we can do it, then we should do it' approach. He put it this way,

> *Open justice is rightly prized as an essential element of our system of justice. Justice must not only be done, but must be seen to be done. There is an obvious tension between the preservation of this fundamental principle and the promotion of virtual, internet-based, systems and processes that enhance efficiency and cost-savings. It is one thing to conduct mediations out of the public gaze. This is already done and there can be no objection to it. But we should not allow advances in technology to lead to secret court determination of disputes. It will be a technical challenge to find a solution to this problem. Technology must be the servant of justice, not its master.*[75]

7.68 Our policy objective is, but cannot simply be, to digitize our justice system. That would be to elevate function over purpose. To render digital the master and not the servant. Equally, modernization's purpose cannot be, as some have suggested, the pursuit of austerity. A more efficient, technology-infused system may be more economical for the state but economy cannot be our overriding aim if the price we are to pay is a reduction in open, accessible, accountable justice. If we are to lead reform, then we must be clear about our policy objective, and the boundaries it places around the use of technology and the pursuit of economy. Thus, in pursuing the policy objective of digitization, we do so because and only to the extent that it furthers open, accessible justice. If it were understood not to do so, we would be duty bound to reject it.

7.69 The second question is then, are the proposed means to implement the policy objective rationally connected to it? We are pursuing digital processing to make filing and managing claims more accessible. That process is to be simpler, more user-friendly for litigants-in-person than our established ways of working. We are pursuing video hearings on the basis that they make it easier, and less daunting, for some litigants to access the system. We pursue this aim because and to the extent that it is able to increase public participation in the justice system by making it more easily accessible.

7.70 The third and fourth questions follow: are the measures to be taken no more than necessary to achieve the policy objective, and do they strike a fair balance between the rights of the individual and the interests of the community? Both are inherent in Lord Dyson's warning. We must ensure we do not go too far. This requires careful planning and the exploration of options for modernization. It requires a critical assessment of the consequences of intended reform. Nobody could properly support, for instance, a use of technology which crucially undermined public participation in justice while promoting individual participation. Nobody could properly support measures aimed at increasing efficiency or promoting economy

---

[75] Lord Dyson MR, 'Delay too often Defeats Justice' (Law Society, April 2015) [30] <https://www.judiciary.uk/wp-content/uploads/2015/04/law-society-magna-carta-lecture.pdf>.

if in doing so they undermined the rights of individuals to be able to access the justice system effectively, or of the public interest in securing the Rule of Law.

7.71 Proper planning and effective implementation of well-planned reforms is not sufficient however to satisfy the third and fourth questions. What is also, and crucially, needed is ongoing scrutiny of implementation. Effective, robust, and statistically sound research is necessary during implementation, that is through re-search-based pilot schemes. It is equally necessary post-implementation—a point inherent in the view expressed earlier this year by Lord Burnett CJ's that modern-ization is a process and not event;[76] a point I made earlier this year when I out-lined the necessity of feedback continuing post-implementation—feedback which will enable us to consider how the reforms work, whether they are achieving their aims. And if they are not where and why they are not, to enable remedial action to be taken in real time rather than once every ten years as has been the historic pattern of reform.[77]

7.72 In our future approach to judicial leadership of the justice system, our approach to developing and implementing reform policies, we cannot but adopt these four clear guiding principles. They must be our rule of reason.[78] And, they must be evidence-led and subject to ongoing evidence-based scrutiny.

7.73 In conclusion, it is plain that we are living through an age of transformations.[79] The delivery of justice is not and cannot be exempt from change. It too must evolve in the light of new technology so as to better secure effective access to justice for all. It must not do so in an unplanned, uncritical way. It must not do so unreflectively. When reforms have been carried out effectively in the past they have been the product of critical consideration. They have been evidence-based, and here the best example of this—and it reaches back in time—is the evidence-gathering exercises that were carried out by the nineteenth century court reformers. Where those reforms succeeded it was because there was clarity of pur-pose, a strong evidence base identifying the source of the problems to be over-come, and considered conclusions concerning how they were to be rectified. It was an era of guided transformation—guided by judicial leadership, which is itself guided by proportionality.

---

[76] Lord Burnett CJ, 'The Age of Reform' (Sir Henry Brooke Lecture, June 2018) [39], 'Modernisation will not stop in 2023. It is not an event but a continuing process. Too often in the past that point, whilst appreciated by the far-sighted, was not acted on by Government, which is why there is now so much to be done in a relatively short time.' <https://www.judiciary.uk/wp-content/uploads/2018/06/speech-lcj-the-age-of-reform2.pdf>.

[77] Sir Ernest Ryder SPT, 'What's Happening in Justice: The View from England and Wales' (UCL Future of Justice Conference, May 2018) [27]–[30] <https://www.judiciary.uk/wp-content/uploads/2018/05/speech-ryder-spt-ucl-may-2018.pdf>.

[78] Ryder (n 70) [32].

[79] Ryder (n 77) [1]

Accordingly, if the judiciary is to harness the full potential of the IT revolution **7.74** to improve the accessibility and accountability of our justice systems, to improve democratic participation in the shared enterprise that is the governance of law, to innovate where innovation improves the delivery of justice, then the judiciary cannot shirk its duty of leadership. Nor can it approach it in anything other than a coherent, considered manner, one which draws on evidence, which weighs it properly, and which continues to draw on it to monitor implementation.

We have therefore, through this book, identified the ten principles which we see **7.75** underpinning judicial leadership, how it and how modernization of our justice system should be carried out:

   i. *Open justice;*
   ii. *Accountability;*
  iii. *Accessible justice;*
   iv. *Democratic participation and civic engagement;*
   v. *Diversity and inclusivity;*
   vi. *Specialism and expertise;*
  vii. *Localism;*
 viii. *Proportionality, including speed and efficiency;*
   ix. *Innovation that is evidence-based and tested; and*
   x. *Coherent governance.*

If we apply these principles, lead consistently with them, we will enable the de- **7.76** livery of a justice system fit for the twenty-first century; a justice system that is fit for the just governance of law for all our citizens.

H. Judicial Leadership Fit for a 'Modern Judiciary'

Judges across the country in courts and tribunals make judgments every day.[80] **7.77** Some are straightforward. Some are non-contentious. At the other end of the spectrum some are highly complex. And some are highly contentious. All are important. Whether the decision is taken in a small, low value claim or whether it is taken in a multi-million pounds claim, it matters. It matters to the parties involved, to their families and friends, and to wider society. Judicial decision-making is an exercise of state power. Irrespective of the nature of the case in which a judge makes a decision, it is and must be the Rule of Law in action. It cannot be underestimated either in its scope or in the effect it has on all our lives.

---

[80] This section was first given by Sir Ernest Ryder, Senior President of Tribunals as a lecture to BASPCAN 10th International Congress at the University of Warwick on 9 April 2018.

7.78 It is often though not exclusively the case that some of the most sensitive decisions a judge has to make are those that arise within the family justice system, particularly those involving children—those who are very often the most vulnerable members of society. Since the publication of the Family Justice Review in 2011, the family justice system has been undergoing a systematic programme of reform, the aim of which is to ensure more and better access to justice for children and their families. That reform programme has seen the creation of a single Family Court through the Crime and Courts Act 2013. It has seen the implementation of the Family Justice Modernisation Programme, aimed at ensuring that the family judiciary and HMCTS have the necessary structures, and leadership and management skills to ensure that the new—now no longer so new—Family Court is able to operate effectively.

7.79 The modernization of family justice remains work in progress. It is a judge-led process. As part of that process it is important to re-visit one aspect of that reform programme, the one focused on decision-making and judicial decision-making as part of the process in which we are all involved: the young person, parents, carers, professionals, and agencies and the judge of the Family Court. In July 2012, as part of the Judicial Proposals for the Modernisation of Family Justice, the report highlighted the need for frameworks of good practice. As described, they covered issues such as the management of individual cases, the leadership of the justice system, and the use of expert evidence, that is empirically validated materials relevant to the issues in a case. This report focused attention on decision-making and made the following point:

> Decision-making is a risk-based judgment call based on principles. That is what we appoint and train our judges to do. They are not alone in performing that task … Judges identify and solve problems which lead to an ultimate decision and the best judges, like the best advocates learn to discard the noise of peripheral disputes and concentrate on the key issues. The art of a quality decision making process is the balance between the risk being taken and the protection against that risk which is part of the process.[81]

7.80 The question of how we can ensure that all judges are in a position to make the best quality decisions they can is not however simply an issue for the family courts. It is as pertinent to the criminal, the civil, and the tribunals justice systems. It is particularly interesting at the present time because of the development of what has been described as a more problem-solving approach to judicial decision-making. This is evident in the present civil justice reforms that are being carried out as a consequence of Sir Michael, now Lord, Briggs' Civil Court Structure Review.

---

[81] E Ryder, 'Judicial Proposals for the Modernisation of the Family Justice System' (July 2012) 9 <https://www.judiciary.uk/announcements/justice-ryder-report-family-justice-modernisation-31072012/>.

As the Master of the Rolls has described it, the developing new approach to the delivery of online civil justice:

> … will be problem-solving in the sense that the [court] … will help the parties find the appropriate solution to their dispute. A problem-solving purpose is the next step in the evolution of the [Civil Procedure Rule's] Overriding Objective, which lies at the heart of modern case management.[82]

A problem-solving approach is well known in the family justice system. That it is **7.81** moving to the heart of civil justice, and has also been a central feature of tribunals justice for many years, emphasizes the importance of ensuring that all judges are properly equipped with the right skills, materials, and knowledge to play that role effectively. It requires a greater emphasis on and understanding of how we continue to attain high quality decision-making.

There is another reason why it is important that we get it right. We often hear **7.82** about the importance of role models. We do not, however, often hear talk of our civic institutions being role models. They are and must be. Our courts and judiciary, as a civic institution, have an important role to play in leading by example. If we set and continue to set high standards, if we demonstrate through our approach that we will not accept less than the application of those standards in what we do, we can hopefully help secure a race by all of us to the top. In terms of evidence-gathering and decision-making in those professions that are involved not only in the judicial process, but also more generally, we may help build on and maintain existing cultures of excellence, while also helping to foster such cultures in new areas. Collaboration in the development of good practice, its dissemination and application should be our acknowledged goal. That the collaboration should involve the views and perceptions of the young people and families involved in our decision-making goes without saying.

This book has examined ways in which we may improve the state of the art, it is **7.83** important to consider the following:

- the principles underpinning our approach; and
- the nature of the evidence that informs judicial decisions.

I. Three Key Principles

As a starting point, our approach must be underpinned by three principles. As we **7.84** develop our approach, more principles will become relevant.

---

[82] Sir Terence Etherton MR, *The Civil Court of the Future* (14 June 2017) [29] <https://www.judiciary.gov.uk/wp-content/uploads/2017/06/slynn-lecture-mr-civil-court-of-the-future-20170615.pdf>.

7.85 The first principle is that the approach to improving and enhancing judicial decision-making must be systematic, evidence-based, and tested. We cannot afford to pluck best practice out of thin air. It is neither whatever is the latest fashion of the day, nor is it what any particular judge finds attractive or interesting; even less the sometimes uninformed and historically hidebound views of those who happen to exercise power. It is no use a judge advising other professionals about their skill and expertise without the benefit of access to evidence-based materials rather than mere common sense or personal preference. Best practice and its development cannot be an exercise in ad-hocery. It must be thought out, considered, and rigorously tested. And when its lessons are implemented, they too must be tested and monitored.

7.86 One of the great flaws of our justice system is that, historically, we did not test reform before implementing it generally. We have tended to rush to implementation, when a more considered approach would have been more advisable. We are now far more used to testing reforms through pilot schemes, so that we can see how they operate in practice, whether they achieve their aims, and whether and if so what unintended consequences they create. In that way we can take steps to rectify any problems before full implementation occurs. In the present courts and tribunals modernization programme, which is digitizing our court and tribunal processes, the use of pilot schemes is embedded. We have learnt. And, we go on learning.

7.87 The central importance of learning from continuous testing ought to be obvious to all. It is inherent in the precedent-based system that underpins the development of the common law. It is always inadvisable for a judge to express opinions about issues that are not decisive on the facts of a case just at is inadvisable to express opinions about the practice of other professions without reliance on evidence that has been tested. If we turn from the individual case to the operation of our justice *systems*, evidence that has been tested is sorely lacking. If there is a need to demonstrate the utility of ongoing testing we need only look to developments in Canada. In British Columbia, they have developed an online tribunal, known as the Civil Resolution Tribunal, for small claims and what we would call landlord and tenant disputes. The online system has been designed to enable users—litigants—to provide feedback at every stage of the process. That feedback is then collated and—importantly—acted upon to refine and improve the system.[83] The same type of feedback process is being employed in the pilots of our court and tribunal reforms.[84] Feedback and refinement cannot stop at the inception of reform.

---

[83] See Tanja Rosteck, 'Happy First Birthday, Strata Solution Explorer!, and Solution Explorer Quarterly Update: 2017 Q4' <https://civilresolutionbc.ca/happy-first-birthday-strata-solution-explorer/>; <https://civilresolutionbc.ca/solution-explorer-quarterly-update-2017-q4/>.

[84] See Sir Terence Etherton MR, 'Civil Justice after Jackson' (15 March 2018) [33]–[35] <https://www.judiciary.gov.uk/wp-content/uploads/2018/03/speech-mor-civil-justice-after-jackson-conkerton-lecture-2018.pdf>.

As Canada is very properly demonstrating it must be an ongoing process. As a first principle, the same type of ongoing testing and refinement must be embedded in our approach to maintaining and improving the quality of judicial decision-making.

Turning to the second principle: reform needs to be implemented through **7.88** rigorous and informed training. It might be said that judges do not need to be given training in how to make decisions. After all judges, both before and after appointment, have spent their careers testing evidence, hypotheses, or theories of the case, and drawing conclusions accordingly. Critical thinking is in the judge's DNA. It is. But there remains much that can be learnt to improve those skills. Lord Neuberger, in a lecture given in 2015, alighted upon the issue at the heart of this principle.[85] He noted how an evidential study of behaviour carried out over ten months in Israel which examined over 1,000 rulings on applications before parole boards came to the conclusion that decision-making differed depending on the time of day. Lord Neuberger noted that the study showed that the decision-makers granted two thirds of the applications in the morning, but as the day went on the number of approvals declined to zero. The approval rate returned to two thirds after the decision-makers came back from lunch.[86] He also noted experimental studies that showed that judicial decision-making can be effected by cognitive bias and heuristics. Anchoring effects, for instance, have been shown to apply to judges.[87] And again, as he pointed out, subconscious bias is something that needs greater consideration than it has had in the past.[88]

The point from this is not to feed decision-makers more often. It is to emphasize **7.89** the importance of ensuring, in developing training and materials to improve judicial decision-making, that we draw on experience from the social sciences, from behavioural psychology, from legal academics who study judicial decision-making and so on. We need to ensure that the approach we take is one that is grounded in robust evidence drawn widely and which has itself been subject to critical scrutiny. As judges we are all trained in the legal method from law school, through our practices as lawyers, and while on the bench. Judges and their judge-craft, cannot however be islands unto themselves. If we are to maintain and enhance the quality of our decision-making we need to broaden the legal method to incorporate insights drawn from other fields where critical thought plays a central role, just as we also need to have a greater understanding and appreciation of the social, economic, and business context of the cases that come before us. As Lord Neuberger rightly pointed out, we needed to develop subconscious bias training so that we

---

[85] Lord Neuberger PSC, ' "Judge not, that ye be not judged": Judging Judicial Decision-making' FA Mann Lecture 2015 <https://www.supremecourt.uk/docs/speech-150129.pdf>.

[86] ibid [25].

[87] ibid [26].

[88] ibid [31].

are aware of it and aware of how to combat it. We have, since his call to arms, developed in the Judicial College an impressive array of induction and advanced training that draws on good practice in this field of knowledge.

7.90 This book has illustrated the importance of drawing insights from other areas by reference to the current civil justice reforms. I noted earlier that those reforms, particularly the Briggs reforms, are intended to introduce a problem-solving focus to the judicial process. This differs from the traditional common law adversarial process in civil proceedings. As such it will necessarily require the application of different skills and approaches than judges have traditionally applied. Its intention is for judges to be more investigative. Investigation requires different skills than forensic analysis in the adversarial context, as those familiar with the family and tribunals justice systems know. Its intention is also to bring mediation and early neutral evaluation into the case management and dispute resolution processes. It thus goes further than Mediation and Information Meetings in the family justice system and will draw on the skills and experience used in financial dispute resolutions hearings, issues resolutions hearings, and settlement conferences which will now be familiar to many and which rely on early neutral evaluation which is a form of risk assessment.

7.91 Again though, care is needed. Just as investigation differs from the cut and thrust of the adversarial process and has its own procedural protections, mediation calls for different skills than early neutral evaluation. While the former can involve evaluation of opposing cases, just as the latter intrinsically does—both foreshadowing what a judge may decide at the end of an adversarial process, the latter needs to be evaluative. Mediation need not, and some may say, should not focus on the assessment of argument, evidence, and rights, but rather should be and properly is a facilitative process which focuses on helping the parties to a dispute to identify the interests that underpin the positions they have taken in the litigation. And having done so, to explore creative—problem-solving—solutions. That is an entirely different approach, calling for different skills. The danger without effective training, without exposing judges and those court or case officers who may carry out such mediation sessions to the range of different approaches to mediation, is that the default process will be an evaluative one. It will be one that does not focus on problem-solving because it could be interpreted and applied within the terms of the adversarial, rights-based, paradigm.

7.92 If we are to enhance judicial decision-making, we will need to draw widely from expertise in facilitative mediation as well as evaluation. We will need to expand the nature of the paradigm within which judges, courts, and tribunals carry out their role, and make decisions concerning individual cases and also match the right kind of decision-making process to the risk that the proceedings are intended to protect against. In the Employment Tribunals there is an impressive track record of early conciliation by ACAS, early neutral evaluation during case management, and the availability of judicial mediation: all before the parties submit their long-term relationship to the process of adversarial decision-making. If we do not enhance our skills in this way, we will not be able to develop this aspect of our reforms as well as we could. Hence the need for a systemic, evidence-based, and tested approach that ensures our training properly draws upon all relevant sources to enhance judicial decision-making. Here the point is that we need to be provided with effective training and experience of facilitative mediation, of principle-based as well as adversarial negotiation, and other problem-solving approaches.

This takes us to the third principle. It is intrinsically linked with the first two. It **7.93** is the need for the provision of high-quality materials to assist judges in carrying out the decision-making role. It should be clear that such materials will be needed for training purposes. We will need to develop and enhance the role played by the Judicial College in preparing training materials and training judges. If we are to provide a systematic approach, it must play an integral part. Expert materials will also, however, need to play a central role in the decision-making process itself. They cannot simply be a means to enhance skills and training. Such materials must also be available to judges when they are in courts and tribunals deciding cases. In the tribunals system a specialist judge or panel is expected to know their specialist material just as the SPT is required to administer the tribunals justice system in a manner that has regard to its expertise and that is innovative.

The nature of evidence is important and can be understood in two ways: the **7.94** evidence that helps inform individual judicial decisions; and the evidence that informs the improvement of the justice system as a whole. The two will of course be interlinked. Work is being carried out to improve both. A recent collaboration between the judiciary, academics led by Professor Broadhurst at Lancaster University, and the Nuffield Foundation has produced real results. The Foundation seeks to develop evidence-based practice to help individuals exercise their rights. It thus promotes civic activity, and seeks to promote the health of society generally. The Family Justice Review identified a gap in our understanding of the family justice system, and particularly concerning how it makes decisions concerning children. It was an evidential gap. We did not have sufficient evidence drawn from the system which could assist judges to make individual decisions or leadership judges to administer the justice system—and that is perhaps a significant understatement. The Nuffield Foundation has agreed to fund the establishment of an organization—the Nuffield Family Justice Observatory—to fill that gap.[89] Its aim is to 'support the best possible decisions for children by improving the use of data and research evidence in the family justice system in England and Wales'.[90]

---

[89] K Broadhurst, T Budd, and T Williams, *The Nuffield Family Justice Observatory for England and Wales: Making it Happen* (The Nuffield Foundation 2018).
[90] ibid 4.

7.95 It is going to achieve this aim in a systematic, evidence-based way drawing on evidence from England and Wales. It will do so through stakeholder engagement and through examining the available data on the operation of the system. As such specialist agencies and bodies, such as CAFCASS, child protection and care organizations and agencies who represent users and professionals who work with them will have an important part to play. This work will be a collaborative exercise. It cannot but be if it is to produce robust, research-led and peer-reviewed materials for judges and other decision-makers to draw upon. The idea behind the Observatory is now being expanded into the administrative justice arena by work being done by the Legal Education Foundation with the Administrative Justice Council, HMCTS, and the Council's academic panel. The ambitious aim is to set up a data lab in HMCTS and to identify principles for the collection, analysis, and use of data about administrative law outcomes.

7.96 The Observatory has an even broader purpose. It will also consider and learn from best practice from abroad. In this respect, it has already noted how the Association of Family and Conciliation Courts has already established a practice of working through interdisciplinary teams drawn from its international membership to consider and reach a consensus on best practice to, for instance, child contact arrangements.[91] Equally, drawing on international experience and evidence related to it could be used to develop a more rigorous application of, for instance, collaborative law techniques, and not least the development of that family dispute resolution process into an interdisciplinary team model where different practitioners—psychologists, child development specialists, mental health practitioners, and so on—from a wide range of fields are integrated into the process to help the parties devise and implement problem-solving solutions, ones that are best for the family and for the children within the family.[92]

7.97 By looking at international developments, at best practice across other jurisdictions and learning from them, these projects will be able to provide a rigorous and evidence-based series of proposals about how the system as a whole can be improved, and in this way how judicial decision-making can consequently be improved. It goes without saying that such an approach ought not to be limited to the family justice system. Rigorous evidence-based reform proposals that draw on best practice from across the world—and subject them to a proper examination of how and in what ways they may be adapted for practice here—are something that ought properly to underpin our approach to reform generally across all of our justice systems. The Observatory will follow the lead of other 'What Works' centres in allied professions and justice systems that are enhancing our knowledge and skills as decision-makers and which can help the judiciary improve

---

[91] ibid.

[92] P Tesler, 'Collaborative Family Law' (2004) 4(3) Pepperdine Dispute Resolution Law Journal 317, 330ff.

the administration of justice. For those who rightly caution the judiciary not to become enmeshed in the politics of executive policy, this is about the operation of the rule of law, its effectiveness and efficiency, which is properly the judiciary's concern.

Moving away from the system level, the Observatory is to look at ways in which the   **7.98**
individual judicial decision-making process can be improved. There will be a number of limbs to this. It will work to 'identify priority issues where empirical evidence may help guide practice'; provide 'reliable summaries of what is, and is not, known from research or administrative data'; combine 'knowledge from empirical research with insights from policy practice and user experience'; and, work with 'system professionals to develop, update and test guidance ... based on [their systems] knowledge'.[93]

First, it will ensure that you as professionals can bring your experience to bear   **7.99**
in the development and testing of any such guidance. In this way, it will ensure that guidance does not just have the rigour of academic study and research, but also benefits from the practical, professional insights of practitioners. Second, it will help to overcome one of the problems that the Observatory brought to light during the initial scoping study, which underpinned the basis of what it determined would be its aim. This problem was that often practitioners were unsure about whether research studies or findings should be placed before the courts. As the scoping study concluded,

> *Although practitioners recognised that their understanding of, and deliberation about, cases was informed by background child welfare knowledge, they were far less confident about making reference to specific research studies to support arguments in court. Social workers feared cross-examination if they made direct reference to research, whereas lawyers, barristers and judges felt that this kind of 'extra-legal' knowledge was best introduced to the court by an expert instructed on the basis of specific expertise.[94]*

Where practitioners also have limited access to such research materials and where   **7.100**
a case may not warrant or justify the appointment of an expert witness, the provision of reliable, rigorous education and information to the judiciary is a key way in which their understanding of specialist issues such as child development may be informed. Indeed, not only is it wrong to proffer expert evidence when it is not necessary, it has always been the case that expert evidence should not be provided where the issue is within the skill and expertise of the court.

In this way we will build on the excellent initiative being carried out by the   **7.101**
Royal Society, the Royal Society of Edinburgh, and the judiciary in which expert primers for judges on specific areas of scientific study are being developed. Two such primers have already been published—the first on Forensic Gait

---

[93] Broadhurst, Budd, and Williams (n 89) 4.
[94] ibid.

Analysis,[95] the second on Forensic DNA Analysis.[96] Those primers seek to provide judges 'with the scientific baseline from which any expert dispute in a particular case can begin'.[97] They provide context and help foster greater understanding, thus improving a judge's ability to get to grips with such evidence as is presented by an expert during a trial. It is hoped that the same will come to be said of the Observatory's research studies. They may play a further role, where there is no expert, of educating the judge about the state of the art in the field which they cover. This will be of particular importance where there have been developments in a particular field. Where the court is a problem-solving tribunal this will be of crucial importance. It is only where a judge has such knowledge that they will be able, with the parties and their representatives, to be in a position to explore all the possible options to resolve the issues in the case before them. They will help underpin the skill and expertise of a specialist judiciary.

7.102 The Observatory will enable us to return to unfinished business from the Family Justice Review. In that review, the conclusions of which were accepted by government and the then LCJ, Lord Judge, it was recommended that as part of the supporting architecture for reform, the judiciary would lead the introduction of at least ten good practice guides. They were to cover:

- Local authority pre-proceedings work;
- Social work evidence;
- The Official Solicitor's capacity guidance;
- The timetable for the child;
- Key issue identification;
- The threshold for intervention by the state in a child's life;
- The use of experts;
- Third-party disclosure and concurrent evidence in proceedings (or hot-tubbing as it is known colloquially);
- Placement and care plan scrutiny; and finally
- The use of research in the court.[98]

7.103 Some of these elements of practice have been well developed but, as yet, insufficient attention has been paid to the collation and analysis of evidence about the practice that is the consequence. The Observatory's work will clearly engage in this and will, in particular, focus on the last of that list: the use of research in

---

[95] See <https://royalsociety.org/~/media/about-us/programmes/science-and-law/royal-society-forensic-gait-analysis-primer-for-courts.pdf>.

[96] See <https://royalsociety.org/~/media/about-us/programmes/science-and-law/royal-society-forensic-dna-analysis-primer-for-courts.pdf>.

[97] Per Lord Hughes JSC <https://royalsociety.org/news/2017/11/royal-society-launches-courtroom-science-primers/>.

[98] E Ryder, *Talking about Reform* (26 June 2012) 5 <https://www.judiciary.uk/wp-content/uploads/JCO/Documents/Speeches/ryder-speech-26062012.pdf>.

court. It will help the development of practice guides so that family courts, judges, and practitioners across the professions are equipped with the materials that the reform programme anticipated. Successful reform requires change to be implemented and constantly reviewed.

We therefore should of course emphasize that the development of practice guides **7.104** and the use and availability of research more generally to judges and practitioners is not a means to bypass expert witnesses and the scrutiny that must be engaged when professionals disagree. As was once said 'we cannot demand of the judges that they have knowledge of every branch of science, of every are and of the mysteries of every profession' (cited in J Jolowitcz, On Civil Procedure, at 225). However, there is no intention to attempt to meet such a demand. It would not be possible to do so. And primers and practice guides are not intended to be an attempt to do so. Expert evidence may not always be necessary, but whether it is necessary on the facts of a particular case is, in part, dependent on the skills and knowledge of the specialist judge. We all need skill and experience to realize that which we do and do not know. Knowledge of the context and research in an area ought always to be available. The primers and guides will ensure that that is the case. They are meant to be educative, and in being so they may be relied upon by judges, but subject of course to challenge in an individual case. To facilitate the possibility of such challenges, which must be a genuine opportunity in order for the courts to maintain a commitment to fundamental principles of procedural justice, primers and guides must be made available publicly. They should therefore be placed on the Judiciary of England and Wales' website so that they are readily accessible to anyone who wishes to know what material is available to judges.

While the intention is not to replace experts, there will be cases where a party **7.105** either will not be in a position to appoint an expert or it will be disproportionate for one to be instructed. Equally, there will be cases where expert evidence will be unnecessary. In those circumstances, the evidence that the judge and the parties may have available to them is that from witnesses, which may be specialist without technically being that of an expert under the Rules, or from specialist agencies involved in the case, and/or the primers or practice guides. The risk in such cases is that there will be no effective—no critical—challenge to the material. Such a challenge may be necessary where, for instance, the guidance does not go into sufficient detail or where there is a case for an alternative view notwithstanding the fact that the guidance has been peer-reviewed and sets out an accepted professional opinion.

In such cases, there is a risk that the primers or guidance may inadvertently mis- **7.106** lead the parties and the judge. In the absence of adversarial scrutiny, that which should be tested may not be. How are we to ensure that judges do not default to simply accepting that which they are familiar with or that which is in front of them? An answer to the problem is the provision of sufficient and effective training in behavioural sciences, so that judges become more aware of how the decision-making process works. It is to instil in them greater awareness of heuristics, confirmation bias, and so on so that they can better approach the material before them with a critical, investigative eye. That is the value of the investigative or inquisitorial approach that has been developed in the tribunals. Secondly, it is to ensure that expert and specialist agencies are appropriately involved in the justice process. If expert practitioners know that the judge has research material before the court, the fear of introducing it or discussing it in evidence will inevitably decrease. If its use is understood to be the norm, then reference to and practitioner challenge to it will also become much more normal. The prospect then of a court not engaging with the material critically will as a result be minimized. In this way we can help to make judicial decision-making a more critical, collaborative exercise: one which draws on practitioner expertise at the macro level through primers and practice guides, and at the micro level through enhanced practitioner involvement in individual cases. There is, of course, much work to be done by the Observatory, the judiciary, and all stakeholders in the justice system to make this work effectively. It is work that if done properly and well, will benefit us all, not least those whose interests we are charged to safeguard. The delivery of justice has to change to meet the needs of those who need it, who use it, and who are judged by it. For a long time, justice was something that was done by the state to its citizens. It was the product of a primarily adversarial process, and one that was party-led, or perhaps more accurately lawyer-led. That adversarial approach is challenged in the context of family justice with its more inquisitorial process, in which the focus must be on safeguarding children by securing their best interests. The retreat from the adversarial model can be seen elsewhere, for example in the criminal context, with the development of problem-solving courts and attempts to introduce restorative justice techniques and processes. It can be seen in the civil context through the Briggs reforms and the intended introduction of investigative and problem-solving approaches to the resolution of money claims in the digital court. It can be seen in the family context, where, as a result of the Family Justice Review, it has been embedded in the approach in the Family Court and through the development of, for instance, the Family Drug and Alcohol Court.[99] And the more investigative, inquisitorial approach has always been at the centre of the approach in the tribunals.

7.107 If we are to ensure that these developments enhance how we deliver justice, we will need to ensure that judges have the training, experience, and materials to enable them to carry out their evolving roles effectively. If we are to continue to make high quality decisions, and decisions in a changing judicial culture, the right training, experience, and materials must be drawn from a multi-disciplinary, peer

---

[99] See, for instance, J Harwin et al, 'After FDAC: Outcomes 5 Years Later Final Report' (2016) <http://wp.lancs.ac.uk/cfj-fdac/files/2016/12/FDAC_FINAL_REPORT_2016.pdf>.

reviewed, and validated research base. To obtain that we must both demonstrate leadership in identifying and putting in place what is necessary and acknowledge that we should draw on the skills and experience of others. Judicial decision-making is an exercise of state power. The state has a duty to ensure that all proper steps are taken to ensure it is capable of being exercised properly, that is justly. If it does so, and we take the steps outlined, then not only will the quality of our decision-making processes improve, but we will ensure that the judiciary is able to maintain and enhance public trust and confidence in the rule of law. And importantly, in making the difficult decisions that judges do on a daily basis, it will help ensure that we make the best ones for the individuals involved. As a society, and as judicial leaders and/or judges, committed to the Rule of Law it is a responsibility we cannot shirk.

J. Concluding Thoughts

Hopefully, our aim at the outset of this book is realized. Let us bring theory and principles together in order to inform practice. **7.108**

Government spending and policy implementation is conditioned by criteria that take effect within spending review periods which are themselves informed by social and fiscal policy. All of that is scrutinized in Parliament and save as respects its legality in an individual case, policy is not a matter upon which the judiciary comment. The LCJ and the SPT however have an obligation to consider and, if appropriate, comment upon those matters involving the judiciary which include financial efficacy and the effect of policy on the administration of justice. The normal mechanism for that comment is through annual reports presented to Parliament and the Lord Chancellor and by written and oral evidence to the Justice Select Committee in the House of Commons and the Constitution Committee in the House of Lords. In practice, and within spending review periods, the Treasury approves the framework within which the judiciary are remunerated and the courts and tribunals are funded. It is, however, the Lord Chancellor and Secretary of State for Justice who has the formal responsibility for the effectiveness and efficiency of the justice system. S/he has the responsibility for the provision of court and tribunal estate (and its physical condition and appropriateness), HMCTS support services (including staff and ICT), and the terms and conditions of service of the judiciary (including their recruitment i.e. their complement, pay, and pensions). **7.109**

HMCTS has an almost unique position within government. Although its senior officers are part of the Ministry of Justice and that department's leadership structures, the service operates under a partnership agreement known as the Framework Agreement which creates the HMCTS Board as a joint venture between the Principals to the Agreement who are the LCJ, the SPT, and the **7.110**

Lord Chancellor. There is an effective duty of mutual cooperation between the Principals that extends to a collaboration where that is not inimical to the independence of the judiciary or other constitutional principles. However, the judiciary recognize that the financing of the justice system occurs within that context and the ever changing political landscape that can make even the most rigorous plans subject to exogenous events. It follows that the senior judiciary are involved in medium term financial planning and an annual budgeting exercise (known as the 'Concordat discussions') both in respect of the sitting days that are presently the currency which determines how many of what kind of JoH sit doing what (and hence the recruitment and deployment/assignment questions that necessarily follow) and also the staff who directly and indirectly support those sittings who are employed by HMCTS. The ability of the Principals to satisfy their statutory duties and of HMCTS to operate efficiently and effectively are underpinned by these negotiations.

7.111 Although the HMCTS Board makes its recommendations to the Principals based on detailed forecasts, business analysis, and business planning, the senior judiciary have to be involved either as the jurisdictional leaders in that process and/or as one of the Board members taking part in the negotiations. Ultimately, the Board recommends to the Framework Agreement Principals an annual settlement which the Principals scrutinize and discuss in order to come to a consensus. The lack of consensus would trigger the cessation of the Framework Agreement, which would ultimately lead to a settlement directed by the Lord Chancellor and an inevitable report to Parliament by the LCJ and the SPT. That has never occurred.

7.112 In order for senior judges to comply with their statutory duties and responsibilities and inform the process described, it is necessary to have a strategic vision and a plan, or rather a series of plans that are regularly refreshed. The judiciary, however, would bring little or nothing to the process, as senior judges, if they did not have regard to the fundamental principles we have described. Earlier in this work we described the tactical, clinical, organizational, and strategic functions of the leadership judiciary. We sought to suggest that the leadership judiciary must have regard to constitutional norms, ethical behaviours, internationally accepted principles that describe the Rule of Law, statutory duties, Rules, and directions which inform their roles. These individual and collective responsibilities provide a principled framework for the decisions that leadership judges have to make in their administration of justice. We have also described broader civic obligations around that core framework that are critically important to the legitimacy of the judiciary, that is the trust, respect, and accountability which are necessary components of the functioning of the judiciary and the Rule of Law.

7.113 In practice, each jurisdiction functions in its own way in part informed by the traditional imperatives and protections of that jurisdiction (see, eg the differences that can be deduced from the overriding objectives of each jurisdiction and the more particular Rules and guidance that exist in each). There are also simple approaches which are adopted by Heads of Jurisdiction which inform, by schemes of delegation, direction, guidance, training, and review, the way in which their leadership judges function. The leadership of the judiciary is a collegiate function—both at a local level and regionally/nationally within and across jurisdictions. It may involve decisions by Heads of Jurisdiction and their delegates which are constitutionally important and as influential to the effective and efficient administration of justice as any decision in an individual case (eg by the use of practice directions) but leadership and management of the administration of justice involves every judge playing their part and contributing to the whole, which is the Rule of Law. Judicial leadership is both collaborative and consensual. It has to be in a system that is built on respect for the independent decision-making of judges and that places obligations on leadership judges in the way they lead, that is the perceptions of their own judiciary are important to internal respect and trust and the legitimacy of the leadership function just as those concepts and the public perception of the judiciary are vital to society.

Moreover, we have described the theoretical bases for leadership and the behaviours that each methodology and style involves. The essence of what works and which style to use will change over time and circumstance. The collegiate structure was for most of recent history hierarchical and directive reflecting the nature of precedent in the common law. Leadership is now much more intuitive and understanding of the need to engage, communicate, and explain albeit that decisions of principle and guidance will be reasoned from first principles. We have also described ten principles derived from high authority by which leadership judges can assess, analyse, and determine questions that relate to the administration of justice (by reference to open justice, accountability, accessibility, democratic participation and civic engagement, localism, proportionality, diversity and inclusivity, specialism and expertise, innovation, and coherent governance). There needs to be an understanding that to apply these principles leadership judges will need reliable data (primary evidence) and empirically validated advice about what works and what is good practice. It is the responsibility of senior leadership judges to commission this, and approve its use by their colleagues. **7.114**

Collegiate and civic leadership also involves positive outreach and engagement, comprehensible language, and above all a mutual understanding of the civic role that the institution of the judiciary should nurture and protect. We have described the importance of this to the health of the institution of the judiciary and to the Rule of Law that they are charged to safeguard. **7.115**

Let us finish with a practical example of the organization of leadership in the context of a judiciary which your authors know very well. In the tribunals, which comprise both the unified reserved jurisdictions of the United Kingdom and the Employment Tribunals and EAT in Great Britain, the methodology of **7.116** governance has become a commonplace. It begins and ends with a vision and strategic imperatives which are reported upon in the SPT's annual report to the Lord Chancellor and Parliament. That report provides a retrospective look at the plans as implemented in the previous year and the reports of each of the fourteen chamber Presidents of the First-tier and Upper Tribunals, the Employment and Employment Appeal Tribunals on their jurisdictions and perspectives from the Presidents of devolved tribunals in Scotland and Wales and the senior Commissioner in Northern Ireland. It also describes the ways in which the SPT exercises his duty of mutual cooperation with his fellow Heads of Jurisdiction, the geographic Chief Justices in the UK. It provides a forward look both across the remaining term of any spending review period and the next financial year. The report sets out headline governance issues that are intended to further the statutory powers and duties of the SPT and enhance the administration of justice by reference to the principles we have described which are themselves intended to safeguard the Rule of Law. The report and its annexures reflect the detailed discussions and advice that have taken place between and been tendered to the SPT by his leadership judges, that is the Presidents in the TJEB, the First-tier and Upper Tribunals Presidents' groups that advise on strategy and assignment (deployment and performance issues), the representatives of the tribunals judicial associations (the Forum of Tribunals Judges who also meet as a Judges Council), and the judges who advise upon the reform programme (the Tribunals Judicial Engagement Group). Each major jurisdiction (eg immigration and asylum or employment) has a jurisdiction board that feeds in to this process and is itself an example of partnership working within HMCTS. The jurisdiction boards are responsible for forecasting and business planning in the jurisdiction, the profile of resources used, and the effective matching of supply and demand including in the use of fee paid JoHs and by recruitment and cross assignment.

7.117 Plainly, there is a very effective process of external and internal collaboration, challenge, scrutiny, and review provided by a number of organizations. The most significant external organization outside Parliament and the executive is the Administrative Justice Council (administered by the charity 'JUSTICE') which is a transparent, independent body comprising of the full Council that identifies and advises both on policy and legal reform and has a thriving academic panel, pro-bono panel, and advice sector panel which identify the priorities for the work that is sponsored by the Council. Internally, both leadership judges and judicial associations are members of the Judges Council and there is a Change Network that seeks and discusses feedback from judges and panel members about the major reform programmes. Communication and engagement (including importantly with courts judges) are provided through regular national bulletins, regional and local leadership groups, the judicial associations in the Forum and a strong, independent academic journal (the *Tribunals Journal* produced by the Judicial College) together with critical friends and networks of both strategy and project judges who are appointed to ensure that what we identify as good practice and improvements are implemented in practice (eg in respect of appraisal, the use of information technology, security, international affairs, training, welfare, and diversity). Examples of the concepts that have been identified, developed, and implemented include: a tribunals reform that is moving towards greater flexibility of deployment of the courts and tribunals judiciary, their joint authorization, training, and the ability to sit concurrently in tribunals and courts jurisdictions without compromising the flexible and informal processes that are the hallmark of the tribunals (known as 'one judiciary'); a reform that identifies best practice improvements to process which bring Rules, practice directions, and guidance closer together, using comprehensible plain language, signposting and assistance for users and a greater reliance on triage, pre-hearing supervision and alternative and ODR methods (known as 'one system'); and an initiative that seeks to iden-tify from empirically validated and/or successfully piloted good practice better quality decision-making both by the decision-makers whose decisions form the subject matter of our proceedings and the decisions of our judges themselves. Some of the issues are of sufficient importance for them to be reported upon separately, for example, the courts and tribunals modernization programme and progress towards the Smith Commission promise of devolution to Scotland of the administration of tribunals justice.

The identification of jurisdictional business plans and their implementation, the **7.118** monitoring of operational performance to match supply and demand, and the in-tegration of improvements into business as usual are major parts of the leadership functions of each national President and their team of leadership judges (whether the change is a major reform project such as process reform and digitization or a minor procedural change by Practice Direction). Agreeing outcome measures, identifying and embedding data, and commissioning its analysis with feedback loop improvements are becoming the norm, as is the commissioning of research about good practice and the success of pilots. It is in this way that the strategic ob-jectives which are agreed at TJEB and directed by the SPT and his Presidents are converted into plans, workstreams, and decisions at a regional and local level that themselves engage the principles we have discussed. The ambitious objectives of the reform programmes will, over time, lead to the development of detailed strat-egies for the use of the tribunals' estate, information technology, service support and user support, and ultimately new, consensually developed ways of working for JoHs.

As this book attests, there are elaborate systems and policies relating to welfare, **7.119** discipline, grievance, recruitment, and assignment which are administered by leadership judges. Given the scale of the tribunals judiciary which numbers over 5,500 people across the UK, leadership involvement in the design and implemen-tation of these policies is significant. Involvement begins with the skills and abil-ities framework for judges which we have earlier referred to, judicial involvement in recruitment based on that framework, and the development of more diverse opportunities in best practice recruitment processes which are now gender and background blind. The coordination of career progression, succession planning, and appraisals processes to open opportunities for a more diverse judiciary is a key leadership function and more recently the development of our judiciary has focussed on social support (both internal and external), adaptability, self-confidence, and purposefulness to improve each individual judge's resilience.

7.120 Leadership is a constant process of collaborative renewal and development, often best seen in the collegiate way our executive functions are performed and the collegiate way we undertake training and development. That is not to say that the systems are good enough. They are not yet. The constitutional settlement of 2004–2005 and 2007–2008 in respect of the tribunals is still work in progress. There are real and interesting issues around the collective responsibility of the judiciary and how and by whom it is exercised and the principles on which our civil service may act for us and with us. There will undoubtedly be opportunities to look again at the organization of the judiciary, in particular the responsibilities for and process by which the judiciary and HMCTS are funded and whether our separation into specialist areas remains fit for purpose, that is capable of responding to society's needs in a digital world. Underpinning all of this, the identification and development of leadership principles, their acceptance and understanding by judges, and the provision of the very detailed functions that leaders and managers must perform will continue to deserve our urgent attention. It is hardly surprising in that context that the need for leadership management and development has never been greater and the time has come to scrutinize whether the leadership judiciary have adequately identified their purposes, objectives, and means of achieving quality outcomes. The governance of the judiciary is no longer an ad hoc enterprise. It is and has to be a process that provides for the application of high principle, reflects and achieves the essential ethical and civic purposes with which the judiciary are engaged, and administers justice in a way that is perceived by the public as safeguarding the Rule of Law. Judicial leaders are not alone in facing these challenges and our responses to them will be significantly improved by an ongoing collaboration between leadership judges, their JoHs, and their training and development advisors across the UK and more broadly across both common law and civilian jurisdictions. As we hope we have described, there is also a great deal to be discovered and benefited from by a new conversation with academic and professional colleagues for whom the concepts of leadership and management, governance and regulation are specialist areas of study and practice which will continue to influence what judicial leaders do.

7.121 Yet, the wealth of skill and experience that these multi-lateral exchanges reveal should be used to better effect. Perhaps the time is ripe for a judicial leadership centre where frameworks of good practice can be shared, discussed, developed, and trialled. The success of leadership involves an acknowledgement of the concept and its component parts. Engagement with JoHs to nurture that acknowledgement will involve them developing an appreciation of the skills needed of their colleagues and the acceptance that followers have a role just as important as leaders, whether they have an inkling to become a leader or not. In a collegiate judiciary that is not only possible, it reinforces the very principles that draw the judiciary together in their common quest to safeguard the Rule of Law in pursuit of their delivery of justice for all.

Judicial College: Leadership & Management Development Programme

Module 1

Leadership and Management Concepts and Definitions

Leadership is a topic that has been discussed and written about in great depth for centuries and whilst academic studies on both leadership and management have multiplied since the 1970s no agreed single definition of either exists. The following models and definitions are drawn from a body of research both academic and practice-based and are presented to inform discussion.

Leadership:

Although leadership has been written about for centuries it is of interest to note that in many respects the skills and abilities that have been identified for an effective leader have changed little over time:

Xenophon (300 BC)	Bass, B. M., & Riggio, R. E. (2006)
Leaders:	*Leaders:*
Inspire others by encouragement	Articulate a vision that is appealing and inspiring
Remind people of the higher purpose	Instill pride, gain respect and trust
Are firm, fair and visible	Provide a role model for highly ethical behaviour
Show humanity	Provide empathy and support

Until the 20th century much of leadership theory was based on a model of military characteristics and a belief that leaders were born, not made. The 18th and 19th centuries in particular were dominated by the notion of the *'heroic'* model of leadership. It was not until the 1950s that Professor John Adair, a renowned British academic, successfully demonstrated that leadership was a set of skills that could be trained, rather than an exclusively innate ability. His work instigated the move away from the *'the great man'* theory of a charismatic, heroic leader who was born to rule, towards behavioural and situational leadership models.

The theory of *'Contingency'* was developed in the 1950s and is still the basis of many of the most rigorous models of leadership. Such models argue that whilst there might be a range of generic leadership skills and abilities, there should also be consideration of the situational variables with which leaders must deal. The 1970s saw the introduction of the *'servant'* model of leadership which emphasised the ethical responsibilities of leaders to their followers.

A report in 2013 by the Centre for Creative Leadership on future trends in leadership has found that the number one priority in leadership development is to support the emergence of more flexible, reflective and sensitive leaders. Without this focus, they argue, leaders will remain incapable of dealing with the complexity of the modern world.

Management:

Management as an area of study separate from Leadership began to be developed in the late 19th century. Much of early management theory is reflected in the definition taken from the Latin 'manus', meaning hand. Theory focussed initially on the practicalities of managing machinery and other resources including people.

Adair's *Action Centred Leadership model*, developed during his tenure at Sandhurst Military Academy, helped to change the perception of management to include the associated abilities of decision-making, communication and time-management. Adair argued that not all leaders are necessarily great managers, but the best leaders will possess good management skills.

James MacGregor Burns' model of Transactional v Transformational Leadership (1978) attempted to distinguish between management and leadership styles. His work has been adapted over time with management emerging as the transactional (practical, functional, contractual) element of leadership.

Definitions of leadership and management:

There is such a wide range of definitions for both leadership and management that to list them all would be self-defeating, overwhelming and probably a waste of time; however there are similarities among the definitions.

Leadership is often defined in one of two ways. Either very simply, such as *'a leader is someone who has followers' (Drucker 1973),* or more fully to include a list of the leader's roles and responsibilities, such as *'leadership defines the future of an organization, aligns people with a vision, and inspires others to make that vision happen, despite obstacles' (Kotter 1996)*

Definitions of management follow the same formula. Either very simply, *'the art of getting things done through people' (Mary Parker-Follett 1926)* or more fully, *'management ensures that organizations run smoothly, keeps things in order, and deals effectively and efficiently with problems as they occur' (John Kotter 1996)*

There are also some judicial definitions that reflect the fuller version, including those offered by Lord Justice Ryder regarding the single Family court in 2013:

> **Leadership**; *'focuses on people; with particular responsibility for the performance and pastoral care of judges and for delivering change and establishing a new culture in the family courts'.*

> **Management:** *'focuses on the process of the family courts which includes deployment (patterning, listing and allocation), the application of the rules and practice directions by HMCTS and relationships with partnership agencies'*

In many ways the differences between leadership and management can be summarised in the words of Admiral Grace Hopper, U. S. Navy (1986) who said:

> *'You manage things; you lead people'*

> Admiral Hopper also said that the most dangerous phrase in the language is *'we have always done it this way'*; which is a helpful introduction to our thinking about leadership and managing change.

Summary:

Leadership and management are separate activities exercised in varying proportions in different roles. There are valuable elements of management not always found in leadership, e.g. administration and managing resources. Leadership also contains elements not necessarily found in management, e.g., inspiring others through the leader's personal enthusiasm and commitment.

Current models of leadership and management suggest the following differences between the roles:

Leadership	Management
Develops and communicates strategy	Understands and implements strategy
Builds and maintains relationships	Builds and maintains relationships
Influences and inspires others	Delegates and instructs
Collaborates	Prioritizes
Communicates	Communicates
Develops talent	Develops individuals and teams

Leadership	Management
Plans for succession	Monitors and reviews
Ensures sustainability	Delivers sustainability
Leads in spite of ambiguity	Manages ambiguity
Leads change including culture change	Manages change
Delivers strategy through others	Ensures delivery of tasks

However it must be noted that for judicial purposes the line between leadership and management is often blurred. There will be differences dependent upon the jurisdiction in which the role sits, the structure of the jurisdiction, the level of the role and the scope of the judicial office holder's responsibilities.

The statement of judicial leadership and management skills describes the skills which can promote successful judicial leadership and the effective management of other judicial office holders.

Judicial College: Leadership & Management Development Programme

Module 2

Stress management behaviours

Management Behaviours	Sub-behaviours	Do ✓ Don't ✗	Examples of manager behaviour
Respectful and responsible: managing emotions and having integrity	Integrity	✓	• Is a good role model • Treats colleagues with respect • Is honest
		✗	• Says one thing, the does something different • Speaks about colleagues behind their backs
	Managing emotions	✓	• Acts calmly in pressured situations • Takes a consistent approach to managing
		✗	• Is unpredictable in mood • Passes on stress to colleagues • Panics about deadlines • Takes suggestions for improvement as a personal criticism
	Considerate Approach	✗	• Makes short term demands rather than allowing planning • Creates unrealistic deadlines • Gives more negative than positive feedback] • Relies on others to deal with problems • Imposes 'my way is the only way' • Shows a lack of consideration for work-life balance

Management Behaviours	Sub-behaviours	Do ✓ Don't ✗	Examples of manager behaviour
Managing and communicating existing and future work	Proactive work management	✓	• Clearly communicates work objectives to others • Develops action plans • Monitors others' workload on an ongoing basis • Encourages others to review how they organise work • Stops additional work being taken on when necessary • Works proactively • Sees projects/tasks through to delivery • Reviews processes to see if work can be improved • Prioritises future workloads
	Problem solving	✓	• Deals rationally with problems • Follows up problems on others' behalf • Deals with problems as soon as they arise
		✗	• Is indecisive at decision-making
	Participative / empowering	✓	• Gives employees the right level of responsibility • Correctly judges when to consult and when to make a decision • Keeps others informed of what is happening in the organisation • Acts as a mentor • Delegates work equally • Helps others develop in their role • Encourages participation • Provides regular meetings
		✗	• Gives too little direction to others
Reasoning / managing difficult situations	Managing conflict	✓	• Acts as mediator in conflict situations • Deals with squabbles before they become arguments • Deals objectively with conflicts • Deals with conflicts head on
		✗	• Acts to keep the peace rather than resolve issues
	Use of organisation Resources	✓	• Seeks advice from other managers when necessary • Uses HR as a resource to help deal with problems • Seeks help from the Judicial Helpline when necessary

182

Management Behaviours	Sub-behaviours	Do ✓ Don't ✗	Examples of manager behaviour
	Taking responsibility for resolving issues	✓	• Follows up conflicts after resolution • Supports others through incidents of abuse • Makes it clear they will take ultimate responsibility if things go wrong
		✗	• Doesn't address bullying
Managing the individual	Personally accessible	✓	• Speaks personally rather than uses email • Provides regular opportunities to speak one to one • Returns calls/emails promptly • Is available to talk to when needed
	Sociable	✓	• Brings in treats • Socialises with colleagues • Is willing to have a laugh at work
	Empathetic engagement	✓	• Encourages colleagues' input in discussions • Listens when colleagues ask for help • Makes an effort to find out what motivates colleagues at work • Tries to see colleagues' point of view • Takes an interest in colleagues' life outside work • Regularly asks 'how are you?' • Treats all colleagues with equal importance
		✗	• Assumes rather than checks that colleagues are okay

Judicial College: Leadership & Management Development Programme

Module 3

Managing yourself as a leader

The aim of this module is to provide Leadership and Management Judges with an opportunity to explore their individual leadership roles, responsibilities and style.

The workshop will provide opportunities for you to develop your ideas and skills in the following areas:

- Your approach to leadership and management
- Managing your time and delegating to others
- Developing your personal resilience

PERSONAL RESILIENCE

"Resilience is the process of, capacity for or outcome of successful adaptation despite challenging or threatening circumstances" (Masten, Best & Garmezy, 1990)

Essentially, this refers to the positive capacity of people to cope when they encounter significant adversity, trauma, tragedy, threats or significant sources of stress. It encapsulates their ability to 'bounce back' due to having effective coping mechanisms.

Resilience is a skill that can be learned and developed. There is a common misconception that people who are resilient do not experience the same negative emotions as others in similar difficult situations and that they are naturally optimistic. In reality evidence suggests that resilient individuals are simply better able to navigate their way around crises, using effective methods of coping.

There are three forms of resilience:

1. **Physical:** the physical ability to respond to stressful events and return to homeostasis. It is possible to influence this consciously. For example by deciding to exercise physically when feeling stressed. This can increase one's production of adrenaline, giving one an endorphin boost and lift one's mood.
2. **Psychological:** the mental ability to recognise, respond to and deal with stressful events. Resilient individuals choose to believe that they have the ability to cope with events and to influence their situation.
3. **Emotional:** the affective ability to respond to stressful events appropriately. Research has shown that it is possible to think or act one's self into a better mood.

Self-organisation

> *'I like work: it fascinates me. I can sit and look at it for hours'* (Jerome K Jerome) - be alert to signs of procrastination and avoidance.

Time management

- **Slow your response time to problems:** Type A personalities think well on their feet. Reacting on your feet can be less helpful, leading to hurt feelings, miscommunication and escalated tension.

- **Create a balanced schedule:** Analyse your schedule, responsibilities, and daily tasks. Try to find a balance between work and family life, social activities and solitary pursuits, daily responsibilities and downtime.
- **Do not over-commit yourself:** Set realistic rather than idealistic goals, it is common to underestimate how long things take. Avoid scheduling things back-to-back or trying to fit too much into one day. Allow time for the unexpected. Drop tasks that are not truly necessary to the bottom of the list or eliminate them entirely.
- **Allow extra time:** Do not add to your stress levels by running late.
- **Plan regular breaks:** Take short breaks (take a walk or get away from your desk at lunch) and clear your mind, it will help you be more productive.

Task management

- **Prioritize tasks:** Make a list of tasks and tackle them in order of importance. Distinguish between the "shoulds" and the "musts." Do the unpleasant and difficult tasks first so that it you do not dread them all day. Avoid frustration by concentrating on those things that you have direct control over or can influence.
- **Break tasks into small steps:** If a task seems overwhelming, make a step-by-step plan. Focus on one step at a time, rather than taking on everything at once.
- **Delegate responsibility:** You do not have to do it all yourself. Let go of the desire to control or oversee every little step. Allow others to do things their way.
- **Anticipate issues:** Prepare for meetings by listing items you want to discuss.

BUILDING RESILIENCE

Please consider what you might start or continue doing in order to build and maintain your levels of resilience. Try and consider those changes that will have the most positive personal impact on your life and concentrate on these. Do not try and tackle too many changes at once. Remember, if you change one thing in your life you have started to make a difference.

Research indicates that having a strong social network not only minimizes stress, it fosters a sense of belonging and boosts self-esteem.

Lifestyle

- **Schedule work:** Try to schedule your work activities so that you avoid taking as much work home. Create space between home and work life.
- **Allow time for hobbies:** plan enjoyable activities which absorb your concentration—these will help you stop thinking about work too much.
- **Review your social life:** identify with whom you feel a sense of connection. Seek out those who you feel comfortable in saying how you really feel.
- **Connect with people:** Diary at least two leisure/social activities each week. Take time to **meet up with friends** or take a few minutes to say hi to the people around you. Ensuring you have people "there for you" when you need it is well worth the time invested
- **Improve your** interpersonal skills: do you need to improve how you listen, understand and respond to others, express feelings and thoughts?
- **Learn to accept support and share your feelings:** is not a sign of weakness and it will not mean you are a burden to others
- **Volunteer:** A study of the effect of altruistic behaviour on mental health showed reduced stress levels in people who dedicated a few hours of their time to caring for others.
- **Keep a diary:** A good way to examine and express your thoughts is to start a journal, or start expressive writing regularly. Writing about your feelings, especially if they are intense and it is done in a time-limited way, can help you to get them out of your head.

APPENDIX 4

Judicial Skills and Abilities Framework—2014

Judicial Office-holder Skills & Abilities	Judicial Office-holder Elements	Leadership & Management Elements	Leadership & Management Skills
Assimilating and Clarifying Information: Quickly assimilates information to identify essential issues, develops a clear understanding and clarifies uncertainty through eliciting and exploring information.	• Possesses the ability to quickly absorb, recall and analyse information, facts and legal argument. • Identifies and focuses on the real issues; is not lost in irrelevant detail. • Properly applies appropriate legal rules and principles to the relevant facts. • Is able to weigh evidence in order to decide the facts of a case.	**Level 1** - Establishes, and communicates the evolving strategic direction in their jurisdiction, chamber or region. **Level 2** - Communicates priorities and leads their court/tribunal through personal example.	Leading the way
Working with Others: Conducts proceedings appropriately, values diversity and shows empathy and sensitivity in building relationships.	• Manages hearings through fair and objective direction and intervention. • Has an awareness of the diversity of the communities which the courts and tribunals serve. • Works constructively with others to encourage co-operation and collaboration when needed. • Treats people with respect, sensitivity and in a fair manner without discrimination; ensuring the requirements of those with differing needs are properly met. • Maintains effective relationships, demonstrating the appropriate balance between formality and informality in hearings and with all contacts. • Is able to recognise and deal appropriately with actual or potential conflicts of interest.	**Level 1** - Acts as the judicial figurehead and builds effective relationships with the centre, agencies and key policy areas across their jurisdiction/chamber or region. **Level 2** - Uses an inclusive approach to develop and maintain the reputation of the court/tribunal within the community.	Working with others

Judicial Office-holder Skills & Abilities	Judicial Office-holder Elements	Leadership & Management Elements	Leadership & Management Skills
Exercising Judgement: Demonstrates integrity and applies independence of mind to make incisive, fair and legally sound decisions.	• Makes timely and appropriate decisions. • Exercises sound judgement and common sense. • Reaches clear, reasoned decisions objectively, based on relevant law and findings of fact. • Demonstrates integrity and independence of mind. • Does not exercise bias or prejudice.	**Level 1** - Works to improve judicial performance across the wider justice system and within the region to ensure it can meet existing and future needs. **Level 2** - Provides support to maintain and improve the performance of the judiciary and the court/tribunal to meet existing and future needs.	**Supporting and encouraging performance**
Possessing and Building Knowledge: Possesses a detailed knowledge of a relevant jurisdiction, law and practice and demonstrates an ability and willingness to learn and develop professionally.	• Possesses a high level of expertise in chosen area or profession. • Possesses an appropriate and up to date knowledge of the relevant law and its underlying principles and procedure. • Shows an ability and willingness to learn and develop.	**Level 1** - Keeps approaches and knowledge up to date to meet evolving requirements within the jurisdiction, chamber or region. **Level 2** - Encourages learning, keeps knowledge up to date and communicates developments within the court/tribunal.	**Building knowledge and learning**
Managing Work Efficiently: Works effectively and plans to make the best use of resources available.	• Runs trials/hearings effectively to facilitate a fair and efficient conclusion. • Prioritises effectively and minimises delays and irrelevancies. • Shows ability to work at speed and under pressure. • Deals effectively with case management. • Undertakes necessary preparatory work.	**Level 1** - Maintains and improves efficiency within the jurisdiction/chamber or region. **Level 2** - Takes personal accountability for the efficient and effective use of judicial and court/tribunal time and resources.	**Delivering an efficient judicial system**

Judicial Office-holder Skills & Abilities	Judicial Office-holder Elements	Leadership & Management Elements	Leadership & Management Skills
Communicating Effectively: Demonstrates good oral and written communication skills and authority.	• Establishes authority and inspires respect and confidence. • Remains calm and authoritative even when challenged. • Explains relevant legal or procedural information in language that is succinct, clear and readily understood by all. • Asks clear, concise, relevant and understandable questions. • Willing to listen with patience and courtesy	**Level 1** - Drives change across their Jurisdiction, chamber or region. **Level 2** - Supports and delivers change within the court/tribunal centre.	Facilitating change

APPENDIX 5

Judicial Leadership Toolkit

Leadership & Management Skills	Leadership and Management Elements	Skill Evidence
Leading the way	Establishes, and communicates the evolving strategic direction in their jurisdiction/chamber or region. Communicates priorities and leads their court/tribunal through personal example.	
Working effectively with others	Acts as the judicial figurehead and builds effective relationships with the centre, agencies and key policy areas across their jurisdiction/chamber or region. Uses an inclusive approach to develop and maintain the reputation of the court/tribunal within the community.	
Supporting and encouraging performance	Works to improve judicial performance across the wider justice system and within the region to ensure it can meet existing and future needs. Provides support to maintain and improve the performance of the judiciary and the court/tribunal to meet existing and future needs.	
Building knowledge and learning	Keeps approaches and knowledge up to date to meet evolving requirements within the jurisdiction/chamber or region. Encourages learning, keeps knowledge up to date and communicates developments within the court/tribunal.	
Delivering an efficient judicial service	Maintains and improves efficiency within the jurisdiction/chamber or region. Takes personal accountability for the efficient and effective use of judicial and court/tribunal time and resources.	
Facilitating change	Drives change across their jurisdiction/chamber or region. Supports and delivers change within the court/tribunal Centre.	

APPENDIX 6

Useful Websites

HEA www.heacademy.ac.uk/

Judicial College www.judiciary.gov.uk/about-the-judiciary/training-support/judicial-college/

Judicial Office www.gov.uk/government/organisations/judicial-office

Ministry of Justice www.moj.gov.uk

NHS Leadership www.leadershipacademy.nhs.uk

SELECT BIBLIOGRAPHY

Acemoglu D and Robinson J, *Why Nations Fail—The Origins of Power, Prosperity and Poverty* (Profile Books 2012).

Adewale OO and Anthonia AA, 'Impact of Organizational Culture on Human Resource Practices: A Study of Selected Nigerian Private Universities' (2013) 5(4) Journal of Competitiveness 115–33.

Alimo-Metcalfe B and Alban-Metcalfe J, 'Leadership: Time for a New Direction?' (2005) 1(1) Leadership 51.

Allinson C and Hayes J, 'The Cognitive Style Index: A Measure of Intuition-Analysis for Organizational Research' (1996) 33(1) Journal of Management Studies 119.

Antonakis J, 'Transformational and Charismatic Leadership' in D Day and J Antonakis (eds), *The Nature of Leadership* (Sage 2012) 119–51.

Antonakis J and House R, 'Instrumental Leadership: Measurement and Extension of Transformational—Transactional Leadership Theory' (2014) 25(4) The Leadership Quarterly 746.

Avolio B, Bass B, and Jung D, *MLQ Multifactor Leadership Questionnaire: Technical Report* (Mindgarden 1995).

Avolio B, Bass B, and Jung D, 'Re-examining the Components of Transformational and Transactional Leadership Using the Multifactor Leadership Questionnaire' (1999) 72(2) Journal of Occupational and Organisational Psychology 441.

Avolio B and Bass B, *Multifactor Leadership Questionnaire: Manual and Sample Set* (3rd edn, Mindgarden 2004).

Avolio B and Gardner W, 'Authentic Leadership Development: Getting to the Root of Positive Forms of Leadership' (2005) 16 The Leadership Quarterly 315.

Avolio B, Walumbwa F, and Weber T, 'Leadership: Current Theories, Research and Future Directions' (2009) 60 Annual Review of Psychology 421.

Avolio B and Yammarino F, 'Reflections, Closing Thoughts and Future Directions' in Avolio B and Yammarino F (eds), *Transformational and Charismatic Leadership: The Road Ahead* (Emerald Group Publishing 2013).

Backhaus K and Liff J, 'Cognitive Styles and Approaches to Studying in Management Education' (2007) 31(4) Journal of Management Education 445.

Barton B and Bibas S, *Rebooting Justice* (Encounter Books 2017).

Bass B, *Leadership and Performance Beyond Expectations* (Free Press 1985).

Bass B, *The Bass Handbook of Leadership Theory, Research, and Managerial Applications* (4th edn, New York Free Press 2008).

Bass BM and Avolio BJ, *Improving Organisational Effectiveness Through Transformationational Leadership* (Sage1994).

Bass B and Riggio R, *Transformational Leadership* (Lawrence Erlbaum Associates 2006).

Bass B and Stogdill R, *Handbook of Leadership* (Free Press 1990).

Betsch C, 'Chronic Preferences for Intuition and Deliberation in Decision Making: Lessons Learned about Intuition from an Individual Differences Approach' in Plessner H, Betsch C, and Betsch T (eds), *Intuition in Judgment and Decision Making* (Lawrence Erlbaum Associates 2008) 231.

Bingham T, *The Business of Judging* (OUP 2001).

Bingham T, *The Rule of Law* (Allen Lane 2010).

Bolden R, Petrov G, and Gosling J, 'Tensions in Higher Education Leadership: Towards a Multi-Level Model of Leadership Practice' (2008) 62(4) Higher Education Quarterly 358.

Brown F, Trevino LK, and Harrison DA, (2005) *Ethical Leadership* (Elsevier 2005).

Browne-Wilkinson N, F Mann Lecture (Oxford 1987).

Burns J, *Leadership* (Harper and Row 1978).

Carroll A, 'The Pyramid of Corporate Social Responsibility: Toward the Moral Management of Organizational Stakeholders' (1991) 34 Business Horizons, 39–48. http://dx.doi.org/10.1016/0007-6813(91)90005-G.

Denison DR, *Corporate Culture and Organizational Effectiveness* (John Wiley & Sons, Inc. 1990), 267 pp.

Dyson L, 'The Application of the Amendments to the Civil Procedure Rules' (2014) 33 CJQ 124.

Eagly AH, Johannesen-Schmidt MC, and van Engen ML, 'Transformational, Transactional, and laissez-Faire Leadership Styles: A Meta-Analysis Comparing Women and Men' (2003) 129(4) Psychological Bulletin, pp. 569–591

Evans L, Homer M, and Rayner S, 'Professors as Academic Leaders: The Perspectives of "the Led"' (2013) 41(5) Educational Management, Administration and Leadership 674.

Fiss O, 'Against Settlement' (1984) 93 Yale LJ 1073.

Forbes, Andrew; and Henley, David (2012). *The Illustrated Art of War*: Sun Tzu. Chiang Mai: Cognoscenti Book

Hadfield G, *Rules for a Flat World* (OUP 2016).

Handy C, *Understanding Organisations* (4th edn, Penguin 1995).

Horner M, *Leadership Theory—Past, Present & Future* (MCB University Press 1997).

Hofstede G, *Culture's Consequences: International Differences in Work-related Values* (Sage Publications 1980).

Judge I (Lord), *The Safest Shield* (Hart Publishing 2015).

JUSTICE, Delivery of Justice in Austerity (2015).

Lumby J, Review Paper: *What do we know about Leadership in Higher Education?* (Leadership Foundation for Higher Education 2012).

Malby R and Fischer M, *Complex Systems Approaches* (Kingsham Press 1996).

Mullins L, *Management and Organisational Behaviour* (Pearson 2007).

Mullins L, *Management and Organisational Behaviour* (11th edn, London: Financial Times 2013).

Northouse P, *Leadership: Theory and Practice* (7th edn, Sage 2016).

Onora O'Neil B, *A Question of Trust: The BBC Reith Lectures* (CUP 2002). http://www.bbc.co.uk/radio4/features/the-reith-lectures/transcripts/2000/.

Pollock F and Maitland FW, *The History of English Law*, Vol 2 (2nd edn, CUP 1967).

Puett M and Gross-Loh C, *The Path: What Chinese Philosophers Can Teach Us about the Good Life* (Simon & Schuster 2016).

Quinn RE, *Beyond Rational Management: Mastering the Paradoxes and Competing Demands of High Performance*. (Jossey-Bass 1988).

Resnik J, 'Precluding Appeals' (1985) 70 Cornell LR 603.

Rhode D, *Access to Justice* (OUP 2004).

Rost JC, *Leadership for the Twenty-First Century* (Praeger 1991).

Schein, E. (1985), *Organizational Culture and Leadership*, Jossey-Bass, San Francisco, CA.

Scouller J, *The Three Levels of Leadership: How to Develop Your Leadership Presence, Knowhow and Skill* (Management Books 2011).

Sethi S Prakash, 'Dimensions of Corporate Social Performance—an Analytical Framework' (1975) 17(3) California Management Review, 58–64.

Shetreet S and Turenne S, *Judges on Trial* (CUP 2013).

Spicker P, '"Leadership": A Perniciously Vague Concept' (2011) 25(1) International Journal of Public Sector Management 34.

Tourish D, *The Dark Side of Transformational Leadership: A Critical Perspective* (Routledge 2013).

Treviño LK, Hartman LP, and Brown ME (2000). *Moral person and moral manager: How executives develop a reputation for ethical leadership*. California Management Review, 42, 128–142

Useem M, *Leading Up* (Penguin 2001).

Van Dooren W, Bouckaert G, and Halligan J, *Performance Management in the Public Sector* (Routledge 2010).

Yukl G, *Leadership in Organizations* (8th edn, Pearson 2013).

INDEX